Forensic Epidemiology in the Global Context

Sana Loue
Editor

Forensic Epidemiology in the Global Context

Springer

Editor
Sana Loue
Department of Bioethics
Case Western Reserve University
Cleveland, OH, USA

ISBN 978-1-4614-6737-3 ISBN 978-1-4614-6738-0 (eBook)
DOI 10.1007/978-1-4614-6738-0
Springer New York Heidelberg Dordrecht London

Library of Congress Control Number: 2013934110

Printed on acid-free paper

Springer is part of Springer Science+Business Media (www.springer.com)

Preface

Epidemiologists are often thought of as the Sherlock Holmes of public health. They are the sleuths who seek to understand why disease or a specific health-related condition might occur in one population and not another, or why it occurs at differential rates across populations (see Last, 1988). Once concerned primarily with communicable diseases such as malaria, the scope of their investigations has broadened to include chronic disease, and environmental and occupational disease, as well as the effects resulting from a wide range of exposures.

It should come as no surprise, then, that legal systems around the world have taken note of epidemiologists' skills and the potential contribution that these skills may offer in the context of litigation. The epidemiologic methods utilized to assess the level of risk among individuals exposed to a specified exposure compared to those who were not so exposed may help to resolve legal disputes relating to diseases and injuries alleged to have resulted from pharmaceutical, environmental, and occupational exposures. An understanding of epidemiologic methods, their potential use in the courtroom setting, and their limitations has become even more critical due to increasing globalization, through which individuals in one country may be exposed to the industry practices of companies from other nations, with potentially resulting benefit or harms.

Chapter 1 sets the stage for an exploration of how epidemiologic methods may be used in the global context through an examination of the Pfizer trovafloxacin drug trial in Kano, Nigeria. Loue notes the difficulties that accompany efforts to right the wrongs done in one country by actors of another and how the procedural provisions of the US civil law ultimately control the conduct of the legal proceedings and the use or nonuse of epidemiologic methods. Chapter 2, authored by Johnson and colleagues, explores the role of the epidemiologist as an expert, whether consulting or testifying, and the processes for expert testimony that are utilized in the US courts. Claire McIvor addresses in Chap. 3 the use of epidemiology in the UK tort law, arguing that the UK courts, much like many US courts, have failed to understand the basic principles underlying epidemiology and the important contribution that such methods may have in efforts to resolve disputes arising from harms alleged to have been caused by specified exposures.

Bădărău and Ioan focus in Chap. 4 on the nascent use of epidemiology in the Romanian legal system, exploring the use of epidemiologic methods to determine liability arising from long-term neurological injury due to an occupational exposure. Chapter 5 focuses on injuries and environmental damage in Ecuador, alleged to have resulted from exposures caused by the actions of the American company Texaco. Loue again illustrates the difficulties that attend efforts to rectify harms in one country that result from the actions of those of another nation.

The final chapter appropriately explores human right violations and the role that can be played by forensic epidemiology. Loff and Cordner focus on how modern forensic medicine in Australia has integrated an epidemiological function as a fundamental aspect of its contribution to both justice and public health. They also explore the role of forensic pathology and related disciplines in the resolution of mass deaths in war, internal conflict, and disaster.

Forensic epidemiology is an ever-growing field, one that allows epidemiologists to truly serve as detectives seeking the cause of disease and injury. As such, the field offers the potential to contribute to the attainment of justice.

Cleveland, OH, USA Sana Loue

Reference

Last, J. M. (1988). *Dictionary of epidemiology*, 2nd ed. New York: Oxford University Press.

Contents

Chapter 1
Forensic Epidemiology in the Global Context: A Case Study of Pfizer and the Trovafloxacin Trial

Sana Loue

Introduction

One needs to only look at the daily news to understand that events in one part of the world often have considerable repercussions and implications not only for those living and working in close proximity to the events but even populations living, working, and traveling far afield from where the original incidents may have occurred. Recent illustrative examples include Pfizer's 1996 clinical trial of trovafloxacin (Trovan) conducted in Kano, Nigeria, the consequences of which continue to reverberate to this day in the nature of chronic adverse health effects to the individuals unknowingly subjected to that experiment and ongoing legal battles; the ongoing oil development in the Amazon basin of Ecuador with resulting long-term adverse health and environmental effects that have ultimately led to the courtroom in an effort to seek justice for those who have been harmed (Donziger, 2004); and the 2011 *Escherichia coli* outbreak in Europe that led to the deaths of at least 49 persons in Europe and the United States (Anon, 2011a), illness among 4,178 individuals throughout Europe (Anon, 2011a), and a likely action by Spain against Germany to recoup economic losses associated with Germany's erroneous attribution of blame for the epidemic to Spanish cucumbers (Abend, 2011; Anon, 2011a, 2011b; Pleitgen & Hsieh, 2011).

This chapter uses the trovafloxacin clinical trial to illustrate both the critical role to be played in such cases by epidemiologists and epidemiologic methods and the legal issues that surround the use of epidemiology in the legal resolution of such cases, that is, the role of forensic epidemiology. The issues relating to oil development in the Ecuadorian Amazon basin will be explored in Chap. 5, which addresses the use of epidemiology in legal proceedings related to environmental justice.

S. Loue, J.D., Ph.D., M.P.H., M.S.S.A., M.A. (✉)
Department of Bioethics, Case Western Reserve University, Cleveland, OH, USA
e-mail: sana.loue@case.edu

S. Loue (ed.), *Forensic Epidemiology in the Global Context*,
DOI 10.1007/978-1-4614-6738-0_1, © Springer Science+Business Media New York 2013

Pfizer and the Trovafloxacin Trial

The Kano Meningitis Epidemic

Meningitis is caused by a virus, fungus, or bacteria; regardless of the underlying cause, it leads to an inflammation of the membranes that protect the brain and spinal cord, known as the meninges (World Health Organization, 2011b). Meningococcal meningitis is caused by bacteria that are transmitted from person to person through respiratory droplets or throat secretions of individuals who are carrying the bacteria. Transmission of the infection is facilitated by close contact with a carrier of the disease, such as sharing utensils or living together in relatively close quarters. Incubation of the disease ranges from 2 to 10 days. Symptoms include a stiff neck, sensitivity to light, headache, fever, vomiting, and confusion, which may progress to long-lasting neurological deficits in up to 20 % of those affected and death in up to 10 % of those with the infection (World Health Organization, 2011b). Meningococcal meningitis caused by the bacteria *Neisseria meningitidis*, in particular, can lead to the relatively rapid deterioration of the body's defenses. Because of the high incidence of long-term disability and the high rate of mortality, meningococcal meningitis "should always be viewed as a medical emergency" and "appropriate antibiotic treatment must be started as soon as possible" (World Health Organization, 2011b).

Nigeria lies within the "meningitis belt" of Africa, with epidemics of the infection occurring every 5–12 years (Lapeysosonnie, 1963). In any given epidemic, up to 10,000 individuals may die due to the disease. Only two antibiotics, a single dose of either oily chloramphenicol or ceftriaxone, are recommended for the treatment of meningococcal meningitis in epidemic conditions in Africa in areas that have limited health care resources and a poor health care infrastructure (World Health Organization, 2011b).

These were exactly the conditions that prevailed at the time of the 1996 meningitis outbreak. The government had made drastic spending cuts during the 1980s and 1990s that led to an inadequate health care infrastructure and insufficient water, electricity, drugs, and equipment to respond to meningitis epidemics (Ejembe, Renne, & Adamu, 1998). At the time of the epidemic, Nigeria was led by a military government that has been characterized as having "one of the world's worst human rights and corruptions records" (Stephens, 2000). Kano, the site of the Pfizer study, is the capital of Kano state, which sits in the north central region of Nigeria. The state is densely populated with a predominantly Muslim population, is highly urbanized, and serves as a major trading route between the northern and southern areas of the country.

At the time of the meningitis epidemic, Kano was experiencing concurrent epidemics of measles and cholera. Immunization rates had decreased, largely due to increasing hostility towards Western medicine. These sentiments stemmed from a campaign launched by radical Muslims claiming that Western countries were attempting to limit African population growth both by infecting Africans with HIV and sterilizing them under the pretense of immunization. One medical practitioner explained the epidemics as being linked to the intensification of Islamic sentiments in several Northern states which have adopted the Sharia and anti-Western feelings due to the widespread perception that the West is opposed to the Islamic legal system:

> For a lot of the ordinary people in mainly Muslim areas, accepting Sharia also means rejecting everything Western, be it education, fashion or medicines. And in the case of medicines the consequences are already being felt in terms of increasing casualties from infectious diseases (IRIN, 2001).

Kano's Infectious Disease Hospital has been described as "a small collection of concrete buildings inside a sandy compound" (Boseley & Smith, 2010). International aid workers have referred to it as "one of the world's most fetid and overburdened hospitals" (Stephens, 2000). A reporter from *The Washington Post* described what could be seen at the hospital: "Rats chew on neglected corpses and patients defecate on the ground. Many wards lack water and electricity; walls are encrusted with excrement and blood." At the time of the epidemic, the medical enclave lacked specialists, adequate equipment, and even a working X-ray machine (Stephens, 2000).

Doctors Without Borders (Médecins sans Frontières) arrived as the epidemic was raging. Its volunteer physicians treated patients with chloramphenicol, one of the drugs recommended for treatment of meningococcal meningitis. Patients were screened by their severity of illness and those who were sickest were provided with the few available beds housed inside the buildings, while those with less serious symptoms were tended to in cots placed in tents outside (Stephens, 2000). At the height of the epidemic in March 1996, the Infectious Disease Hospital was admitting 50 patients a day (Ojewale, 1996). More than two-thirds of Kano's meningitis cases involved children less than 16 years of age (World Health Organization, 1996).

By the end of Nigeria's epidemic, at least 8,000 people had died, many of whom were children, and more than 75,000 had been infected (World Health Organization, 2011a). The mortality rate during the epidemic reached a peak of 20 % (Pfizer, n.d.). Pfizer has claimed that it has long maintained a commitment to the people of Nigeria (Pfizer, n.d.), and that its goal in Kano was to study the safety and effectiveness of Trovan and to pioneer a new treatment for the Third World (Stephens, 2000).

Pfizer's Clinical Trial

At the time that Pfizer initiated its Trovan study in Nigeria, Pfizer was attempting to obtain the approval of the US Food and Drug Administration (FDA) for the drug. Trovan belonged to a class of antibiotics known as quinolones. Trovan had been demonstrated, at least on a preliminary basis, to be effective in the treatment of various infections including bronchitis, sinusitis, gonorrhea, and pneumonia. Its use in children, however, was questionable because it had been shown to lead to severe joint damage in studies conducted with young rabbits and puppies. If the drug were approved, it would be one of the most financially successful new drugs in its class in years (Stephens, 2000).

Pfizer's research team, led by Scott Hopkins, assumed the care over a period of 2 to 3 weeks of approximately 198 children, ranging in age from only a few months to 18 years of age. Pfizer has depicted its efforts in Kano as philanthropic, a characterization that has been challenged by a researcher who noted that the experiment allowed Pfizer to understand better how the drug works and potentially paved the way to receive FDA approval, which would then allow the US-based physicians to prescribe it (Stephens, 2000).

The experimental protocol specified that one-half of the children were to receive Trovan by tablet, in an oral solution, or in an intravenous formulation that could bypass the digestive system. The second half of the patients was to receive ceftriaxone, an antibiotic treatment that had been approved for use in the United States for children suffering from meningitis. This second group of children was to serve as a comparison group against which the effectiveness of Trovan would be assessed. Children were to have their blood tested at the time of diagnosis and again after 5 days of treatment in order to determine if they were responding to the drug. If the child was not responding well to Trovan, he or she was supposed to be switched to treatment with ceftriaxone.

However, the administration of ceftriaxone did not comport with the standards that had been established for its use. The drug is to be administered by injection into a vein or a muscle. However, Pfizer staff abandoned this procedure in an effort to save time and, instead, injected the drug into the children's buttocks and thighs, resulting in such pain that the children became fearful of the injections. In order to reduce the injection-associated pain level, Pfizer staff then reduced the dosage of the drug to one-third of the recommended dosage, claiming that it was sufficient to combat the infection. However, the medical director of Hoffman-La Roche, which manufactures ceftriaxone, has asserted that "a high dose is essential" and that the low dosing may have led to clinical failures and possibly the deaths of some children (Stephens, 2000).

The procedure used for the experiment similarly failed to comport with commonly accepted standards for the testing of experimental drugs for meningitis. Industry guidelines indicate that a spinal tap is to be conducted approximately 1 day following the initiation of treatment in order to ascertain whether the treatment is working. However, Pfizer staff chose not to conduct these examinations. Additionally, the blood tests that were to have been conducted were abandoned due to staff shortages. As a result, the Pfizer team was unable to determine whether the medication that had been administered was actually effective apart from visible clinical signs of a child's deteriorating health.

Later data indicated that 45 of the 198 children received treatment that deviated from the experimental protocol. Five children who received Trovan and six children who received low doses of ceftriaxone died. Seven children who received Trovan and seven children who received the comparison drug were found to have full-blown arthritis. Fifteen of the children in the Trovan group experienced joint pain while on the drug, a rate that was three times higher than that among the children receiving ceftriaxone (Stephens, 2000). Others suffered blindness, deafness, and paralysis. Numerous discrepancies in the data were noted by the FDA during its inspection of Pfizer's documents, including variations in the recording of lab results. The FDA did not approve the use of the drug in children, but on December 19, 1997, authorized its use in the treatment of 14 illnesses in adults (Stephens, 2000).

Between the time of its approval and mid-1999, sales of Trovan exceeded $160 million. However, following reports of death in 14 patients and liver problems in 140 patients taking Trovan, approval of the drug was revised to limit its use to patients with serious diseases in which the risks of their disease outweighed the risk of liver damage.

Pfizer has claimed both that it received the approval of the Nigerian Government to conduct the experiment following independent review by an ethics review committee and that no such review was required or conducted (Pfizer, 2007). The company also claimed that all participants were informed in the local language that they were being enrolled in a clinical trial, and that all participants provided their oral or written informed consent (Pfizer, n.d.). To date, no informed consent documents translated into the local language of Hausa have been located (Stephens, 2000). Although Pfizer later claimed that the staff had obtained informed consent from the families for their children's participation in the study (Pfizer, 2007), an investigation by a committee appointed by the Nigerian Ministry of Health disputed that claim (Federal Ministry of Health, 2001). Pfizer's representation that it had received the approval of an ethics committee in Nigeria to conduct the experiment was also found to be inaccurate; it appears that the hospital did not have an ethics committee at the time the study was conducted and the approval letter may have been drafted 1 year after the trial had been concluded (Federal Ministry of Health, 2001; Wise, 2001). Publications resulting from the study listed the Nigerian Principal Investigator selected by Pfizer, Isa Dutse, as the first author, although he did not have access to the data and was not consulted in the preparation of these manuscripts (Statement of Defence, 2007).

Reports following the conclusion of the trial also indicate that a Nigerian physician in Kano had attempted to halt the trial due to various concerns (Federal Ministry of Health, 2001). In addition, Juan Walterspiel, who had been a Pfizer infectious disease specialist, claimed that he had been fired due to his repeated warnings to the company regarding the scientific and legal flaws of the study (Malakoff, 2001; Silverman, 2011). Walterspiel's allegations included charges that Pfizer had bribed foreign officials in order to gain permission to conduct the study; had never obtained parental consent to enroll the children in the study; had falsified documents that were submitted to the FDA; had failed to meet professional and legal standards for its physicians to practice medicine in Nigeria; had assigned Pfizer physicians to the study who had limited experience in the evaluation and treatment of meningitis; and had compromised the validity of the study by having the same individuals responsible for participant selection, recruitment, evaluation, treatment, observation, and recording of the findings (*Abdullahi v. Pfizer, Inc., Adamu v. Pfizer, Inc.*, Order, 2011).

Legal Battles

Survivors of the Trovan experiment who believed that they had been harmed brought suit against Pfizer. Rather than filing their claims against Pfizer in Nigeria with a legal system that had never defined the parameters of informed consent and a court system that was widely believed to be corrupt, they filed their complaint in the United States District Court for the Southern District of New York (*Abdullahi v. Pfizer*, 2002) ("Abdullahi I"). The plaintiffs alleged that five children who had received Trovan had died and that six children who had been randomized to the low-dose ceftriaxone had also died. Pfizer filed a motion to dismiss pursuant to Federal Rule of Civil Procedure 12(b)(6),[1] arguing that the plaintiffs hadn't demonstrated that Pfizer as a private party could be liable for the "law of nations." The court, though, found that because Pfizer claimed to have had the permission of the Nigerian Government to move forward with the research, Pfizer had acted as a "de facto state actor." However, the court did dismiss the lawsuit on the grounds of *forum non conveniens*,[2] finding that Nigeria was an adequate alternative forum despite the plaintiffs' concerns about corruption. The court additionally held that the "Gilbert factors" supported a transfer of the case to Nigeria. The court granted Pfizer's motion to dismiss conditioned on Pfizer's consent to suit and acceptance of process[3] in Nigeria. Pfizer further waived problems associated with the statute of limitations[4] and agreed to return to the United States if the Nigerian courts found that there was no jurisdiction.[5]

Both Pfizer and the plaintiffs appealed the district court's decision to the Court of Appeals for the Second Circuit (*Abdullahi v. Pfizer*, 2003) ("Abdullahi III"). Pfizer appealed from the court's denial of its motion to dismiss premised on Federal Rule of Civil Procedure 12(b)(6) and plaintiffs appealed from the order dismissing their case. The Second Circuit found that although under normal circumstances Nigeria might serve as an appropriate forum for the litigation, a motion to dismiss premised on *forum non conveniens* should be denied if the plaintiffs could demonstrate that they would not obtain basic justice due to conditions in that other forum, in this case Nigeria. The court specifically noted that the plaintiffs had produced letters from the United States Department of State and the United Nations that supported their characterization of the Nigerian judiciary as corrupt (*Abdullahi III*). In the interim, a lawsuit that had been filed in a Nigerian court against Pfizer, *Zango v. Pfizer*, had been dismissed following the removal of one judge and a second judge's declination of jurisdiction (*Zango v. Pfizer*, 2001). The Court of Appeals for the Second Circuit vacated the earlier decision of the district court on the basis of *forum non conveniens* and remanded (sent back) the case to the district court, with instructions to consider the impact of *Zango v. Pfizer* on the issue of *forum non conveniens*.

Upon remand, the district court found that the *Zango v. Pfizer* litigation did not preclude dismissal of the case on the basis of forum non conveniens and granted Pfizer's motion to dismiss that was premised on Federal Rule of Civil Procedure 12(b)(6) (*Abdullahi v. Pfizer*, 2005) ("Abdullahi III"). The court again held that Nigeria offered an adequate judicial forum for the litigation, notwithstanding plaintiffs' continuing allegations of corruption within the judiciary and the Nigerian court's dismissal of *Zango v. Pfizer.*

The court also analyzed whether the plaintiffs had stated a cause of action under the Alien Tort Claims Act. That US legislation allows federal courts in the United States to hear alien tort claims for violations of international law in relatively limited circumstances. The court found that Pfizer had not violated customary international law because the Nuremberg Code (1949),[6] the Declaration of Helsinki (1964, 2008),[7] and the documents promulgated by the Council of Organizations for Medical Sciences (2002)[8] represent only general statements of policy and do not authorize a private cause of action. The court additionally held that the International Covenant on Civil and Political Rights (1966)[9] is not self-executing and that, rather than imposing obligations as a matter of international law, the Universal Declaration of Human Rights[10] is "merely aspirational."

The case of *Adamu v. Pfizer* (2005) was also filed in the United States District Court for the Southern District of New York. The court considered plaintiff's claims brought under the Connecticut Unfair Trade Practices Act and the Connecticut Products Liability Statute. The court found that Nigerian substantive law controlled the case and accordingly dismissed the lawsuit, both on this ground and based on *forum non conveniens*.

The Second Circuit Court of Appeals has since heard a consolidated appeal from the *Abdullahi III* and the *Adamu* cases (Abdullahi v. Pfizer, 2009) ("Abdullahi IV"). The Second Circuit reversed the holdings of the district court, finding that (1) the court had subject matter jurisdiction under the Alien Tort Statute because the "prohibition against nonconsensual human medical experimentation was a universally accepted "norm of customary international law," and (2) that the plaintiffs had alleged a sufficiently close nexus between Pfizer's conduct as a private actor in conducting the Kano trial and the Nigerian Government's provision of hospital facilities to consider that Pfizer could be fairly treated as an agent of the State. The Second Circuit reversed the holding of the district court and again remanded the case for further proceedings based on its analysis of customary international law.

The Government of Nigeria filed a lawsuit against Pfizer on June 5, 2007, claiming that Pfizer had never obtained the approval of the Nigerian Government to carry out the experiment. The lawsuit sought $6.95 billion dollars in damages. Former US president Jimmy Carter and the former Nigerian leader Yakubu Gowon brokered an out-of-court settlement between the Nigerian Government and Pfizer in the amount of $75 million. Of the promised $75 million, $30 million has been distributed to the Kano State Government and $10 million has been paid to the lawyers representing the state government in its case against Pfizer (Shuaibu, 2011). The family of each claimant was to receive $175,000 (Smith, 2011).

An April 20, 2009, cable disclosed by WikiLeaks indicates that Pfizer made efforts to discredit Nigerian Attorney General Michael Aondoakaa in an attempt to dissuade him from pursuing Nigeria's litigation against the company (Edwards, 2011; Silverman, 2010b). The confidential cable notes that articles damaging to Aondoakaa were published in February and March of that year, and quoted Enrico Liggeri, Pfizer's country manager, as saying that Pfizer had engaged private investigators to uncover corruption links to Aondoakaa in order to pressure him to withdraw the lawsuit and that Pfizer was passing on this information to local media. Liggeri further alleged that the charges against Pfizer were political in nature because Doctors Without Borders had also administered Trovan to children, a claim that Doctors Without Borders denied and that Pfizer later retracted (Médecins sans Frontières, 2011).

In June 2010, the United States Supreme Court denied Pfizer's petition for a writ of certiorari,[11] refusing to review the ruling of the Second Circuit Court of Appeals that had reinstated the lawsuits (*Pfizer v. Abdullahi*, 2010). In July 2010, 192 plaintiffs filed a new lawsuit in Nigeria. The plaintiffs challenged the provision of the Nigeria–Pfizer settlement agreement that required the collection and testing of DNA samples prior to payment of the victim or his or her family (Silverman, 2010a). The plaintiffs alleged that Pfizer could switch the DNA samples and deny compensation. Pfizer claimed in response that it had received claims from more than double the number of persons who had participated in the Trovan trial and that therefore DNA results were needed to establish the validity of each claim.

As of October 2011, only four families had received full payment and four others had received only partial payment (Shuaibu, 2011). Other victims have died while awaiting the payments from the Healthcare Meningitis Trust Fund, established jointly by Pfizer and the Kano State Government to manage the disbursement of the compensation. Alhaji Mustapha Mai Sikeli, who chairs the Trovan Victims Forum which represents 192 of those enrolled in the Trovan trial, alleged in March 2011 that Pfizer had breached most of the agreements that it had entered into with the victims and was delaying the release of the DNA testing that served as a basis for the identification of Trovan experiment participants (Shuaibu, 2011). It has been alleged as well that many of the victims had agreed to a payout from Pfizer of $5,000 in exchange for withdrawing their lawsuit, and this payment was not to be considered part of the $175,000 promised compensation.

Assessing Responsibility: Enter Forensic Epidemiology

It is readily admitted that deaths during the meningitis epidemic were inevitable, regardless of who provided what type of care (Stephens, 2000). The question thus presented is whether the death of or injuries to subjects in the Trovan experiment are attributable to their participation in that study, or whether their deaths or injuries were the result of the underlying disease, notwithstanding their participation in the experiment. In essence, this requires the application of a population-based science—epidemiology—to determine the effect of a specified exposure on particular individuals. Such an application is fraught with significant challenges and rests not only on epidemiologic principles but also on the legal conceptualization of causation, which differs significantly from the epidemiologic understanding of causation as well as policy determinations.

Causation in epidemiology rests on a multidimensional assessment that encompasses study design; the sampling strategies employed; the use or nonuse of randomization and blinding; sample size and statistical power; the extent to which confounding, bias, and effect modification have been identified and controlled for; and the reliability and validity of measures used. This analysis of a hypothesized link between a specified exposure and effect extends far beyond a mere assessment of statistical significance.

The discovery of an association between an exposure and an effect cannot, however, be equated to causation. Whereas it was once believed that causation required a one-to-one correspondence between the cause and effect, such that the factor under examination is the only and only cause of the disease under investigation (Kleinbaum, Kupper, & Morgenstern, 1982), we now understand that many diseases, if not most, result from the combined effects of multiple factors (Rothman, 1986). However, because the identification of all factors that contribute to a disease is often impossible, epidemiologists utilize statistical techniques and probability theory to assess the risk of disease resulting from exposure to specified factors (Rothman, 1986).

Using an inductive approach, Bradford Hill enunciated the criteria to be considered in identifying causal associations: strength, consistency, specificity, temporality, biological gradient, plausibility, coherence, experimental evidence, and analogy (Morabia, 1991). The *strength* of an association between the putative causal factor and the effect depends upon the relative prevalence of other component causes. This criterion encompasses two separate issues: the frequency with which the factor under investigation is found in cases of a specific disease and the frequency with which the factor occurs in the absence of the disease (Sartwell, 1960). *Consistency* refers to the repeated observation of an association between the putative causal factor and the effect in varied populations at varied points in time and under different circumstances (Susser, 1991). Inconsistency, however, does not necessarily negate a causal relationship because all causal components must exist to bring about the effect and some may be absent. *Specificity* refers to the association between a postulated cause and a single effect (Rothman, 1986). Hill specifically cautioned against overemphasizing the importance of this particular element (Hill, 1965).

Temporality requires that the cause precedes the effect in time (Rothman, 1986). Although a dose–response curve, or a biological gradient, is to be considered, it does not necessarily indicate causation due to the effects of confounding factors. *Plausibility* requires that the hypothesized relationship between the causal factor and the effect be biologically plausible. This is clearly limited by the state of our knowledge at any given point in time. *Coherence* requires that a postulated causal association be consistent with our knowledge of the natural history and biology of the disease in question. *Analogy* posits that reference to known examples may provide insights into other causes (Rothman, 1986).

One approach to determining whether the administration of Trovan was associated with a statistically significant increase in deaths or injuries among the study subjects would be to conduct a study using a case–control design. In this type of study, individuals with the disease (or who died), known as the cases, are compared with individuals without the disease (or who remain alive), known as the controls, as illustrated below. (Other study designs and approaches to analysis may, however, be utilized.)

	Cases	Controls	Totals
Exposed	a	b	$a+b$
Not exposed	c	d	$c+d$
Total	$a+c$	$b+d$	$a+b+c+d$
Proportions exposed	$a/a+c$	$b/b+d$	

If the exposure is associated with the disease, the proportion of cases exposed ($a/a+c$) would be expected to be greater than the proportion of the controls who were exposed ($b/b+d$) (Gordis, 1996). Here, if exposure to Trovan is associated with death, we would expect that the proportion of those dying who were exposed to Trovan would be greater than the proportion of those who did not die who were exposed to Trovan. Applying this to Trovan, we have the following:

	Cases (individuals who died)	Controls (individuals who did not die)	Totals
Exposed to Trovan	5	94	99
Not exposed to Trovan	6	93	99
Total	11	187	198
Proportions exposed to Trovan	5/11	94/187	

A cursory analysis suggests that a lesser proportion of those who received Trovan died in comparison with those who received ceftriaxone: 5/11 = 45.5 %; 94/187 = 50.3 %.

However, this is only the first step in the analysis. It is important to also assess the odds of dying. The odds of an event have been defined as "the ratio of the number of ways the event can occur to the number of ways the event cannot occur" (Gordis, 1996, p. 145). This can be written as (the probability an event will occur)/(the probability that an event will not occur) or $P/(1-P)$ (Gordis, 1996, p. 146). The calculation of the odds ratio in a case–control study is done by calculating: odds that a case was exposed/odds that a control was exposed. Applying this to the table yields $(a/c)/(b/d)$ or ad/bc. Using this formula with the data from the Trovan trial, we have $(5\times93)/(6\times94)=465/564=0.82$. The odds ratio is less than 1.0, suggesting that treatment with Trovan was protective against death in comparison to treatment with ceftriaxone, a result consistent with the initial examination of the proportion of individuals who die. Further analysis would require calculations to determine if this difference between the two treatment groups was statistically significant, taking into account additional factors that might have influenced the outcome, such as severity of illness at the time of treatment, preexisting illness, age, etc.

Despite the indication from an initial examination of the proportions and the odds ratio that treatment with Trovan was protective from death, these calculations provide an inadequate basis on which to conclude epidemiologically that Trovan was beneficial. The treatment administered to 45 of the children in the experiment deviated from the protocol, but the details of those deviations and the children affected are not publicly available. As a result, necessary adjustment in the analysis cannot be made, such as whether the data derived from the children whose treatment deviated from the prescribed protocol should be excluded from the analysis. Additionally, data relating to relevant factors, such as those noted above, are similarly unavailable, precluding the conduct here of additional necessary analyses.

The establishment of causation in the legal context does not rest only on epidemiologic conclusions. While epidemiologic findings may be relevant, it is the structure of the legal proceedings and the rules of evidence that ultimately determine what evidence, including evidence gleaned from the use of epidemiologic methods, can be considered in determining causation. This basic precept underscores the importance of forensic epidemiology in the global context: not only can events involving epidemiologic investigation have global consequences, but also the forum in which the court sits and the law that is applied have significant bearing on the outcome of the litigation.

In the context of an action in tort, such as the Trovan experiment where one party (the plaintiff) is claiming injury due to the actions of another (the defendant), the plaintiff must establish that the defendant owed a duty to the plaintiff, that duty was breached, that the breach of the duty resulted in harm to the plaintiff (cause in fact), that there was a nexus between the defendant's conduct and the plaintiff's injury (proximate case), and that the plaintiff is seeking damages. Depending upon the legal jurisdiction in the United States, the plaintiff must demonstrate either that the claimed injury would not have occurred but for the action or inaction of the defendant or, alternatively, that the defendant's conduct is a substantial factor in bringing about the harm that the plaintiff suffered (Keeton, Dobbs, Keeton, & Owen, 1984).

The term proximate cause is actually a misnomer because it refers to a policy determination rather than an actual assessment of causation. Whether proximate cause will be determined to exist in a particular situation rests on an assessment of the foreseeability of the plaintiff, the foreseeability of the manner in which the breach of duty occurred, and the foreseeability of the result. If there is no duty owed to the plaintiff, the issue of foreseeability, however, will never be reached. Jurisdictions may differ with respect to whether a duty is owed to an unforeseeable plaintiff. In some jurisdictions, if a duty is owed to anybody, it is owed to everybody. In other jurisdictions a duty may not be owed to foreseeable plaintiffs who fail to establish a sufficiently close connection between the defendant's conduct and the suffered harm or to unforeseeable plaintiffs.

Accordingly, in the Trovan experiment, the plaintiffs are claiming that Pfizer and its staff owed them specific duties related to their status as research participants; that Pfizer breached those duties; and that as a result of that breach, individuals suffered harm, such as arthritis and death. In support of their position, the plaintiffs have pointed to the various international documents that enunciate the obligations of researchers conducting research involving human participants.

Some US courts have held that epidemiologic evidence will not be admissible unless the odds ratio is statistically significant at a 95 % confidence level, and have equated the scientific standard with the legal standard (Poole, 1987). Other US courts have required a relative risk or odds ratio of 2.0 before epidemiologic evidence will be admitted, explaining that a twofold increase in risk is necessary to meet the legal standard of a preponderance of evidence (*Marder v. G.D. Searle & Co.*, 1986).

(For a discussion of similar pronouncements by the UK courts, see Chap. 3 in this volume.) Several courts, however, have recognized that the absence of statistical significance does not preclude the existence of a causal relationship between the exposure of interest and the alleged resulting injury (*Allen v. United States*, 1984; *In re TMI Litigation Cases Consolidated II*, 1996).

This discussion of a threshold requirement based upon the magnitude of relative risk or attributable fraction can be analogized to the concepts of sensitivity and specificity in epidemiology (Loue, 1999), used in conjunction with screening tests. Sensitivity refers to the proportion of individuals who truly have a specific characteristic that is correctly classified by the screening strategy as having that characteristic. Specificity refers to the proportion of individuals who do not have a specific characteristic that is correctly classified by the screening strategy as not having that characteristic. Sensitivity and specificity are related in that attempts to reduce the proportion of individuals incorrectly classified as having a characteristic (false positives) may result in an increase in the proportion of individuals misclassified as not having that characteristic (Roht, Selwyn, Holguin, & Christensen, 1982).

Accordingly, in the context of litigation, a high threshold requirement, such as a relative risk of 3.0, would result in a lesser proportion of unharmed individuals being erroneously classified as harmed, but would also result in a larger proportion of truly harmed individuals being misclassified as unharmed, thereby precluding recovery for those injuries. Conversely, formal adoption of a lower relative risk as a threshold requirement would result in misclassification of a greater proportion of the unharmed individuals as harmed (Figs. 1.1 and 1.2).

The establishment of a threshold requirement can be likened to the issue of Type I and Type II errors. Assume, for instance, that the null hypothesis (H_0) states that a risk ratio of less than or equal to 2.0 indicates no causal association in the legal and epidemiological contexts, while the alternative hypothesis (H_A) states that a risk ratio of greater than 2.0 indicates that a causal association exists. In any specific situation, one of the following must be true:

1. The null hypothesis is rejected when it is true and, as a result, a Type I error is committed. This means, for instance, that a jury may conclude that a causal association exists and damages should be awarded when, in fact, there is no such causal relationship.
2. The null hypothesis is rejected when the alternative hypothesis is true, i.e., a correct decision has been made. In this case, the jury concludes correctly that a causal association exists.
3. The null hypothesis is not rejected when the alternative hypothesis is true. This constitutes a Type II error. Practically, this means that the jury may conclude that there is no causal association and no damages should be awarded when, in fact, such a relationship does exist.
4. The null hypothesis is not rejected when the null hypothesis is true. In this situation, the jury correctly concludes that no causal relationship exists and, appropriately, no award is granted.

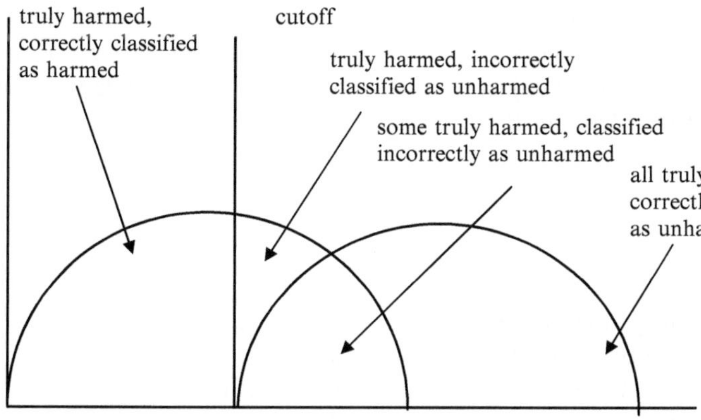

Fig. 1.1 Standards for determining causation: high standard

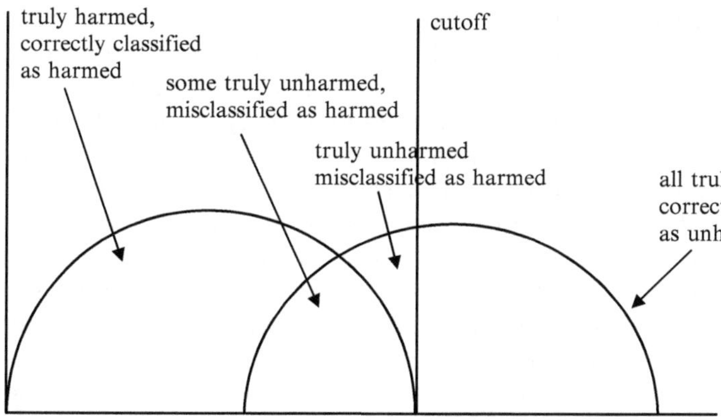

Fig. 1.2 Standards for determining causation: low standard

Both Type I and Type II errors are serious. A Type I error would result in an award to an allegedly injured party when in actuality the putative exposure is not causally associated with the disease or the injury. As a result, individuals would be compensated for their injuries alleged to have resulted from the exposure when, in fact, they should not be entitled to such an award. A Type II error would result in the denial of an award to an individual whose injury or disease may be associated with the exposure under examination.

Whether a Type I or a Type II error can be considered to be more serious in this context rests on a policy determination. It is critical, in this regard, to note that as a society the United States has recognized and accepted numerous other situations in which compensation schemes fail to reflect a perfect synchronicity between injury and compensation, e.g., workmen's compensation for employment-related injuries and no-fault automobile insurance (Macklin, 1999). The resolution of this policy determination rests, at least in part, on how we resolve the underlying ethical dilemma: Is it more unjust to fail to compensate individuals whose exposures did, in fact, result in injury or more unjust to collect damages from a company for unwarranted liability? (See Macklin, 1999.)

Conclusion

The Pfizer Kano litigation is illustrative in several aspects. First, the proceedings demonstrate the interplay between law and epidemiology. Clearly, the legal forum in which a case proceeds determines in large degree whether and the extent to which findings of an epidemiologic investigation will be admitted into evidence in a trial and how the court will view that evidence.

Second, the case highlights the increasing internationalization of epidemiologic and clinical investigations. Research in one country conducted with residents of that country may be conducted and/or funded by researchers and sponsors of one or more other countries, with varying levels of financial support and/or endorsement by the respective governments. The harms and benefits resulting from such research may well reverberate beyond the boundaries of the country in which the research is being conducted. This is not a new insight; we have known for decades at least that discoveries in one locale, such as a vaccine, may be beneficial to diverse populations in distant locales. However, the Pfizer Kano research and litigation underscore the potential impact of those events well outside of the usual medical and scientific arenas and the growing need for governments to establish through consensus acceptable mechanisms to evaluate alleged research-related injuries and develop appropriate compensatory schemes and processes.

Third, the court's recognition of the relationship between Pfizer's conduct and the provisions of various human right accords and declarations suggests that the field of forensic epidemiology must move beyond consideration of only the uses of epidemiology in litigation and other legal functions to address, as well, issues of human rights and ethics. (See Chap. 6 in this volume for a discussion of some of these important issues.)

Notes

1. A motion to dismiss Rule 12(b)(6) of the Federal Rules of Civil Procedure requests that the court dismiss the complaint that was filed by the plaintiff to initiate the lawsuit because it fails to state a claim for which relief can be granted. In deciding whether or not to dismiss the case, the court will assume for the purpose of deciding the motion only that all facts stated by the plaintiff are true, and then will assess those facts to determine if they state claim for which relief can be granted. If the court grants the motion, the case is dismissed.

2. Forum non conveniens is the power of a court to dismiss a case because another forum is considered more appropriate for the hearing of the legal matter. The court will generally not grant a dismissal if another forum is inappropriate or if there is no other forum available. Factors that the court will consider in deciding whether to dismiss a case on this basis ("Gilbert factors") include the location of the events underlying the cause of action, the residence of the parties to the action, the location of evidence and witnesses, the burden on the court, the familiarity of the forum with the relevant law, and how the dismissal would affect the parties involved. Courts may sometimes attach conditions to the dismissal, such as requiring the defendant to agree to the jurisdiction of the other court.
3. Service of process establishes the jurisdiction of the court over the person. The acceptance of service of process indicates that party to the lawsuit is willing to accept jurisdiction of the court.
4. The concept of statute of limitations refers to the maximum time that can elapse from an event for the filing of a lawsuit. The concept applies in both civil law and criminal law. A defendant in a civil lawsuit or criminal trial may raise the statute of limitations as a defense against an action.
5. Jurisdiction refers to the power of the court. This applies to the person (whether the court has jurisdiction over the person), the subject matter of the proceeding, and the rendering of a particular judgment. For example, a court in the United States does not have jurisdiction over a person in Nigeria who has no connection to the United States (jurisdiction over the person) and a small claims court does not have the authority to review bankruptcy cases (subject matter jurisdiction).
6. The Nuremberg Code provides for the following:

   (a) Voluntary consent is essential.
   (b) The experiment must yield fruitful results for the good of society.
   (c) The experiment should be based on the results of animal experimentation and a knowledge of the natural history of the disease under study to justify performance of the study.
   (d) The experiment should be conducted to avoid all unnecessary physical and mental suffering and injury.
   (e) In general, no experiment should be conducted where there is a priori reason to believe that death or disabling injury will occur.
   (f) Proper precautions must be taken to provide adequate facilities to protect the participant against the risk of injury, disability, or death.
   (g) The experiment may be conducted by only scientifically qualified persons.
   (h) The participant may end the experiment.
   (i) The researcher must be prepared to end the experiment at any time.

   These precepts have given rise to three principles governing the conduct of research with human participants: respect for persons, which encompasses the requirements of autonomy and special protection for vulnerable participants;

beneficence, referring to the maximization of good; and justice, which refers to distributive justice. The concept of beneficence is sometimes further delineated as two principles, that of beneficence and that of nonmaleficence, or the obligation to minimize harm.

7. The Declaration of Helsinki further elaborates on the protections due to and the rights of participants in human experimentation. The initial version of the Declaration distinguished between clinical and nonclinical research.
8. The Council of Organizations for Medical Sciences has promulgated guidelines for the conduct of both biomedical research and epidemiologic research (http://www.cioms.org). These documents specifically address issues that may arise in the context of international research, the protections that should be in place for the research participants, and the ethical obligations of the researchers. Specific attention is paid to issues relating to obtaining voluntary informed consent.
9. Article 7 of the International Covenant on Civil and Political Rights provides: "No one shall be subjected to torture or to cruel, inhuman or degrading treatment or punishment. In particular, no one shall be subjected without his free consent to medical or scientific experimentation."
10. The Universal Declaration of Human Rights provides in Article 5: "No one shall be subjected to torture or to cruel, inhuman or degrading treatment or punishment."
11. A petition for a writ of certiorari is a petition by the losing party in a lawsuit to the United States Supreme Court, asking the Court to review the lower court decision.

Acknowledgements Portions of this chapter have previously appeared in Loue, 1999, 2002.

References

Abdullahi v. Pfizer, Inc., ("Abdullahi I"), 2002 U.S. Dist. LEXIS 17436 (S.D.N.Y., September 17, 2002).

Abdullahi v. Pfizer, Inc., ("Abdullahi II"), 77 Fed. Appx. 48, 2003 U.S. App. LEXIS 20704 (2d Cir. N.Y., October 8, 2003).

Abdullahi v. Pfizer, Inc., ("Abdullahi III"), 2005 U.S. Dist. LEXIS 16126 (S.D.N.Y., August 9, 2005).

Abdullahi v. Pfizer, Inc., ("Abdullahi IV"), 562 F.3d 1163 (2d Cir. 2009).

Abdullahi v. Pfizer, Inc., Adamu v. Pfizer, Inc., Order. Case 1:01-cv-08118-WHP, Document 102, filed February 3, 2011. Pauley, W.H., Judge. (S.D.N.Y.). Retrieved May 13, 2012, from http://freepdfhosting.com/8c846926b7.pdf.

Abend, L. (2011). Pain in Spain: The E. coli outbreak's lousy timing. *Time*, June 2. Retrieved July 8, 2011, from http://www.time.com/printout/0,8816,2075333,00.html.

Adamu v. Pfizer, Inc., 399 F. Supp. 2d 495 (S.D.N.Y. 2005).

Allen v. United States, 588 F. Supp. 247 (d. Utah 1984), *reversed on other grounds*, 816 F.2d 1417 (10th Cir. 1987), *cert. denied*, 484 U.S. 1004 (1988).

Anon. (2011a). E. coli outbreak blamed on Egyptian fenugreek seeds. *The Guardian*. Retrieved May 11, 2012, from http://www.guardian.co.uk/world/2011/jul/05/ecoli-outbreak-egyptian-fenugreek-seeds.

Anon. (2011b). *Spain may sue over cucumber E. coli claim. Public Service Europe*, June 1. Retrieved July 8, 2011, from http://www.publicserviceeurope.com/article/418/spain-may-sue-over-cucumber-e-coli-claim.

Boseley, S., & Smith, D. (2010, December 9). *As doctors fought to save lives, Pfizer flew in drug trial team*. Guardian.co.uk. Retrieved December 1, 2010, from http://www.guardian.co.uk/business/2010/dec/09/doctors-fought-save-lives-pfizer-drug/print.

Council of Organizations for Medical Sciences. (2002). *International ethical guidelines for biomedical research.* Geneva, Switzerland: Author.

Donziger, S. R. (2004). Rainforest Chernobyl: Litigating indigenous rights and the environment in Latin America. *Human Rights Brief, 11*(2), 1–4.

Edwards, J. (2011). *Pfizer bribed Nigerian officials in fatal drug trial, ex-employee claims. CBS MoneyWatch.* Retrieved May 12, 2012, from http://www.cbsnews.com/8301-505123_162-42847372/pfizer-bribed-nigerian-officials-in-fatal-drug-trial-ex-employee-claims/.

Ejembe, C.L., Renne, E.P., & Adamu, H.A. (1998). The politics of the 1996 cerebrospinal meningitis epidemic in Nigeria. *Africa, 68*(1), 118–134.

Federal Ministry of Health. (2001). *Report of the investigation committee on the clinical trial of Trovan by Pfizer, Kano*. Retrieved May 12, 2012, from http://www.washingtonpost.com/wp-srv/world/documents/Clinical_Trial_Report.pdf.

Gordis, L. (1996). *Epidemiology*. Philadelphia, PA: W.B. Saunders Company.

Hill, A. B. (1965). The environment and disease: Association or causation? *Proceedings of the Royal Society of Medicine, 58*, 295–300.

International Covenant on Civil and Political Rights, G.A. res. 2200A (XXI), 21 U.N. GAOR Supp. (No. 16) at 52, U.N. Doc. A/6316 (1966), 999 U.N.T.S. 171, *entered into force* Mar. 23, 1976.

IRIN. (2001, May 28). Nigeria: IRIN focus on worsening epidemics in the north. Retrieved May 12, 2012, from http://www.irinnews.org/Report/21805/NIGERIA-IRIN-Focus-on-worsening-epidemics-in-the-north.

Keeton, W.P., Dobbs, D.B., Keeton, R.E., & Owen, D.G. (1984). *Prosser and Keeton on the law of torts* (5th ed.). St. Paul, MN: West Publishing.

Kleinbaum, D. G., Kupper, L. L., & Morgenstern, H. (1982). *Epidemiologic research: Principles and quantitative methods*. New York: Van Nostrand Reinhold.

Lapeysosonnie, L. (1963). La méningte cérébrospinale en Afrique. *Bulletin of the World Health Organization, 28*, 1–114.

Loue, S. (1999). *Forensic epidemiology: A comprehensive guide for legal and epidemiology professionals*. Carbondale, IL: Southern Illinois University Press.

Loue, S. (2002). *Case studies in forensic epidemiology*. New York: Kluwer Academic.

Macklin, R. (1999). Ethics, epidemiology, and the law: The case of silicone breast implants. *American Journal of Public Health, 89*, 487–489.

Malakoff, D. (2001). Nigerian families sue Pfizer, testing the reach of U.S. law. *Science, 293*(5536), 1742.

Marder v. G.D. Searle and Co., 630 F. Supp. 1087 (D. Md. 1986), *affirmed* 814 F.2d 655 (4th Cir. 1987).

Médecins sans Frontières. (2011). *Press release: Statement: Pfizer falsely claims MSF involvement in the company's unethical 1996 drug trials in Nigeria; Pfizer retracts allegations against MSF*. Retrieved May 13, 2012, from http://www.doctorswithoutborders.org/press/release_print.cfm?id=4941.

Morabia, A. (1991). On the origin of Hill's causal criteria. *Epidemiology, 2*, 367–369.

Nuremberg Code. (1949). *United States v. Brandt, Trials of war criminals before the Nuremberg Military Tribunals under Control Council Law no. 10* (Vol. 2, pp. 181–182). Washington, DC: United States Government Printing Office.

Ojewale, O. (1996). Stemming the tide. *Newswatch, 23*(12), 21–22.

Pfizer. (2007, July). *Summary*. Retrieved May 12, 2012, from http://www.pfizer.com/files/news/trovan_statement_defense_summary.pdf.

Pfizer Inc. v. Abdullahi, 130 S.Ct. 3541 (June 29, 2010).
Pfizer. (n.d.). *Trovan fact sheet*. Retrieved May 12, 2012, from http://www.pfizer.com/files/news/trovan_fact_sheet_final.pdf.
Pleitgen, F., & Hsieh, E. (2011, June 11). *Warning lifted against Spanish cucumbers suspected in E. coli outbreak*. CNN.com. Retrieved May 11, 2012, from http://www.cnn.com/2011/WORLD/europe/06/01/spain.germany.e.coli/index.htm.
Poole, C. (1987). Beyond the confidence interval. *American Journal of Public Health, 77*, 195–199.
Roht, L. H., Selwyn, B. J., Holguin, A. H., & Christensen, B. L. (1982). *Principles of epidemiology: A self-teaching guide*. New York: Academic Press.
Rothman, K. J. (1986). *Modern epidemiology*. Boston, MA: Little, Brown, & Company.
Sartwell, P. E. (1960). On the methodology of investigations of etiologic factors in chronic disease: Further comments. *Journal of Chronic Diseases, 11*, 61–63.
Shuaibu, I. (2011). *Still no compensation for Trovan victims as Pfizer cuts corners*. Retrieved May 12, 2012, from http://www.thisdaylive.com/articles/still-no-compensation-for-trovan-victims-as-pfizer-cuts-corners/101123/.
Silverman, E. (2010a). *Pfizer sued by Nigerians for $384b over Trovan*. Retrieved May 12, 2012, from http://www.pharmalot.com/2010/07/pfizer-sued-by-nigerians-for-384b-over-trovan/.
Silverman, E. (2010b). *Pfizer used dirty tricks in Nigerian settlement/Pharmalot*. Retrieved May 12, 2012, from http://www.pharmalot.com/2010/12/pfizer-used-dirty-tricks-in-nigerian-settlement/.
Silverman, E. (2011). *Former Pfizer doc renews his Trovan allegations/Pharmalot*. Retrieved May 12, 2012, from http://www.pharmalot.com/2011/02/former-pfizer-doc-renews-his-trovan-allegations/.
Smith, D. (2011). *Nigeria: Pfizer pays out to Nigerian families of meningitis drug trial. Child Rights International Network*. Retrieved May 12, 2012, from http://www.crin.org/resources/infodetail.asp?id=25778.
Statement of Defence. (2007). Attorney General of Kano State v. Pfizer International Incorporated et al. High Court of Kano State, Suit No. K/233/2007. Retrieved May 13, 2012, from http://www.pfizer.com/files/news/trovan_litigation_statement_defense.pdf.
Stephens, J. (2000). The body hunters: Where profits and lives hang in balance; Finding an abundance of subjects and lack of oversight abroad, big drug companies test offshore to speed products to market. *Washington post*, December 17. Retrieved May 12, 2012, from http://www.washingtonpost.com/wp-dyn/content/story/2008/10/01/ST2008100101390.html?sid=ST2008100101390.
Susser, M. (1991). What is a cause and how do we know one? A grammar for pragmatic epidemiology. *American Journal of Epidemiology, 133*, 635–648.
In re TMI Litigation Cases Consolidated II, 922 F. Supp. 997 (M.D. PA. 1996).
Universal Declaration of Human Rights. G.A. res. 217A (III), U.N. Doc A/810 at 71 (1948).
Wise, J. (2001). Pfizer accused of testing new drug without ethical approval. *British Medical Journal, 322*(7280), 194.
World Health Organization. (1996). Cerebrospinal meningitis in Africa. *Weekly Epidemiological Record, 71*(12), 89–90.
World Health Organization. (2011a). End of a century-long scourge? *Bulletin of the World Health Organization, 89*(8), 550–551. Retrieved May 12, 2012, from http://www.who.int/bulletin/volumes/89/8/11-020811/en/.
World Health Organization. (2011b). *Meningococcal meningitis: Fact sheet no. 141, December*. Retrieved May 12, 2012, from http://www.who.int/mediacentre/factsheets/fs141/en/index.html.
World Medical Association. (2008). Declaration of Helsinki. (Adopted 1964 by G.A. Res., amended 1975, 1983, 1989, 1996, 2000, 2008). Retrieved May 12, 2012, from http://www.wma.net/en/30publications/10policies/b3/index.html.
Zango v. Pfizer International, Inc., 2001 Suit No. FHC/K/CS/204/2001 (Nigeria).

Chapter 2
The Epidemiologist as an Expert in Litigation

Brandy L. Johnson, Ryan C. Turnage, and Jennifer L. Woulfe

Introduction

A tort is a private or civil wrong or injury for which the court may provide a remedy in the form of an action for damages (Torts, *Black's Law Dictionary*, 1990, p. 1489). Toxic tort litigation involves civil actions asserting demands for damages due to exposure to a chemical substance, emissions, or product that caused physical or psychological harm (Cetrulo, 2011; O'Reilly, 2012). Examples of toxic tort claims include litigation arising out of the malfunctioning of a medical device, the harmful effects of a drug, catastrophic events like the chemical plant explosion in Bhopal, India, and exposure to commercial products like asbestos, products like cigarettes, or toxic substances like pesticides (Cetrulo, 2011).

In litigation involving toxic torts and environmental law, a causal connection between the damages and the alleged exposure must be established or disproved. Typically, expert evidence is necessary to prevail (Bois, 2011f). An expert is often defined as a person who has acquired expertise through knowledge, skill, experience, training, or education.

Epidemiologists are uniquely suited to serve as experts in these types of cases, as they study ways to ascertain and control the causes of disease, trauma, or other health conditions (Buncher, 2012a). Epidemiological testimony can play a role in several legal contexts, but the utilization of epidemiology to prove, or disprove, a casual connection between an exposure and a disease or injury can result in litigation that is both complex and controversial (Black, Jacobson, Madeira, & See, 1997). Epidemiological evidence would be probative, for example, in cases where

B.L. Johnson (✉)
Feirich/Mager/Green/Ryan, Carbondale, IL, USA
e-mail: bjohnson@fmgr.com

R.C. Turnage • J.L. Woulfe
Rynearson, Suess, Schnurbusch, & Champion, LLC, St. Louis, MO, USA

S. Loue (ed.), *Forensic Epidemiology in the Global Context*,
DOI 10.1007/978-1-4614-6738-0_2,

there is an alleged causal connection between a chemical exposure and lung cancer or a birth defect and a prescription medication such as Zoloft or Accutane.

This chapter provides an overview of different aspects of the litigation process, the roles of experts in the litigation, and the obligations and duties of such experts. It is beyond the scope of this chapter to address these issues in great depth, and the reader is referred to additional sources for a more detailed discussion. Additionally, as it is not possible address the laws of every country, this chapter focuses on the laws of the United States.

Types of Experts

Categorizations of Experts

In litigation, experts are hired for two basic functions: (1) a scientific function and (2) a forensic function (Sapir, 2007). When fulfilling the scientific function, the expert is needed to collect information/evidence, conduct testing, evaluate evidence, form opinions, offer advice, and help the attorney to understand the scientific elements of the case (Sapir, 2007). On the other hand, when the expert is fulfilling the forensic role, he or she is responsible for communicating his or her opinions, and the basis for them, to the finder of fact (the jury or judge, depending on the specific case) in a manner that is understandable (Sapir, 2007).

Whether a consulting expert or a testifying expert, the professional can be further categorized by whether he or she is a generalist or specialist. A generalist is someone who uses his or her knowledge to form opinions and testify in a wide range of cases (Harrell, 1993). An engineer, for example, who is a "forensic engineer" will appear as an expert in virtually any type of product case (Harrell, 1993). A specialist, conversely, is a professional that is much more qualified in his or her particular area of expertise and, often, serves as an expert in only specific types of cases (Harrell, 1993).

A generalist may be seen as a professional witness and face the danger of being viewed as a hired gun and, as a result, given less credibility (Jones, 2012). However, generalists can be less expensive, familiar with legal terminology, and savvy witnesses (Harrell, 1993). Specialists may have more credibility, in-depth knowledge on the subject at issue, and prove a compelling witness (Jones, 2012). As specialists do not regularly serve as experts, they may require more time in preparation, have a lack of understanding of the legal context of his or her opinions, and be more likely to offer conflicting inconsistent testimony (Harrell, 1993).

Finally, testifying experts will be recognized as either retained or non-retained witnesses. Most experts will be deemed retained and will have been hired by one of the parties for the purpose of litigation. At times, though, an expert may be non-retained. Such experts will often be an employee of one of the parties. If a pharmaceutical company were being sued, one of its scientists may serve as a non-retained expert. The rules of civil procedure (rules that govern how trials and the processes leading up to them are to be conducted) in many jurisdictions will set forth different discovery requirements for retained and non-retained experts.

When Are Experts Retained and What Can They Do for an Attorney?

When an expert is retained may depend on various factors, including the type of expert and the purpose the expert will serve in the litigation. However, when possible, parties to litigation will often want to hire their primary experts as early in the cases as possible. This will allow the attorneys to benefit from the professionals' expertise to the fullest extent possible.

For the plaintiff's attorney, retaining an expert before the suit is even filed permits the attorney to discuss causation with the expert, formulate theories of liability, and/or the specific claims that could be exerted (Bois, 2011a, 2011c; Halebian & Scott, 2011). An epidemiologist can assist the plaintiff's attorney in ascertaining whether there is a relationship between a medical condition and the exposure at issue (Buncher, 2012b). The defendant's attorney, in turn, may utilize an expert early in the litigation to help understand and assess the plaintiff's allegations and theories of liability (Bois, 2011b, 2011c; Halebian & Scott, 2012). An expert can also assist the defendant's attorney in determining viable defenses and/or affirmative defenses that can be asserted (Bois, 2011b, 2011c).

Experts for both the plaintiff and the defendant often continue to assist the attorneys throughout the litigation. While the expert may be asked to review evidence/data, conduct tests, and offer opinions on specific issues in the case, they can also of be of great assistance to the attorney throughout the discovery process. Experts with specialized knowledge in a particular field are in a unique position to help attorneys determine the types of information, documents, data, and items that should be requested from the opposing counsel (Halebian & Scott, 2012).

Additionally, experts can be used to help the attorney determine when the development of the case would benefit from obtaining the services of other experts and/or information, data, or documents from third parties (Halebian & Scott, 2012). The experts can be relied upon to offer recommendations with regard to what specific types of additional expertise, studies, data, or third party services/information would be beneficial. As an example, an epidemiologist who is assisting an attorney to better understand the results of clinical trials conducted by a pharmaceutical company to investigate the efficacy of a new drug might suggest to the attorney that he or she also consult with a pharmacologist to better understand the specific mechanism underlying the use of that drug.

It should be noted the role the expert will play in the litigation may be dependent upon whether they are a consulting or testifying expert. The consulting expert will play more of a role in helping the attorneys understand the evidence, develop factual and legal theories, and develop strategy (Halebian & Scott, 2011). In environmental or toxic tort litigation, consulting experts are often asked to evaluate sensitive data, perform experiments, participate in strategy sessions, assist in developing the scope of the work for testifying experts, and even manage other experts involved in the litigation (Bois, 2011d). The consulting expert's identity and participation does not usually have to be disclosed to opposing counsel and, therefore, he or she can be utilized behind the scenes in an advisory capacity (Halebian & Scott, 2012).

The testifying expert, on the other hand, may perform some of the services for the attorney discussed above, but his or her primary purpose is to offer expert testimony at trial (Halebian & Scott, 2011). As a result, it is important that the testifying expert ensure they have a firm understanding of the evidence, speak plainly to a jury, and appear authoritative and, at the same time, likeable. Further, testifying experts need to invest time into ensuring they present with an even temperament and good demeanor (Jones, 2012).

The Litigation of a Case

Litigation begins before a suit is actually filed. Investigation must be done and experts may be involved in this process. However, once a case has been filed, the parties generally begin the discovery phase. During this phase, each side to the litigation attempts to "discover" facts, documents, and other pieces of evidence held by the other side that may be relevant or helpful to the preparation of its own case. Attorneys will also have the opportunity to file motions, in which they seek a court's ruling on specifically identified issues prior to proceeding to trial. One such motion, known as a *Daubert* motion in limine (discussed in greater detail later in this chapter), permits a party to the litigation to question the legal reliability of scientific evidence that is to be presented. While some motions that are filed may be dispositive of the case, a case that survives them will ultimately be tried. In complex litigation, such as toxic torts, products liability, and environmental cases, the assistance of experts will be necessary in both the discovery and trial phases of the case.

Discovery

Interrogatories and Requests for Production. Interrogatories are a set or series of written questions that, as part of the discovery process, are exchanged between parties [the plaintiff(s) and the defendant(s)] to litigation or for a witness to the case (Interrogatories, *Black's Law Dictionary*, 1990, p. 819). The answers to the interrogatories are usually given under oath, as the person answering the questions signs a sworn statement that the answers are true.

Interrogatories can address any matter that is discoverable. This would exclude matters that are protected by a privilege, such as the attorney–client privilege or the work product doctrine, and issues that are not relevant to the claims and defenses of any party. The attorney–client privilege refers to the confidential nature of communications between an attorney and his or her clients that were made for the purpose of furnishing or obtaining legal advice or assistance (Attorney–Client Privilege, *Black's Law Dictionary*, 1990, p. 129). The work product doctrine refers to a legal rule, under which, any notes, working papers, memoranda, certain correspondence, and similar materials that are prepared in anticipation of litigation are protected from disclosure in discovery (Work Product Rule, *Black's Law Dictionary*, 1990, p. 1606). Typically, the requests must be reasonably calculated to lead to the discovery of admissible evidence (Federal Rules of Civil Procedure, 2010a). The purpose of interrogatories is to both limit and refine the controversies and issues in the pending litigation. Many jurisdictions limit the number of interrogatories that can be compounded upon the opposing party. The Federal Rules of Civil Procedure, for example, state the following:

(1) *Number*. Unless otherwise stipulated or ordered by the court, a party may serve on any other party no more than 25 written interrogatories, including all discrete subparts. Leave to serve additional interrogatories may be granted to the extent consistent with Rule 26(b)(2).
(2) *Scope*. An interrogatory may relate to any matter that may be inquired into under Rule 26(b). An interrogatory is not objectionable merely because it asks for an opinion or contention that relates to fact or the application of law to fact, but the court may order that the interrogatory need not be answered until designated discovery is complete, or until a pretrial conference or some other time (Federal Rules of Civil Procedure, 2010b).

The limitation on the number of questions helps prevent parties from overwhelming the opposing party with an overly burdensome number of requests for information.

Interrogatories will explore the opposing party's claims and defenses and attempt to obtain information that will help determine the strengths and/or weaknesses of the other party's case. Interrogatories can help identify possible lay witnesses (non-expert), individuals with information, studies performed, and relevant documents like medical records. The answers to interrogatories can, at times, be utilized to strengthen the opposing counsel's case.

Requests for Production of Documents are another discovery device that is utilized in conjunction with interrogatories. Where interrogatories request answers, a Request for Production of Documents seeks documents related to the case. As with interrogatories, the use of a Request for Production of Documents is governed by the rules of civil procedure. The Federal Rules of Civil Procedure indicate the following:

(a) In General. A party may serve on any other party a request within the scope of Rule 26(b):

    (1) To produce and permit the requesting party or its representative to inspect, copy, test, or sample the following items in the responding party's possession, custody, or control:

(A) Any designated documents or electronically stored information—including writings, drawings, graphs, charts, photographs, sound recordings, images, and other data or data compilations—stored in any medium from which information can be obtained either directly or, if necessary, after translation by the responding party into a reasonably usable form; or
(B) Any designated tangible things; or

(2) To permit entry onto designated land or other property possessed or controlled by the responding party, so that the requesting party may inspect, measure, survey, photograph, test, or sample the property or any designated object or operation on it.

(b) Procedure.

(1) *Contents of the Request*. The request:

(A) Must describe with reasonable particularity each item or category of items to be inspected;
(B) Must specify a reasonable time, place, and manner for the inspection and for performing the related acts; and
(C) May specify the form or forms in which electronically stored information is to be produced (Federal Rules of Civil Procedure, 2010c).

When served with a Request for the Production of Documents, the receiving party must find all the requested documents and/or evidence for disclosure to the opposing party. The responding party, however, does not have produce documents protected by privilege or that is not relevant to the litigation. Again, the Requests must be reasonably calculated to lead to the discovery of admissible evidence.

The Answers and Responses to interrogatories and Requests for Production can be utilized at trial subject to the rules of evidence applicable to the jurisdiction. The Answers and Responses can be used to impeach (discredit) witnesses. Thus, experts should be aware of this possibility and try to prevent the provision of any contradictory information that the opposing counsel can present for impeachment purposes at trial. If, during the discovery process, any changes in the expert's findings and/or opinions occur, supplemental reports should be prepared and disclosed.

Additionally, a party can obtain information concerning the opposing party's expert and his or her opinions through interrogatories. An example of an interrogatory addressing expert witnesses includes the following:

Interrogatory: State the name and address of each person Defendant expects to call as an expert witness at trial and state the general nature of the subject matter on which the expert is expected to testify.

Interrogatory: State the name and address of each person Defendant expects to call as a non-retained expert witness at trial and state the general nature of the subject matter on which the person is expected to testify.

Similarly, Requests for Production of Documents will seek documents related to the party's expert. By way of illustration, a Request for Production of Documents may include statements such as the following:

Request: All documents, evidence, and/or photographs identified in Defendant's Answers to Interrogatories.

Request: All documents and materials furnished, given, or provided to Plaintiff or on behalf of the Plaintiff to any expert that Plaintiff plans to call at trial.

Request: Any and all written reports of each and every expert witness Plaintiff plans to call at trial.

Request: Any and all documents reviewed and/or relied on by each and every expert witness Plaintiff plans to call at trial.

Request: A current curriculum vitae for each and every expert witness Plaintiff plans to call at trial.

Both consulting and testifying experts are often utilized in the preparation of interrogatories and Request for Production of Documents. Experts, because of their specialized knowledge, can be of great assistance to attorneys while formulating the wording of discovery requests when highly technical information is being sought or the phrasing of the request could have an effect on what the opposing party has to disclose. An epidemiologist would be extremely helpful to an attorney in the drafting of questions that refer to particular control measures used or rejected by the opposing party (Danner & Varn, 1994). Likewise, the epidemiologist's knowledge of the process used to generate use, store, and dispose of substances would assist the attorney in identifying information and documents to be requested (Danner & Varn, 1994).

An expert, similarly, can help the attorney that retained him/her understand the responses, documents, data, information, and other evidence disclosed by the opposing party. This would include the opposing party's expert's report, methodology, and conclusions. Epidemiologists, for example, could be asked to point out the limitations, defects, and alerting subtle characteristics of a study being relied upon by the opposing side and other experts (Buncher, 2012b).

Depositions. Depositions are another tool used during the discovery phase of litigation. Depositions are proceedings during which a witness or party to litigation is questioned orally by the attorneys involved in the case (Deposition, *Black's Law Dictionary*, 1990, p. 440). Depositions are taken outside of the courtroom, usually in the office of the attorney or expert, and are under oath. The deposition will be attended by a court reporter who will transcribe, word for word, the testimony of the deponent. Some depositions may be recorded so the video can be viewed at a later date or presented at trial. Additionally, depositions can include written questions that have been submitted for the deponent to answer.

As with other discovery tools, the rules for depositions vary by jurisdiction. Illinois, for example, provides for both discovery and evidence depositions. Illinois Rule of Civil Procedure 202 provides the following:

> Any party may take the testimony of any party or person by deposition upon oral examination or written questions for the purpose of discovery or for use as evidence in the action. The notice, order, or stipulation to take a deposition shall specify whether the deposition is to be a discovery deposition or an evidence deposition. In the absence of specification a deposition is a discovery deposition only. If both discovery and evidence depositions are desired of the same witness they shall be taken separately, unless the parties stipulate otherwise or the court orders otherwise upon notice and motion. If the evidence deposition of

> a witness is to be taken within 21 days of trial, a discovery deposition is not permitted unless the parties stipulate otherwise or the court orders otherwise upon notice and motion (Illinois Rules of Civil Procedure, 2006).

Thus, the designation of the type of deposition being taken determines how it can be used in an Illinois court. Other jurisdictions, including the federal court, do not make a distinction between discovery and evidence depositions.

Generally, only the parties, testifying experts and other key witnesses will be deposed. When an expert is deposed, he or she should expect to be questioned about his or her qualifications, education, training, practice, publications, studies, and prior service as an expert (Halebian & Scott, 2011). He or she will be questioned concerning the materials he or she reviewed or studies performed as part of the formation of his or her opinions. The expert's report will be reviewed and the results, findings, methodology used, and foundation for his or her opinions will be explained and challenged. The opposing counsel will take the deposition as an opportunity to ascertain as fully as possible the expert's opinion, the scope of the opinion, the reasons/basis of the opinion, and what concessions and admissions the expert is willing to endorse (Halebian & Scott, 2012).

In preparing for his or her deposition, the expert should review his or her file and relevant publications, literature, and studies (Halebian & Scott, 2011). This is especially true of adverse documents and information. The opposing party's expert's report and, if he or she has been deposed, the transcript of the proceeding should also be reviewed. The expert's preparation should include a review of subjects such as (1) the names and identities of who he or she talked to, other than the attorney, and what was said; (2) meetings, other than those with the attorney, the expert attended and what was reviewed; (3) the documents reviewed prior to the deposition; (4) prior testimony in other cases and the substance of it; and (5) the extent of the expert's involvement in the case (Danner & Varn, 1994).

The expert should be as honest as possible during the deposition. An expert's deposition may come back to haunt him or her if inconsistent testimony is offered at trial. When an expert testifies in a manner that contradicts or is inconsistent with his or her deposition testimony, opposing counsel will seek to attack the credibility of the expert and impeach him or her with the deposition testimony. This is, in essence, a question of "Are you lying now or were you lying then?"

Due to the importance of the expert's deposition's testimony, experts should consider insisting on the ability to review the deposition transcript. In most jurisdictions, a deponent at the end of the deposition is given the option of waiving signature or reviewing the deposition and then signing with any corrections noted on a corrections sheet (i.e., errata sheet) (Harrell, 1993). Waiving signature is a common practice. However, reviewing the transcript permits experts to correct typographical mistakes. While such errors do not make a lot of difference in most cases, the correction of the use of the word Toradol, for instance, when the expert said Tramadol could ultimately make a difference in a case.

Another consideration is how the expert will appear at the deposition. One of the purposes of deposing an expert is to assess how the expert would present as a witness at trial. Thus, it is important that the expert present his or her testimony much as if he or she were sitting before the jury. The expert should be aware of his or her own temperament, appearance, demeanor, likeability, and ability to relate to his or her audience. The expert should appear professional, but remember ego has no real place in the litigation (Kolezynski, 1997). If the expert does not present well during the deposition, the attorney may be forced to consider settlement or refrain from calling the expert at trial. Conversely, a strong performance by an expert may cause the opposing counsel to more seriously consider what they would be willing to pay/accept to settle the case (Halebian & Scott, 2011).

Experts should also be aware of how they present during the deposition, as the deposition may be used at trial in lieu of live testimony. This occurs especially when the expert will be unavailable for trial. Thus, the testimony of an epidemiologist who serves as an expert in a case in Missouri may be offered through his deposition due to the fact he resides in Hawaii. Under such circumstances the deposition testimony, or a portion of it, may be read into the record before the jury at trial. It is also not uncommon for the expert's deposition to be recorded and the video shown at trial when the expert is not going to testify live. Whenever possible, however, experts should be prepared to testify live at trial. A live appearance helps the expert to better develop that essential connection to the jury. Further, attorneys who simply have the deposition read into the record risk boring the jury and/or the jury not fully comprehending the expert's opinions. By testifying live, the expert is in a better position to keep the jury engaged and ensure that his or her opinions and findings are effectively communicated.

The involvement of experts in depositions is not limited to the role of deponent. Consulting and testifying experts can also play a role in preparing for deposition. Experts are in a superior position to assess the qualification of the opposing parties' expert, determine his or her reputation in the professional's field, and acquire studies and publications in which he or she was involved (Danner & Varn, 1994). This information and material can be used to prepare for the opposing expert's deposition (Danner & Varn, 1994).

Attorneys also rely on experts to aid in compose deposition questions (Bois, 2011a; Halebian & Scott, 2012). An expert's familiarity with specific aspects of their field places them in a superior position to advise an attorney about the types of information each witness may possess. The retaining attorney may even request an expert attend the depositions of other witnesses and experts (Halebian & Scott, 2012). By doing so, the expert would be on hand to explain, when necessary, the deponent's responses, identify obscure implications of the testimony, the validity of the methodology or process being described, and advise on follow-up questions.

Trial

At a trial, each party has the opportunity to present its witnesses and evidence. The opposing party is also given the opportunity to challenge the witnesses and evidence.

Expert evidence and its presentation to the trier of fact can make or break a case and, therefore, it is important the expert be prepared for both direct examination and cross-examination.

Serving as an Expert at Trial. Expert testimony at trial is extremely vital to any lawsuit involving injuries/diseases and the value of such testimony to establish, or disprove, causation cannot be overstated. Experts must remain mindful that jurors often anticipate expert testimony to be complicated and confusing. At trial, any expert's ultimate job is to simplify complicated evidence and captivate the jury. In jury trials, the jury is often described as the "factfinder." Judges are required to decide which matters of law are to be presented to a jury. The jury, in turn, determines which facts are credible, applies these facts to the law, and then issues a verdict. Obviously, experts have a huge impact on persuading the "factfinder" and influencing the verdict. For this reason, it is crucial that the experts, their findings, and their opinions appear credible.

Consideration of the reaction of juries to expert testimony has led to the identification of five areas of concern (Mauet, 2010). These areas of concern include the following:

1. Juror assumption that expert testimony is complicated and confusing
2. Juror expectation that expert testimony will be boring
3. Doubts as to whether the expert is really an expert
4. Questions as to whether the expert is biased
5. Juror belief that the expert will be condescending

Mauet (2010) advises that experts must keep these concerns in mind while preparing for direct and cross-examination at trial. The ability to balance these concerns with the scientific and medical aspects of their testimony is a hallmark of efficient expert testimony. Epidemiological expert testimony should focus on establishing, or refuting, an association between an agent and injury/disease, addressing sources of error in the epidemiological study, and addressing the relationship between the agent and the disease (Green, Freedman, & Gordis, 2011).

Direct Examination. Direct examination is the expert's opportunity to serve his or her primary function in the trial. The attorney who has retained the expert will have an opportunity to ask the expert a series of questions to explain the expert's findings to the jury. The expert's role as a witness is akin to any witness at a trial: to assist the jury by showcasing the "who, what, where, why, and when" through testimony. The use of technical language is a common pitfall in expert testimony. An effective expert avoids this language, as it will not impress the jury (Bain & Myer, 2010). Despite television's over-sensationalism of jury trials, jurors are often bored during all aspects of the trial. Be aware that jurors typically remain seated for long periods of time throughout a trial with occasional short breaks. Furthermore, jurors are not permitted to discuss the trial until after closing arguments and all evidence has been submitted. All of these conditions contribute to a jury's possible short attention span.

Experts should intend to captivate the jury with credible and verifiable testimony. Techniques such as voice inflection and eye contact are crucial to captivating testimony. For instance, after the attorney asks a question on direct examination, the expert witness should always make eye contact with the jurors during the answer. Effective testimony should appear conversational, although it will also resemble a soliloquy (Bain & Myer, 2010). The expert is essentially playing a featured role in a scene and the jury serves as the audience (Bain & Myer, 2010). The jury should not be distracted by the attorney asking questions, objections by the opposing attorney, or the judge.

First, experts must be aware of any pretrial rulings that may limit the scope of their testimony. Prior to the start of the trial and, in some instances, during the trial, attorneys have an opportunity to argue for motions in limine. The term "limine" is Latin for "at the threshold" (Limine, *Black's Law Dictionary*, 1990, p. 787) For instance, a granted motion in limine may limit an epidemiological expert's testimony to only general causation and bar testimony on specific causation. General causation covers whether the specified exposure is capable of causing the alleged disease outcome. The attorney who has retained the expert should prepare the expert prior to his or her testimony to avoid violating a motion in limine ruling.

Generally, the attorney "directing" the witness will ask open ended questions, such as "What were the results of your findings?" Obviously, there are endless answers to this question, but a well-prepared expert will narrow this answer to a short response outlining the expert's conclusions (Hennet, 2010). A skilled attorney will then ask narrower questions to discuss the expert's process in obtaining these findings. In discussing the process, the expert will need to explain whether the process is generally accepted in his or her field of study. For example, an epidemiologist would explain that the process used is generally accepted in the field of epidemiological studies.

Most attorneys, regardless of their experience level, will prepare an outline for an expert's direct examination. The outline's format and contents will vary among attorneys, but it will serve as a roadmap for the expert's testimony. A typical outline will begin with establishing the expert's credibility with the jury. This includes the expert's educational background, employment history, titles of relevant publications, relevant lecture topics, and any other generally relevant contributions the expert has made to the particular field (Bain & Myer, 2010). The outline will then narrow the testimony to briefly define the expert's field, such as epidemiology, and apply that definition to the expert's involvement in the case (Bain & Myer, 2010).

The expert can keep the jury engaged during this portion by continuing to use simple language, being personable, and remembering that this is the expert's introduction to the jury. The expert's first impression with the jury is extremely important and the expert must be personalized and not likened to words in a textbook. For instance, the expert may briefly explain how and why he or she became interested in epidemiology. An expert's credentials may intimidate the jury, so the expert must come across as a human being who is approachable and relatable rather than just an expensive mouthpiece who rattles off mundane scientific jargon. Finally, the expert's introduction should also include a highlight of what the expert will discuss with the jury that day. This will explain the parameters of the testimony and inform the jury of what the expert did or did not do. This, for example, would permit the jury to know early on that an epidemiologist did not treat the Plaintiff, but that his or her practices are accepted as a credible method to evaluate the effects of disease.

The introductory portion of the expert's testimony may also address any potential bias that is assumed because the expert receives compensation. The opposing counsel may attempt to portray the expert as biased, but a skilled attorney will address compensation during the direct examination to overcome this hurdle. Other methods the opposing attorney will generally use to show bias are to establish whether the expert consistently provides consultation for Plaintiffs or Defendants. No matter what the expert's consulting history shows, the expert's testimony should appear as objective and supported by verifiable facts and practices in their field (Hennet, 2010). In fact, an expert with vast consulting experience will want to showcase to the jury that courts have accepted his or her expertise and he or she is a reliable source of information.

When describing his or her actual experience, the expert should have accurate numbers on how long he or she has researched the particular injury/disease at issue. If he or she is a treating physician, an estimate of the number of patients he or she has treated and whether he or she has researched other similar injuries/diseases will aid the jury. Likewise, the number of publications he or she has written, lectures he or she has given, and the amount of times he or she has been qualified as an expert in court for the injury/disease at issue, or other related diseases, should be discussed. The expert should be aware that one of the attorney's main goals in this preliminary phase of the direct examination is to establish the expert's credibility with the jury. After personalizing the expert and identifying the expert's training and experience, the expert will discuss his or her opinions regarding the case. Some jurisdictions will require the expert's opinion to be expressed to a "reasonable degree of medical or scientific certainty" (Mauet, 2010). In these jurisdictions, the expert's testimony can be objected to as speculative. In general, a speculation objection seeks to bar unsupported factual or conclusive statements. The expert, like any witness, can always avoid the speculation objection by providing facts and opinions as support for his or her statements. As a general practice, the expert's testimony should *always* be supported by a "reasonable degree of medical or scientific certainty" when possible (Bain & Myer, 2010). The following is an example of how this testimony may be elicited on direct examination.

Question: Dr. Taylor, do you have an opinion regarding the affects of XYZ tobacco products on a smoker with a 20-year smoking history?
Answer : Yes.
Question: Is your opinion regarding these affects to a reasonable degree of medical certainty?
Answer : Yes.
Question: Please tell the jury your opinion.
Answer : My opinion is that there is a causal connection between John Doe's lung cancer and his history of using XYZ tobacco products.

Note in the above example, the attorney asked the witness to address the jury. This method of direct examination encourages the witnesses to include the jury in the testimony since they are the primary audience and should remain as the focus.

Even if the attorney's questions do not include the magic language, "to a reasonable degree of medical or scientific certainty," the expert should volunteer this information when it is true to maintain credibility with the jury. Questions concerning the basis of the opinion can then follow.

While supporting his or her findings through opinion or otherwise, as allowed by Rule 702, the expert should use firm and certain terminology, such as "I concluded" or "the findings confirmed/revealed" instead of "I thought." Here is another example:

Question: Dr. Taylor, what did you conclude about the effects of exposure to XYZ tobacco products when comparing individuals in the exposed group and unexposed group?

Answer : I concluded that the exposed group was more likely to develop lung cancer and adverse respiratory symptoms than was the unexposed group. The results and findings from my various studies confirm this conclusion.

There a few things to note in this example. The expert has now introduced the jury to his or her opinion, without using the word "opinion" and also introduced the jury to some of his or her methods that support his or her opinion. The attorney will now have the expert explain to the jury the purpose of comparing an exposed group and an unexposed group and the benefits of various study designs. Remember, the expert's duty is to fascinate the jury with process and introduce the jury to a simplistic explanation of this process (Mauet, 2010).

Demonstrative exhibits are wonderful tools that revive a bored jury and connect the expert's findings with a visual stimulant (Kolezynski, 1997). Since epidemiological experts deal with statistical data, graphs and charts are highly appropriate and effective. When possible, the expert's visual aids should be enlarged and important distinctions should be in color. For instance, a chart showing results from an exposed group and a nonexposed group should be color-coded between all differences between each group, especially in the case of stark differences and disparities between the groups. The demonstrative visual aid should be placed either on an easel in front of the jury or on a screen in more modern courtrooms. During preparation, the expert should practice with the visual aid in the same format that it will be shown to the jury. An effective expert will not distract the jury with technological errors in operating the courtroom's machines or easel. Remember, the expert must maintain credibility with the jury. If a technical difficulty occurs, the attorney directing the expert should either request a brief recess or be prepared to use an easel with enlarged exhibits.

When it is applicable and the court permits the witness to move around the courtroom, the expert should leave the witness stand and interactively reveal his or her findings while using the exhibit. The witness' movement will engage the jury, but the expert must not become so distracting or animated that his or her credibility suffers.

After briefly highlighting the conclusions, the expert will discuss different sources that have contributed to the conclusion. At this point, the expert is showing the jury why her conclusions are reliable. This testimony can include an explanation of what epidemiological studies were performed and whether other colleagues in that epidemiological field of study use those methods. The expert's credibility is enhanced because the testimony is verified by accepted scientific and medical sources of information and methods that led to this information.

For instance:

Question: Dr. Taylor, what sources of information assisted you in developing your conclusions on the effects of XYZ tobacco products?

Answer : I used several sources of information. I relied on cohort studies that monitored exposure to XYZ tobacco products for 20 years and compared individuals who were exposed to tobacco products for varying lengths of time and individuals who were never exposed to tobacco products. I also measured the association between XYZ tobacco products and lung cancer by calculating the relative risk.

Question: Dr. Taylor, explain to the jury what you mean by relative risk.

Answer : Sure. Relative risk is a ratio we use in my field of study. We determine the number of new lung cancer cases that arise in an exposed population in a given period of time and then divide that by the number of new lung cancer cases that arise in an unexposed population in the same given period of time. This ratio is used by epidemiologists to assess the relationship between XYZ tobacco and lung cancer.

Question: Is this method generally used by epidemiologists when evaluating the cause of lung cancer in our population?

Answer : Yes.

Question: Was this information adequate to evaluate the causal relationship between XYZ tobacco products and lung cancer to a reasonable degree of medical or scientific certainty?

Answer : Yes.

Question: Was there any additional information you needed to assist you in evaluating the relationship between XYZ tobacco and lung cancer?

Answer : The computation of this relative risk ratio is used to determine the strength of a causal relationship. I also look at the number of individuals that participate in each study, which allows me to assess whether the relationship between tobacco products and lung cancer is statistically significant; whether the findings are consistent across studies; whether individuals' tobacco exposure preceded their development of lung cancer, and whether there is a plausible biological explanation for a causal relationship between lung cancer and prior exposure to tobacco products.

When discussing mathematical formulas and calculations like relative risk or other methods, a visual aid will be extremely effective in teaching the jury about the expert's process.

Generally, experts are also allowed to obtain second opinions from their colleagues and also rely on learned treatises to verify their findings. In some instances, a young and inexperienced expert can avoid the opposing counsel's attack by relying on an older, well-respected and heavily relied upon learned treatise.

Direct examination of any type of expert, whether epidemiological or otherwise, is a vast topic that can be exhaustively covered. The expert should keep these goals in mind when preparing to give expert testimony. First, remain as an effective communicator. Do not ponder or narrate when answering questions. Keep your answers to roughly 12–15 seconds when explaining a concept. Avoid technical terms, but use simple and vivid language with common analogies, metaphors, and examples that will appeal to any juror regardless of their background (Kolezynski, 1997). Overall, remember that epidemiological experts are qualified witnesses and are essential to establishing, or disproving, a causal relationship between the injury/disease and the exposure.

Cross-Examination. While direct examination is the opportunity for the expert witness to showcase to the jury the expert's opinions and findings, cross-examination is an opportunity for the opponent to attack the expert's direct examination testimony. While attorneys are typically uninitiated to the field of epidemiology, many attorneys prepare for expert witness cross-examination through consulting their expert, reading appropriate epidemiological literature, copies of the opposing directing expert's publications, the expert's prior testimony, and the expert's curriculum vitae or resume (Bain & Myer, 2010). Experts should be aware that attorneys will attempt to research all publications to find adverse information and the expert should be prepared to discredit, distinguish, or counter the adverse information (Bain & Myer, 2010).

The crossing attorney's primary goals are to elicit favorable testimony and somehow impeach the expert by showing that the expert is not qualified or is biased (Bain & Myer, 2010). The expert's goals are the same as those set for direct examination. The witness must appear credible, honest, forthcoming, and qualified. This is achieved by remaining calm when the expert's findings and direct examination testimony is challenged. An angry, rattled, and emotional expert will not maintain credibility and will appear as if he or she is hiding something from the jury (Bain & Myer, 2010). As a general note, the expert should remain pleasant and polite throughout the trial and, especially during cross-examination, remember the questioning is a continuation of the direct examination and the jury is intently listening (Bain & Myer, 2010).

Attorneys are trained to maintain control over the witness on cross-examination and attempt to only elicit points that are favorable to their client (Bain & Myer, 2010). The expert witness on cross-examination must know that the directing attorney will have a second opportunity to repair any damage from the cross examination.

An expert's preparation for cross-examination must include reviewing the opposition's deposition, expert reports, the findings of other experts, and adverse publications. The attorney retaining the expert should provide the expert with the deposition testimony, or a summary of the deposition, expert reports, and other sources of information that support his or her testimony. Likewise, the expert should be aware that the cross-examining attorney's expert will have likely reviewed the expert's deposition testimony from the same case, other cases where he or she testified as an expert, and other relevant materials.

The expert should not be surprised if the crossing attorney directly interrogates him or her on changes between the trial testimony and his or her deposition testimony. For this reason, cross-examination preparation and all general trial preparation must include review of the expert's deposition testimony from the same case. Depositions are sworn testimony and, if an expert's trial testimony deviates from the deposition, then the expert will appear as lacking credibility. At the expert's deposition, the opposition will likely ask the expert to disclose all sources that aided in the formation of his or her conclusions (Bain & Myer, 2010). If the expert discloses new sources that should have been disclosed at the deposition, this will also affect the expert's credibility. All potential for conflicting testimony must be discussed with the directing attorney prior to the trial and addressed on direct examination. When the crossing attorney points out new information during his or her examination, the jury may feel insulted and misled because the expert did not disclose the new information during the direct examination. As an expert in the particular epidemiological field, the expert should be well aware of weak points in her arguments. These weak points should also be addressed during the direct examination in conjunction with all of the evidence that supports the expert's conclusions. The danger of introducing this evidence on cross examination gives the opposition an opportunity to combine all of the harmful testimony in one package for the jury's consideration. If the jury has previously heard the weak points, the blow of the opposition's questions on the weak points is greatly diminished.

Just as the directing attorney may use an outline, it is not uncommon for the crossing attorney to also develop an outline. First, the opposition may attempt to attack the expert's qualifications, including his or her experience, training, and consulting background. For instance, if the epidemiological expert has more experience as a treating physician than researching public health and the cause of diseases in populations, then the crossing attorney will attempt to point this out to the jury. In some instances, a treating expert is more beneficial than an academic expert. If the expert is attacked on this issue, the expert merely needs to rely on the experience and training that was utilized to qualify him or her as an expert to testify before the court. For example:

Question: Dr. Taylor, you're a physician at Green Hospital, correct?
Answer : Yes.
Question: And you have not published any articles on the causal connection between tobacco products and stimulants in the past 10 years since you obtained your degree, correct?
Answer : Yes.

While it is obvious the cross-examiner is attempting to attack the expert's credentials and qualification to testify on this topic, the expert must truthfully answer the question and expect the direct examiner to reestablish any credibility that has been lost with the jury.

Another common attack during cross examination is to expose any potential expert bias (Bain & Myer, 2010). This concept was briefly discussed in the section on direct examination. The expert should recall that during the discovery process prior to trial, the expert may, depending on the jurisdiction, be required to provide a written report detailing every time the expert testified in a trial or deposition in the past. In federal court, for instance, the expert will need to disclose every time he or she has testified in a trial or deposition during the prior 4 years (Federal Rules of Civil Procedure, 2010a). This information should include whether the expert has testified for Defendants or Plaintiffs. If the expert has consistently testified for one side, then the cross-examining attorney will address this to show bias from the expert. Nevertheless, the expert will be rehabilitated by the directing attorney and should not overreact to this tactic. If the expert consistently provides consulting services for one side, then the expert can appear as having specialized knowledge in establishing his or her conclusions.

Bias may also appear if the expert's prior writings in publications were written solely for defense counsel or plaintiff's attorneys. The expert should continue to rely on the empirical and statistical data and other medical and scientific methods that have led him or her to establish an opinion "to a reasonable degree of medical certainty." Naturally, the opposition's experts will have potential biases as well and skilled attorneys will attempt to attack any expert's credibility on these grounds.

The expert must also be aware that the opposing attorney will attempt to uncover any assumptions that were involved in any of the studies utilized. A well-prepared expert should be able to inform the jury that assumptions are a part of studies and are a necessary facet of any scientific method. If the expert must agree that other factors can contribute to the causal relationship between an agent and a disease, then the expert must remain credible and honest. The directing attorney will have an additional opportunity through redirect examination to reestablish the causal connection and the general accepted practices in the studies that contribute to the expert's testimony.

The common theme in providing expert testimony during direct or cross-examination is that the expert witness must be well-prepared (Bain & Myer, 2010). Preparation includes maintaining a working file on the case that tracks the case's development. This file should include the following: all expert depositions that relate to the expert's testimony, expert disclosures under the Federal Rules of Civil Procedure, depositions from the plaintiff and defendant, court rulings limiting testimony and/or epidemiological issues, and any other legal documents the retaining attorney believes is pertinent. This is in conjunction with all documents that support the expert's testimony and documents that an opposing expert may use to refute expert findings and conclusions. The expert should meet with the retaining attorney weeks prior to trial if possible depending on the length of the testimony and rehearse direct examination and cross examination. While the expert does not want to sound too well rehearsed, the expert must develop a good conversational interaction with the retaining attorney to maintain jury captivation. The expert witness must remember that the jury is the target audience and he or she may be the most important witness the jury will encounter.

Qualifying the Expert

Before an individual can testify as an expert in a legal case, he or she must be qualified as an expert. The requirements an individual must meet to be qualified as an expert will vary depending on whether the case is being litigated in state or federal court. The requirements also vary from state to state. The following is a brief discussion of different requirements in both federal and state proceedings.

Codification of Requirements to Qualify an Expert

Federal Requirements. The qualification of experts in federal proceedings is governed by Rule 702 of the Federal Rules of Evidence. Rule 702 states the following:

A witness who is qualified as an expert by knowledge, skill, experience, training, or education may testify in the form of an opinion or otherwise if:

(a) The expert's scientific, technical, or other specialized knowledge will help the trier of fact to understand the evidence or to determine a fact in issue;
(b) The testimony is based on sufficient facts or data;
(c) The testimony is the product of reliable principles and methods; and
(d) The expert has reliably applied the principles and methods to the facts of the case (Federal Rules of Evidence, 2011).

Thus, under the federal rules, an individual must be shown to have gained expertise through knowledge, skill, experience, training, or education. Rule 702 has, however, been interpreted liberally by some federal courts and a broad range of knowledge, skill, and training has been held enough to satisfy the requirements for qualifying as an expert (*Pineda v. Ford Motor Co.*, 2008; Faigman et al., 2011). Rule 702 liberalizes the traditional common law practice of limiting expert testimony to "some science, profession, business or occupation…beyond the ken of the average layman," (McCormick, 1992). Nevertheless, an expert must have such knowledge or experience in his or her field of calling as to make it appear his or her opinions or inferences will probably aid the trier of fact in the search for truth (*U.S. v. Hicks*, 2004).

State Requirements. Each state has its own rules that address the requirements that must be made to qualify as an expert in a legal proceeding. Generally, most states' rules mirror or are similar to the federal rule. The table below shows how various states have formulated their expert requirements (Table 2.1).

Although the above statutes are similar to Federal Rule 702, the statutes can differ slightly in wording or application. For example, Pennsylvania Rule of Evidence 702 limits their rule by adding the language "beyond that possessed by a lay person." (*Commonwealth v. Dunkle*, 1992). In Texas, the courts focus more on the expert's particular skills, experience, and training concerning the specific issue being litigated than under the federal system (Precella & Bailey New, 2009).

An International View. As would be expected, the standard for qualifying an expert varies from jurisdiction to jurisdiction. However, like we see with the numerous different jurisdictions in the United States, the standards utilized in other countries often have similar requirements.

By way of illustration, in Canada, a properly qualified expert is a witness who has particular knowledge thorough study or experience in the matter at issue (*Cleveland v. Hamilton Health Science Corp.*, 2009; *Regina v. Mohan*, 1994). Likewise, in Australia, experts are qualified if they have training or practical experience in an area of knowledge beyond that possessed by the trier of fact, and of apparent assistance to it (Australian Law Reform Commission, n.d.).

Table 2.1 State requirements for reliance on expert witnesses

Alaska Rule of Evidence 702	If scientific, technical, or other specialized knowledge will assist the trier of fact to understand the evidence or to determine a fact in issue, a witness qualified as an expert by knowledge, skill, experience, training, or education, may testify thereto in the form of an opinion or otherwise
Arkansas Rule of Evidence 702	If scientific, technical, or other specialized knowledge will assist the trier of fact to understand the evidence or to determine a fact in issue, a witness qualified as an expert by knowledge, skill, experience, training, or education, may testify thereto in the form of an opinion or otherwise
California Rule of Evidence 720	A person is qualified to testify as an expert if he has special knowledge, skill, experience, training, or education sufficient to qualify him as an expert on the subject to which his testimony relates. Against the objection of a party, such special knowledge, skill, experience, training, or education must be shown before the witness may testify as an expert
Connecticut Code of Evidence 7-2	A witness qualified as an expert by knowledge, skill, experience, training, education or otherwise may testify in the form of an opinion or otherwise concerning scientific, technical or other specialized knowledge, if the testimony will assist the trier of fact in understanding the evidence or in determining a fact in issue
Delaware Uniform Rule of Evidence 702	If scientific, technical or other specialized knowledge will assist the trier of fact to understand the evidence or to determine a fact in issue, a witness qualified as an expert by knowledge, skill, experience, training or education may testify thereto in the form of an opinion or otherwise, if (1) the testimony is based upon sufficient facts or data, (2) the testimony is the product of reliable principles and methods, and (3) the witness has applied the principles and methods reliably to the facts of the case
Florida Statutes 90.702	If scientific, technical, or other specialized knowledge will assist the trier of fact in understanding the evidence or in determining a fact in issue, a witness qualified as an expert by knowledge, skill, experience, training, or education may testify about it in the form of an opinion; however, the opinion is admissible only if it can be applied to evidence at trial
Hawaii Rule of Evidence 702	If scientific, technical, or other specialized knowledge will assist the trier of fact to understand the evidence or to determine a fact in issue, a witness qualified as an expert by knowledge, skill, experience, training, or education may testify thereto in the form of an opinion or otherwise
Idaho Rule of Evidence 702	If scientific, technical, or other specialized knowledge will assist the trier of fact to understand the evidence or to determine a fact in issue, a witness qualified as an expert by knowledge, skill, experience, training, or education, may testify thereto in the form of an opinion or otherwise
Illinois Rule of Evidence 702	If scientific, technical, or other specialized knowledge will assist the trier of fact to understand the evidence or to determine a fact in issue, a witness qualified as an expert by knowledge, skill, experience, training, or education, may testify thereto in the form of an opinion or otherwise
Kentucky Rule of Evidence 702	If scientific, technical, or other specialized knowledge will assist the trier of fact to understand the evidence or to determine a fact in issue, a witness qualified as an expert by knowledge, skill, experience, training, or education, may testify thereto in the form of an opinion or otherwise

(continued)

Table 2.1 (continued)

Louisiana Rule of Evidence 702	If scientific, technical, or other specialized knowledge will assist the trier of fact to understand the evidence or to determine a fact in issue, a witness qualified as an expert by knowledge, skill, experience, training, or education, may testify thereto in the form of an opinion or otherwise
Michigan Rule of Evidence 702	If the court determines that scientific, technical, or other specialized knowledge will assist the trier of fact to understand the evidence or to determine a fact in issue, a witness qualified as an expert by knowledge, skill, experience, training, or education may testify thereto in the form of an opinion or otherwise
Minnesota Rule of Evidence 702	If scientific, technical, or other specialized knowledge will assist the trier of fact to understand the evidence or to determine a fact in issue, a witness qualified as an expert by knowledge, skill, experience, training, or education, may testify thereto in the form of an opinion or otherwise
Mississippi Rule of Evidence 702	If scientific, technical, or other specialized knowledge will assist the trier of fact to understand the evidence or to determine a fact in issue, a witness qualified as an expert by knowledge, skill, experience, training, or education, may testify thereto in the form of an opinion or otherwise
Missouri Revised Statutes 490.065.1	In any civil action, if scientific, technical or other specialized knowledge will assist the trier of fact to understand the evidence or to determine a fact in issue, a witness qualified as an expert by knowledge, skill, experience, training, or education may testify thereto in the form of an opinion or otherwise
Montana Rule of Evidence 702	If scientific, technical, or other specialized knowledge will assist the trier of fact to understand the evidence or to determine a fact in issue, a witness qualified as an expert by knowledge, skill, experience, training, or education may testify thereto in the form of an opinion or otherwise
Nebraska Code §27-702	If scientific, technical, or other specialized knowledge will assist the trier of fact to understand the evidence or to determine a fact in issue, a witness qualified as an expert by knowledge, skill, experience, training, or education, may testify thereto in the form of an opinion or otherwise
Nevada Revised Statutes 50.275	If scientific, technical or other specialized knowledge will assist the trier of fact to understand the evidence or to determine a fact in issue, a witness qualified as an expert by special knowledge, skill, experience, training or education may testify to matters within the scope of such knowledge
New Hampshire Rule of Evidence 702	If scientific, technical, or other specialized knowledge will assist the trier of fact to understand the evidence or to determine a fact in issue, a witness qualified as an expert by knowledge, skill, experience, training, or education, may testify thereto in the form of an opinion or otherwise
North Carolina General Statute 8C-702	If scientific, technical or other specialized knowledge will assist the trier of fact to understand the evidence or to determine a fact in issue, a witness qualified as an expert by knowledge, skill, experience, training, or education, may testify thereto in the form of an opinion, or otherwise

(continued)

Table 2.1 (continued)

North Dakota Rule of Evidence 702	If scientific, technical, or other specialized knowledge will assist the trier of fact to understand the evidence or to determine a fact in issue, a witness qualified as an expert by knowledge, skill, experience, training, or education, may testify thereto in the form of an opinion or otherwise
Ohio Rules of Evidence 702	A witness may testify as an expert if all of the following apply: (A) The witness' testimony either relates to matters beyond the knowledge or experience possessed by lay persons or dispels a misconception common among lay persons; (B) The witness is qualified as an expert by specialized knowledge, skill, experience, training, or education regarding the subject matter of the testimony
Oregon Revised Statutes 40.410	If scientific, technical or other specialized knowledge will assist the trier of fact to understand the evidence or to determine a fact in issue, a witness qualified as an expert by knowledge, skill, experience, training or education may testify thereto in the form of an opinion or otherwise
Pennsylvania Rule of Evidence	If scientific, technical or other specialized knowledge beyond that possessed by a layperson will assist the trier of fact to understand the evidence or to determine a fact in issue, a witness qualified as an expert by knowledge, skill, experience, training or education may testify thereto in the form of an opinion or otherwise
South Carolina Rule of Evidence 702	If scientific, technical, or other specialized knowledge will assist the trier of fact to understand the evidence or to determine a fact in issue, a witness qualified as an expert by knowledge, skill, experience, training, or education, may testify thereto in the form of an opinion or otherwise
South Dakota Codified Laws 19-15-2	If scientific, technical, or other specialized knowledge will assist the trier of fact to understand the evidence or to determine a fact in issue, a witness qualified as an expert by knowledge, skill, experience, training, or education, may testify thereto in the form of an opinion or otherwise
Texas Rule of Evidence 702	If scientific, technical, or other specialized knowledge will assist the trier of fact to understand the evidence or to determine a fact in issue, a witness qualified as an expert by knowledge, skill, experience, training, or education, may testify thereto in the form of an opinion or otherwise
Utah Rule of Evidence 702	Subject to the limitations in paragraph (b), a witness who is qualified as an expert by knowledge, skill, experience, training, or education may testify in the form of an opinion or otherwise if the expert's scientific, technical, or other specialized knowledge will help the trier of fact to understand the evidence or to determine a fact in issue
Washington Rule of Evidence 702	If scientific, technical, or other specialized knowledge will assist the trier of fact to understand the evidence or to determine a fact in issue, a witness qualified as an expert by knowledge, skill, experience, training, or education, may testify thereto in the form of an opinion or otherwise
Wisconsin Statutes 907.02(1)	If scientific, technical, or other specialized knowledge will assist the trier of fact to understand the evidence or to determine a fact in issue, a witness qualified as an expert by knowledge, skill, experience, training, or education, may testify thereto in the form of an opinion or otherwise

Getting an Expert Qualified

Who decides whether an expert is qualified? When an expert is presented to the court, the presenting party has the burden of showing that the statutory criteria has been satisfied by a proponent of the evidence (*Corpus Juris Secundum*, 2012a). The decision concerning whether an expert meets the qualification criteria rests in the providence of the court (Dore, 2012a).

Voir Dire. The challenge to the qualifications of an expert usually occurs during what the legal profession calls *voir dire*. "Voir dire" is French for "to speak the truth" (Voire-dire, *Black's Law Dictionary*, 1990, p. 1575). The purpose of voir dire is to allow an expert's background and abilities to testify on particular matters to be examined (Dore, 2012a). Some jurisdictions allow this voir dire process where the court is able to preview the expert's qualifications prior to testimony in front of the jury. During voir dire, the competency, knowledge, and credentials of the expert will be presented and examined (Dore, 2012a; Sapir, 2007). The counsel for the opposing party is also provided the opportunity to challenge the qualifications (Sapir, 2007). As the opposing counsel does have the opportunity to challenge the expert's qualifications, experts are cautioned not to exaggerate or mislead with respect to their background, experience, or in their curriculum vitae. Especially in high dollar cases, opposing counsel will investigate the expert and any exaggeration and/or dishonesty could result in the individual's disqualification as an expert.

Additionally, when the litigation involves toxic torts, products liability, or environmental law, the qualification process can be more complex. In such cases, the expert qualifications will differ for each area of scientific expertise presented in the case (Dore, 2012a). The qualifications for an epidemiologist will be established with different proof than a toxicologist or biologist (Dore, 2012a). The expert must be qualified to express opinions on the issues to which his or her testimony would pertain. Thus, while an epidemiologist would be qualified to perform studies and explain the implications of the studies, he or she may not be qualified to serve as an expert on the issue of causation (Dore, 2012a).

The qualification process solely determines whether the expert meets the statutory criteria to testify as an expert. The expert does not even have to be the most highly qualified person to testify on a given issue. As recognized the District Court for the Fifth Circuit, differences in expertise "bear chiefly on the weight to be assigned to the testimony by the trier of fact, not its admissibility" (*Huss v. Gayden*, 452, 2009).

In some cases, the voir dire process is unnecessary. If there is little to no doubt an expert is qualified to testify on an issue, the opposing party may waive any objections and stipulate to the expert's qualifications. If the opposing party offers no objection to the introduction of the expert's testimony or stipulates to his or her qualifications, the court should find the expert qualified (*Corpus Juris Secundum*, 2012b).

What is considered when determining whether an individual is an expert? When examining a proposed expert, the court will look at several factors. Some of the areas examined include the individual's education, licensure, certification, background, and training. The individual's work, research, studies, publications, presentations, and practical experience are considered. The court may also consider the individual's membership and/or participation in professional societies and associations. An individual does not have to possess a license in a particular field to qualify as an expert (American Law of Products Liability, 2012; *Corpus Juris Secundum*, 2012c).

Typically, the standard by which to measure the qualifications of individuals with special skills or knowledge is not well defined beyond the general requirement their capacity must be commensurate with the reasonable requirements needed for the nature of the subject matter (*Corpus Juris Secundum*, 2012c). When the case involves subject matter that is complex, the courts will be more prone to require advanced degrees, training, and experience (Brown & Campbell, 2009a). In areas like toxic torts or product liability, epidemiologists with an advanced degree in epidemiology will be qualified, especially if they also have experience in the field, to testify on issues such as the comparative risk of prescription drugs or another expert's methodology (Brown & Campbell, 2009b).

An epidemiologist's education and training becomes more important when offering a causation opinion. In the past, many courts required the expert who addressed issues of causation in toxic tort cases to have a medical degree (Jones & Pogue, 2012). While not every court now requires a medical degree to focus on causation, there will be less of a challenge to the expert if the expert has both a medical degree and training as an epidemiologist (Danner & Varn, 2012; Jones & Pogue, 2012). However, an epidemiologist with a Ph.D. in a field relevant to the litigation can be found to be qualified to address the causation of diseases often associated with exposure to toxic substances (Danner & Varn, 2012).

Further, experts that actually practice in the field at issue can be seen as being better witnesses (Jones 2012). Practitioners have been recognized as being more compelling witnesses, as the trier of fact may find them more convincing because they can testify from firsthand knowledge about their own observations, experiments, and analysis (Jones, 2012).

In litigation involving epidemiologists as experts, courts would have a specific interest in information concerning the epidemiologist's participation in any research that pertained to the toxic substance or injury/disease at issue in the litigation (Dore, 2012a). The titles of any published articles by the epidemiologist examining the specific toxic substance at issue, its effects on humans, and/or the injury/disease at issue should be disclosed to the court (Dore, 2012a). The qualification of an epidemiologist as an expert in the litigation would also be aided by showing his or her familiarity with the scientific literature and studies addressing the particular disease/injury involved in the litigation (Dore, 2012a).

The rules in both federal and state courts usually require an individual to have knowledge, skill, experience, training, *or* education to qualify as an expert. It is important to note the use of the word "or" indicates the individual being offered as an effort does not have to satisfy all five areas. However, an individual who does meet most, or all, of the five areas is more likely to defeat a challenge of his or her qualification to testify as an expert in the litigation.

Qualifying the Expert's Testimony

As discussed above, a qualified expert is someone who has been found to have the requisite expertise through education, training or experience, necessary to give an opinion on a particular subject. However, the qualification of an expert does not automatically mean that expert's opinions and testimony will be deemed admissible. Therefore, once an expert has been qualified, his or her opinions and testimony must also be evaluated to determine their admissibility. An expert may testify in a case when "the expert's scientific, technical or other specialized knowledge will help the trier of fact to understand the evidence or to determine a fact in issue" (Federal Rule of Evidence, 2011).

Determining the Admissibility of an Expert's Testimony

The Federal Requirements: The Frye Standard. In 1923, the US Supreme Court handed down the decision of Frye v. United States. In that case, the Court established a method for determining whether expert testimony was reliable and thereby admissible (*Frye v. United States*, 1923). Under that test, expert testimony is admissible when the methods and procedures employed by the expert have gained "general acceptance in the particular field in which is belongs" (*Frye v. United States*, 1923, p. 1014).

Over the next 70 years, the *Frye* "General Acceptance" standard reined in the federal courts as the method for determining the admissibility of expert testimony. The codification of the Federal Rules of Evidence in 1972, including a rule dealing specifically with expert testimony, did not initially effect any change in the federal standard for admitting expert testimony. The change did not come about until 1993 in the seminal case of *Daubert v. Merrell Dow Pharmacueticals, Inc.*

The Federal Requirements: The Daubert Standard. In *Daubert v. Merrell Dow Pharmaceuticals, Inc.*, two infants and their guardians *ad litem* sued a pharmaceutical company for birth defects alleged sustained by their mothers' use of an antinausea drug, Bendectin, during pregnancy (*Daubert v. Merrell Dow Pharmaceuticals*, 1993). At the trial level, the plaintiffs attempted to submit the testimony of eight experts who based their conclusion that Bendectin caused birth defects on animal studies, chemical structure analysis, and the unpublished reanalysis of previously published human statistical studies (*Daubert v. Merrell Dow Pharmaceuticals, Inc.*, 1993). The trial court held this expert testimony inadmissible under the *Frye* Standard (*Daubert v. Merrell Dow Pharmaceuticals, Inc.*, 1993). The trial court reasoned that, because of the large amount of epidemiological studies regarding

Bendectin, non-epidemiological studies, such as the animal cell studies, live animal studies and chemical structure analyses relied upon by the plaintiffs were not a "generally accepted" methodology for evaluating Bendectin and, thus, failed under the *Frye* test (*Daubert v. Merrell Dow Pharmaceuticals*, 1993). The court further concluded that the plaintiff's epidemiological reanalyses were not generally accepted because they had not been published or subject to peer review (*Daubert v. Dow Merrell Pharmaceuticals*, 1993). The trial court, therefore, refused to admit plaintiffs' expert testimony, and the appellate court affirmed (*Daubert v. Merrell Dow Pharmaceuticals*, 1993).

The case eventually reached the United States Supreme Court where a majority of the justices held the Federal Rules of Evidence superseded the *Frye* standard for admission of expert testimony (*Daubert v. Merrell Dow Pharmaceuticals*, 1993). The Court noted that the text and drafting history of Federal Rule of Evidence 702 governing expert testimony made no mention of a "general acceptance" standard for determining the admissibility of expert testimony (*Daubert v. Merrell Dow Pharmaceuticals*, 1993). Rather, Rule 702 required the trial judge to ensure an expert's testimony was both reliable and relevant (*Daubert v. Merrell Dow Pharmacueticals*, 1993). The Supreme Court found this reliability standard in the Rule's use of the term "scientific…knowledge" (*Daubert v. Merrell Dow Pharmaceuticals*, 1993, p. 580). "Scientific," the Court held, "implies a grounding in the methods and procedures of science," while "'knowledge' connotes more than subjective belief or unsupported speculation" (*Daubert v. Merrell Dow Pharmaceuticals*, 1993, p. 590).

To aid the trial judge in determining whether proffered expert opinion constituted "scientific knowledge" the Supreme Court provided a list of factors that should be considered. While not exhaustive, these factors are meant to assist the trial judge in determining whether the methodology employed by the expert is reliable (*Daubert v. Merrell Dow Pharmaceuticals*, 1993). In considering these factors the trial judge is to focus on the methodology employed by the expert and not upon his conclusions (*Daubert v. Merrell Dow Pharmaceuticals*, 1993). The factors propounded by the Supreme Court include the following:

(1) Whether the theory or technique can be (and has been) tested;
(2) Whether the theory or technique has been subjected to peer review and publication;
(3) The theory or technique's known potential error rate and the existence and maintenance of standards controlling its operation; and
(4) Whether the theory or technique has attracted widespread acceptance within a relevant scientific community (*Daubert v. Merrell Dow Pharmaceuticals*, 1993)

The Supreme Court remanded the case so that the lower courts could apply the newly articulated standard to the proffered expert testimony (*Daubert v. Merrell Dow Pharmaceuticals*, 1993). Applying the new Supreme Court standard, the Ninth Circuit Court of Appeals determined that plaintiffs' expert testimony had to satisfy two prongs: (1) it had to be reliable, "scientific knowledge" and (2) it had to be relevant in that it aided the trier of fact in reaching a conclusion (*Daubert v. Merrell Dow Pharmaceuticals*, 1995).

Under the first prong, the court found the factors set down by the Supreme Court were not exclusive (*Daubert v. Merrell Dow Pharmaceuticals*, 1995). In particular, the court considered the fact that the research prepared by the experts was only done in anticipation of litigation to weigh against reliability (*Daubert v. Merrell Dow Pharmaceuticals*, 1995). Further, it noted that the methodology utilized by the plaintiffs' experts had not been subjected to peer review or publication (*Daubert v. Merrell Dow Pharmaceuticals*, 1995). Finally, the court noted that the plaintiffs' experts failed to explain their methodology or reference an external source to validate their opinions and provide an assessment of the reliability of their methods (*Daubert v. Merrell Dow Pharmaceuticals*, 1995). The Ninth Circuit, thus, determined plaintiffs had failed to satisfy the first prong for the admission of expert testimony (*Daubert v. Merrell Dow Pharmaceuticals*, 1995). After further discussion, the court found plaintiffs' proffer of expert testimony failed the second prong Rule 702's requirement for the admission of expert testimony (*Daubert v. Merrell Dow Pharmaceuticals*, 1995). Therefore, even after applying the new *Daubert* standard, the Ninth Circuit affirmed the district court's exclusion of plaintiffs' expert testimony (*Daubert v. Merrell Dow Pharmaceuticals*, 1995).

Federal Standard: Post-Daubert Developments; One question left open by the *Daubert* decision was the standard of review appellate courts were to apply when considering a district judge's decision to admit or deny expert testimony. The Supreme Court answered this question 4 years later in *General Electric v. Joiner*, settling on an abuse of discretion standard, the same standard used for all evidentiary decisions (*General Electric v. Joiner*, 1997). The "abuse of discretion standard" means the reviewing court looks to see if the lower court's decision: (1) was clearly unreasonable, arbitrary, or fanciful; (2) was based on an erroneous conclusion of law; (3) was clearly erroneous; or (4) the record contains no evidence upon which the court rationally could have based its decision (Casey, Camara, & Wright, 2001–2002). In that opinion, the Court emphasized that while *Daubert* permitted the admission of a greater range of expert opinion, it still left in place the gatekeeper role of the judge in determining the reliability and relevance of such testimony (*General Electric v. Joiner*, 1997). The Court thus affirmed the district court's exclusion of the expert testimony in this case, determining that the animal study in this case was too factually remote from the actual facts of the case and the epidemiological studies either did not have significant results or contained exposures to other carcinogens not at issue in the case (*General Electric v. Joiner*, 1997).

Finally, in *Kumho Tire Co. v. Carmichael*, the Supreme Court addressed the question of whether *Daubert* applied to all expert testimony or only expert testimony based on "hard" science, such as biology and chemistry. The Court noted Rule 702 of the Federal Rules of Evidence encompassed all forms of expert testimony, including "scientific, technical or other specialized knowledge" (*Kumho Tire Co. v. Carmichael*, 1999). Thus, the Court concluded the trial judge's gatekeeping role applied to all forms of expert testimony, not just testimony based on "hard" science (*Kumho Tire Co. v. Carmichael*, 1999). Therefore, the *Daubert* standard of admissibility would apply to all forms of expert testimony (*Kumho Tire Co. v. Carmichael*, 1999).

States' Requirements. The previous section considered the federal standard for the admission of expert testimony, as now governed by *Daubert*. However, because *Daubert* is based on the Federal Rules of Evidence rather than a constitutional provision, the states are free to apply their own standards in assessing the reliability and, thus, admissibility of expert testimony.

As one would expect, the applicable standard varies by the state. However, the states' approaches can generally be divided in four different categories: (1) those applying the *Daubert* standard, (2) those applying the *Frye* standard, (3) those applying a *Daubert-Frye* hybrid, and (4) those applying their own standard. Experts are cautioned to ensure they become familiar with the standard for the state in which they are testifying and the manner said standard has been applied by the courts.

As of 2011, the states that follow the *Daubert* standard include the following: Alaska, Arizona, Arkansas, Colorado, Connecticut, Delaware, Georgia, Hawaii, Idaho, Indiana, Iowa, Kentucky, Louisiana, Maine, Massachusetts, Michigan, Mississippi, Montana, Nebraska, New Hampshire, New Mexico, Ohio, Oklahoma, Oregon, Rhode Island, South Dakota, Tennessee, Texas, Utah, Vermont, West Virginia, Wisconsin, and Wyoming (Blinka, 2011; Budd, Cottle, & Hutchinson, 2012). It should be noted that some of states following the *Daubert* standard have adopted distinctions that differ from the federal standard (Budd, Cottle, & Hutchinson, 2012).

A handful of states have chosen to continue to follow the *Frye* Standard. These states include Alabama, California, the District of Columbia, Florida, Illinois, Kansas, Maryland, Minnesota, New York, Pennsylvania, and Washington (Budd, Cottle, & Hutchinson, 2012).

While some states have adopted either the *Frye* or *Daubert* standard, others have developed a hybrid of the two or their own unique approach. These states, as of 2011, included Missouri, Nevada, New Jersey, North Carolina, North Dakota, South Carolina, and Virginia (Budd, Cottle, & Hutchinson, 2012).

An International View. Clearly, the courts of the United States are not the only tribunals faced with the difficulty of determining whether or not to admit expert testimony and what standards to apply in making this determination. The differences in the standards used across varying locations may have serious implications for the outcome of a trial in the context of international litigation. As an example, Loue discusses in Chap. 5 of this volume, a case involving a lawsuit against an American corporation doing business in Ecuador and a challenge by the defendant corporation of the methods utilized by the expert witness in the litigation in Ecuador.

The following will consider the approach to this question employed by some other countries for a comparative look at the admission of expert testimony on an international scale.

England: Pro-Admissibility. In general, opinion testimony is inadmissible in English courts (Browne, Williamson, & Barkacs, 2002). However, expert testimony is admissible under an exception to this general rule which allows expert testimony to prove "matters of specialized knowledge, on which the court would be unable [to] properly reach a conclusion unaided" (Murphey, 1992, p. 302). Under the English system, expert testimony is admissible where it is sufficiently well-established that it would pass the ordinary tests of relevance and reliability (*R v. Dallagher*, 2002). While this standard seems relatively similar to that propounded in *Daubert*, in practice, the English courts have been more liberal in admitting expert testimony (Dempsey, 2004). For additional discussion of the standard in England, see the chapter by Claire McIvor in this volume.

South Korea: *Court-Controlled Experts*. In South Korea, the court, not the parties, chooses an expert witness (Browne, Williamson, & Barkacs, 2002). In choosing an expert, the court may instruct the parties to nominate an expert witness, may provide a list from which the parties can choose, or may choose an expert on its own (Browne, Williamson, & Barkacs, 2002). Unlike the United States, a Korean expert will have obtained a specialized degree or certification; accumulated knowledge and experience are insufficient (Lee, 1997). Thus, Korean experts will generally hold such professions as physicians and engineers, and the courts will not permit testimony from, for example, mechanics and construction workers (Lee, 1997). Once the expert is chosen, the court will give the expert his or her assignment (Browne, Williamson, & Barkacs, 2002). The expert then prepares a report which the court is free to accept or reject (Browne, Williamson, & Barkacs, 2002). The expert is exempt from pretrial discovery and can only be examined in court by leave of the judge (Lee, 1997).

The parties may also obtain their own, non-court-appointed experts, but because such experts are generally considered biased, parties rarely obtain such experts (Lee, 1997). Occasionally, the court will adopt the opinion of a party-retained expert over that of the court-appointed expert (Lee, 1997). Because of the unique position occupied by experts in Korean courts, the question of admissibility of testimony does not really arise. It is the judge who hears the expert report and the judge alone who decides whether to accept or to reject the testimony of the expert.

France: *The Expert-Judge Team*. Like South Korea, French courts appoint their own experts (Browne, Williamson, & Barkacs, 2002). An expert is appointed in one of three ways: (1) one of the parties requests an expert; (2) the judge appoints the expert on his or her own motion; or (3) the judge is required by statute to appoint an expert (Browne, Williamson, & Barkacs, 2002). The idea is for the expert witness and the judge to work together, and the judge ensures that the parties to the litigation cooperate with the expert (Taylor, 1996). Once the expert has completed the assignment, he or she files a written report with the court which the judge is free to accept or reject (Browne, Williamson, & Barkacs, 2002). Once again, the question of admissibility does not really arise in French courts. The judge, not the parties, controls the expert and the scope of his or her testimony (Taylor, 1996). Thus, an expert in French court does not face the threshold barrier of whether his testimony is admissible.

Serving as an Expert

As discussed above, experts can serve as consultants and/or testifying witnesses. When serving in either role, the expert is best served by gaining, up font, a clear understanding of his or her obligations and the litigation process in general.

Objectivity

Unlike an attorney, whose job is to persuade, the role of an expert is to explain (Kolezynski, 1997). Consequently, experts should strive for objectivity (Kolezynski, 1997). In some countries, such as England, Wales, Canada, and New Zealand, experts even have an obligation to the court to provide objective, unbiased opinions (Civil Rules & Practice Directions, 1999; Federal Court Rules, 2010; Judicature Act 1908, 2009).

Ethical Rules and Guidelines

In the United States and other countries, some professional fields have published position statements with ethical guidelines or rules of professional conduct. For example, the American Medical Association and American College of Occupational and Environmental Medicine both have ethical guidelines that pertain to its professionals who serve as expert witnesses. Such rules help professionals understand what constitutes ethical conduct in the litigation context (Kolezynski, 1997). Such guidelines often address the association or society's stance with regard to the goal of expert testimony, qualifications, objectivity, compensation, and the conduct of expert witnesses (Dore, 2012b).

Further, professionals serving as experts should be aware of the American Bar Association's Model Rules of Professional Conduct and the state's rules governing an attorney's professional conduct. Experts retained by attorneys become the agents of those attorneys (*Restatement (Second) of Agency*, 1958). Therefore, the attorney may be held responsible for a breach, by the expert, of the ethical obligations applicable to attorneys (Kolezynski, 1997). Moreover, experts that cause an attorney professional embarrassment during the litigation will find other attorneys are reluctant to retain their services in the future (Kolezynski, 1997).

Experts also have an ethical obligation to comply with the oath they take before testifying. Though the oaths vary by jurisdiction, they all require the witness to swear or affirm he or she will offer only truthful testimony under the penalty of perjury. However, as experts offer opinions, the "truth" of the opinion is open to debate (Kolezynski, 1997). Thus, the most probable consequence of offering "false" testimony is that the trier of fact will disregard the expert's opinion (Kolezynski, 1997).

Experts in litigation have an obligation to exercise reasonable care and skill. While experts have enjoyed immunity from litigation arising from the written and spoken word they have offered, this is beginning to change (Dore, 2012b; Masterson, 1998). Courts have begun to reexamine the breadth of an expert's immunity and permit claims, such as malpractice, to be brought against experts (Dore, 2012b; Hanson, 1996; *Murphy v. A.A. Matthews*, 1992).

Deadlines and Confidentiality

Experts who are retained in litigation have an obligation to meet the deadlines given to them. Once a case is underway, various deadlines can be enforced upon the attorneys. Depending on the jurisdiction, litigation will often involve a case management or discovery schedule. As it applies to experts, most jurisdictions have rules that dictate the parties' deadline for disclosing experts and their reports. Federal Rule of Procedure 26(a)(2)(D), for example, states the following:

(D) *Time to Disclose Expert Testimony*. A party must make these disclosures at the times and in the sequence that the court orders. Absent a stipulation or a court order, the disclosures must be made:

1. At least 90 days before the date set for trial or for the case to be ready for trial; or
2. If the evidence is intended solely to contradict or rebut evidence on the same subject matter identified by another party under Rule 26(a)(2)(B) or (C), within 30 days after the other party's disclosure (Federal Rule of Civil Procedure, 2010a).

The parties are required to meet the deadlines of the schedule. An expert's inability to conduct research, analyze records, and compile a report in a timely manner can complicate an attorney's job and, if after the deadline, prohibit the attorney from utilizing the expert's findings (Bois, 2011c; Jones, 2012). Therefore, it is important for the expert and attorney to discuss these deadlines and determine whether the expert can reasonably meet them.

A retained expert should also be aware of the duty of confidentiality. Attorneys are required to maintain and preserve a client's confidences. As discussed above, retained experts are agents of the attorney and, as such, should adhere to the same rules of confidentiality. The contract that the expert and attorney enter into will also often address the issues of confidentiality, creating a contractual obligation to maintain confidentiality. Thus, once an expert is retained, he or she has an obligation to treat information and documents from the attorney or on the client's behalf as confidential (Kolezynski, 1997). If during the course of the expert's evaluation of a case, he or she discovers unfavorable evidence, the duty of confidentiality requires the expert to only discuss this evidence with the retaining party (Kolezynski, 1997). Further, the duty of confidentiality would extend to any of the expert's staff, subcontractors, or coworkers that are engaged to assist in the matter. Experts should further be aware the duty of confidentiality expends beyond the conclusion of the case (Kolezynski, 1997).

Recordkeeping

When serving as an expert, especially a testifying expert, one should be conscious of record keeping and preserving evidence. It is likely that, sometime during the litigation of the case, a testifying expert's entire file will have to be produced for scrutiny by opposing counsel (Bois, 2011e). Experts would be wise when conducting their evaluations to remember this eventuality and strive to maintain minimal and objective record keeping (Bois, 2011g). The experts should also refrain from destroying any evidence and/or records they do manufacture, utilize, and/or consider (Bois, 2011e).

The Expert's Report

It is important to note the expert's role will vary from case to case. Therefore, it is important for the expert to ascertain exactly what is being expected of him or her. Likewise, the content of the expert's report will vary, as the rules regarding the contents of a report vary from jurisdiction to jurisdiction and country from country.

In the United States, an expert's report in a federal proceeding must comply with Federal Rule of Civil Procedure 26(a)(2). This Rule states the following:

(B) *Witnesses Who Must Provide a Written Report.* Unless otherwise stipulated or ordered by the court, this disclosure must be accompanied by a written report—prepared and signed by the witness—if the witness is one retained or specially employed to provide expert testimony in the case or one whose duties as the party's employee regularly involve giving expert testimony. The report must contain:

1. A complete statement of all opinions the witness will express and the basis and reasons for them;
2. The facts or data considered by the witness in forming them;
3. Any exhibits that will be used to summarize or support them;
4. The witness's qualifications, including a list of all publications authored in the previous 10 years;
5. A list of all other cases in which, during the previous 4 years, the witness testified as an expert at trial or by deposition; and
6. A statement of the compensation to be paid for the study and testimony in the case (Federal Rules of Civil Procedure, 2010a).

In England, Part 35.10 of the Rules & Practice Directions requires reports to contain the following:

(1) An expert's report must comply with the requirements set out in Practice Direction 35.
(2) At the end of an expert's report there must be a statement that the expert understands and has complied with their duty to the court.
(3) The expert's report must state the substance of all material instructions, whether written or oral, on the basis of which the report was written.
(4) The instructions referred to in paragraph (3) shall not be privileged against disclosure but the court will not, in relation to those instructions –

  (a) Order disclosure of any specific document; or
  (b) Permit any questioning in court, other than by the party who instructed the expert, unless it is satisfied that there are reasonable grounds to consider the statement of instructions given under paragraph (3) to be inaccurate or incomplete (Civil Rules & Practice Directions, 1999).

Given that the report requirements may vary depending on the locale of litigation, experts would be well served to become familiar with the requirements of the court in which the litigation is pending. Experts should also be aware that many courts have local rules that also apply.

In general, an expert should consider a report that includes elements such as (1) the expert's background and qualifications; (2) a summary of his or her opinions; (3) the objectives of the evaluation; (4) the tests performed to verify the opinions; (5) a review of the principles, methodologies, and analyses utilized; (6) the evidence considered; (7) the publications and studies considered; (8) the peer review of the methods employed; (9) indicia of reliability relied upon by the expert; and (10) the expert's conclusions (Bois, 2011g; Brown & Campbell, 2009c).

Conclusion

To prevail in complex litigation, especially litigation involving toxic torts, products liability, or environmental issues, the attorneys for both parties must effectively utilize experts. Thus, the expert witness becomes an essential and important factor in the litigation. The litigation of such complex cases is most successful when the attorneys and experts function as a team.

An expert must have a firm grasp on both his or her field of practice and the law. Expert must understand what is expected of them and the legal rules that must be followed. When an expert proves competent, honest, and knowledgeable, it is more likely he or she will be successful, increase his or her professional acclaim, and be repeatedly retained.

References

32 *Corpus juris secundum.* (2012a). Burden and manner of presenting proof of competency, Section 707.

32 *Corpus juris secundum.* (2012b). Generally, Section 706.

32 *Corpus juris secundum.* (2012c). Scope of requisite expertise; licensing, Section 702.

Alaska Rule of Evidence 702. (1997).

American law of products liability, 3rd ed. (2012). Qualification as expert—Requisites for qualification, Section 54:80.

Arkansas Rule of Evidence 702. (2010).

Australian Law Reform Commission (n.d.). 9. Opinions based on specialized knowledge. *Uniform evidence law (ALRC Report 102)/9*. Retrieved October 13, 2012, from http://www.alrc.gov.au/publications/9.%20The%20Opinion%20Rule%20and%20its%20Exceptions/opinions-based-specialised-knowledge.

Bain, A., & Myer, P. (2010). Direct and cross-examination of expert witnesses in civil litigation: Where art meets science. *Expert Witnesses, 1*(58), 24–35.

Black, B., Jacobson, J., Madeira, E., & See, A. (1997). *Expert evidence: A practitioner's guide to law, science, and the FJC Manual*. American Law Institute—American Bar Association Continuing Legal Education, St. Paul, MN: West Group.

Blinka, D. (2011). The *Daubert* standard in Wisconsin: A primer. *Wisconsin Lawyer, 84*(3). Retrieved October 13, 2012, from http://www.wisbar.org/AM/Template.cfm?Section=Wisconsin_Lawyer&template=/CM/ContentDisplay.cfm&contentid=100905.

Bois, T. (2011a). When to retain the plaintiff's expert. *Expert Witnesses Environmental Cases*, Section 4:2.

Bois, T. (2011b). When to retain the defendant's expert. *Expert Witnesses Environmental Cases*, Section 4:3.

Bois, T. (2011c). Introduction. *Expert Witnesses Environmental Cases*, Section 4:1.

Bois, T. (2011d). Nontestifying consulting experts. *Expert Witnesses Environmental Cases*, Section 5:7.

Bois, T. (2011e). Expert communications. *Expert Witnesses Environmental Cases*, Section 3:1.

Bois, T. (2011f). Introduction. *Expert Witnesses Environmental Cases*, Section 5:1.

Bois, T. (2011g). Practice tip—Six reliability requirements of expert reports. *Expert Witnesses Environmental Cases*, Section 4:10.

Brown, L., & Campbell, C. (2009a). Case law regarding qualifications. *Expert Witnesses: Products Liability Cases*, Section 1.7.

Brown, L., & Campbell, C. (2009b). Education and training. *Expert Witnesses: Products Liability Cases*, Section 3.4.

Brown, L., & Campbell, C. (2009c). Structure. *Expert Witnesses: Products Liability Cases*, Section 3.18.

Browne, N., Williamson, C., & Barkacs, L. (2002). The perspectival nature of expert testimony in the United States, England, Korea, and France. *Connecticut Journal of International Law, 18*, 55–99.

Budd, T., Cottle, E., & Hutchinson, C. (2012). *Expert witness answer book 2012*. New York, NY: Practicing Law Institute.

Buncher, C. (2012a). What is the role of the epidemiologist? *Toxic Torts Practice Guide, 1*(4), 1.

Buncher, C. (2012b). What can epidemiologist do for attorneys? *Toxic Torts Practice Guide, 1*(4), 2.

California Evidence Code §720. (1967).

CanLII 59152 (ON SC).

Casey, K., Camara, J., & Wright, N. (2001–2002). Standards of Appellate Review in the Federal Circuit: Substance and Semantics. *Federal Circuit Bar Journal, 11*, 279. Retrieved October 6, 2012, from http://www.stradley.com/library/files/krc-standards.pdf.

Cetrulo, L. (2011). Toxic tort litigation: a functional description. *Toxic Torts Litigation Guide, 1*(1), 2.
Cleveland v. Hamilton Health Science Corp. (2009).
Code of Conduct for Expert Witnesses, Federal Court Rules, Rule 52.2. (2010).
Code of Conduct for Expert Witnesses, Judicature Act 1908, Schedule 4. (2009).
Commonwealth v. Dunkle. (1992). 529 Pa. 168, 602 A.2d 830.
Connecticut Code of Evidence 7-2. (2000).
Courts; Rules of Evidence, Nebraska Statutes 27-702. (1975).
Danner, D., & Varn, L. (3rd Ed. 2012). Qualifications—Education. *Expert Witness Checklist.* (3)14:52.
Danner, D., & Varn, L. (1994). Toxic experts. *American Jurisprudence Trials*. (52) 473:8.
Daubert v. Merrell Dow Pharamaceuticals, 43 F.3d 1311. (9th Cir. 1995).
Daubert v. Merrell Dow Pharmaceuticals, 509 U.S. 579. (1993).
Delaware Uniform Rules of Evidence 702. (2001).
Dempsey, M. (2004). Experts witness testimony in the prosecution of domestic violence. *CPS DV Expert Witness Report.*
Dore, M. (2012a). Expert qualifications. *Law of Toxic Torts, 5*(30), 4.
Dore, M. (2012b). Professional obligations of the expert witness. *Law of Toxic Torts, 5*(30), 12.
Evidence, Missouri Revised Statutes 490.065. (2003).
Evidence, North Carolina General Statutes 8C-702. (2011).
Evidence Code, Florida Statutes 90.702. (2010).
Evidence Code, Oregon Revised Statutes 40.410. (1981).
Evidence -Opinion and Expert Testimony, Wisconsin Statutes 907.002. (2011).
Experts and Assessors, Civil Rules & Practice Directions, Part 35. (1999).
Faigman, D., Blumenthal, J., Cheng, E., Mnookin, J., Murphy, E., & Sanders, J. (2011). Bases of exclusion—Lack of qualifications. *Modern science evidence: The law and science of expert testimony, 3*(26), 13.
Federal Rules of Civil Procedure 26. (2010a).
Federal Rules of Civil Procedure 33. (2010b).
Federal Rules of Civil Procedure 34. (2010c).
Federal Rules of Evidence 702. (2011).
Frye v. United States, 293 F. 1013. (D.C. Cir. 1923).
General Electric v. Joiner, 522 U.S. 136. (1997).
Green, M., Freedman, M., & Gordis, L. (2011). *Reference guide on epidemiology. The reference manual on scientific evidence* (3rd ed.). Washington, DC: The National Academies Press.
Huss v. Gayden, 571 F.3d 442. (5th Cir. 2009).
Halebian, J., & Scott, J. (2011). The use of expert witnesses. *Practicing Law Institute* (859) 451.
Halebian, J., & Scott, J. (2012). The use of expert witnesses. *Practicing Law Institute* (884) 213.
Hanson, R. (1996). Witness immunity under attack: Disarming "hired guns". *Wake Forest Law Review, 31*, 497.
Harrell, P. (1993). A new lawyer's guide to expert use. *Practical Lawyer, 39*(2), 55–63.
Hawaii Rules of Evidence 702. (1992).
Hennet, R. J.-C. (2010). Working with lawyers: The expert witness perspective. *Expert Witnesses, 1*(58), 14–17.
Idaho Rules of Evidence 702. (1985).
Illinois Rules of Civil Procedure 202. (2006).
Illinois Rules of Evidence 702. (2011).
Jones, J., & Pogue, R. (2012). Who can testify as an expert? *Toxic Torts Practice Guide, 2*(16), 3.
Jones, J. (2012). How is the expert chosen? *Toxic Torts Practice Guide, 2*(16), 2.
Kentucky Rules of Evidence 702. (2007).
Kolezynski, P. (1997). Ethical challenges for experts in civil litigation. *ExpertPages*. Retrieved October 6, 2012, from http://expertpages.com/news/ethical_challenges_for_experts_i.htm.
Kumho Tire Co. v. Carmichael, 526 U.S. 137. (1999).

Lee, E. (1997). Expert Evidence in the Republic of Korea and under the U.S. Federal Rules of Evidence: A comparative study. *Loyola of Los Angeles International and Comparative Law Review, 19*, 585–632.
Louisiana Code of Evidence 702. (1989).
Masterson, L. (1998). Witness immunity or malpractice liability for professionals hired as experts. *The Review of Litigation, 17*, 393–418.
Mauet, T. (2010). *Trial techniques* (8th ed.). New York, NY: Aspen.
McCormick, C. (4th ed. 1992). *McCormick on evidence*, § 13.
Michigan Rules of Evidence 702. (2004).
Minnesota Rules of Evidence 702. (2006).
Mississippi Rules of Evidence 702. (2000).
Montana Rules of Evidence 702. (1977).
Murphey, P. (1992). *A practical approach to evidence* (4th ed.). Vancouver, BC: Blackstone.
Murphy v. A A Matthews, 841 S.W.2d 671. (Mo. en banc 1992).
New Hampshire Rules of Evidence 702. (2011).
North Dakota Rules of Evidence 702. (2007).
O'Reilly, J. and Board of Contributors (2012). How are toxic torts defined? *Toxic Torts Practice Guide*, 1(2), 1.
Ohio Rules of Evidence 702. (1994).
Opinion and Expert Testimony, South Dakota Codified Laws 19-15-2. (2011).
Pennsylvania Rules of Evidence 702. (2004).
Pineda v. Ford Motor Co., 520 F.3d 237. (3rd Cir. 2008).
Precella, K., & Bailey New, H. (September 10–11, 2009). Federal and state expert testimony under Daubert and Robinson: what's the difference? 23rd Annual Advanced Civil Appellate Practice Course, State Bar of Texas.
R v. Dallagher, 1 Cr. App. R. 12. (2002).
Regina v. Mohan, 1994 CanLII 80 (SCC).
Restatement of agency (second): Agency; Principal; Agent, § 1. (1958).
Sapir, G. (2007). Qualifying the expert witness: A practical voir dire. *Forensic Magazine*, Retrieved October 6, 2012, from http://www.forensicmag.com/article/qualifying-expert-witness-practical-voir-dire?page=0,0.
South Carolina Rules of Evidence 702. (2011).
Taylor, R. (1996). A comparative study of expert testimony in France and the United States: Philosophical underpinnings, history, practice, and procedure. *Texas International Law Journal, 31*, 181–220.
Texas Rules of Evidence 702. (1998).
The Publisher's Editorial Staff. (1990). *Black's law dictionary* (6th ed.). St. Paul, MN: West.
United States v. Hicks, 389 F.3d 514. (5th Cir. 2004).
Utah Rules of Evidence 702. (2011).
Washington Rules of Evidence 702. (1979).
Witnesses, Nevada Revised Statues 50.275. (1971).

Chapter 3
The Use of Epidemiological Evidence in UK Tort Law

Claire McIvor

Introduction

The UK courts are highly sceptical of epidemiological evidence and, consequently, they are reluctant to rely on such evidence in determining issues of causation in personal injury litigation. This is a matter of regret since the UK courts could benefit greatly from epidemiology and, in particular, from the routine use of epidemiological expert witnesses. This chapter will demonstrate that the current UK judicial approach to assessing causation in complicated disease cases is beset with fundamental legal and scientific errors. Epidemiology could help the UK courts to address these problems in two principal ways: (1) by providing the courts with statistical information that is both scientifically robust and pertinent to the causal issues at stake, and (2) by proving the courts with guidance on how to use and interpret such information.

This chapter is divided into three main sections. Section I looks at recent applications of epidemiology in UK tort law. Through an examination of several key tort cases, it both illustrates the general hostility of the courts towards epidemiological evidence and identifies the reasons underlying this hostility. It shows that lasting damage to the reputation of epidemiology resulted from the judicial reasoning evident in the case of *XYZ v. Schering Health Care Ltd* (2002). It further demonstrates that much of the hostility is predicated upon a general lack of judicial understanding of epidemiology as a discipline. Focusing on the recent UK Supreme Court (formerly the House of Lords) decision in *Sienkiewicz v. Greif* (2011), Section II addresses, and seeks to correct, three common judicial misconceptions of epidemiology: (1) that epidemiology is concerned solely with "naked statistics"; (2) that epidemiologists treat evidence of a "doubling of the risk" as sufficient proof of causation; and (3) that if accepted in court, epidemiological evidence would have to

C. McIvor (✉)
Birmingham Law School, University of Birmingham, Birmingham, UK
e-mail: c.mcivor@bham.ac.uk

S. Loue (ed.), *Forensic Epidemiology in the Global Context*,
DOI 10.1007/978-1-4614-6738-0_3, © Springer Science+Business Media New York 2013

be regarded as determinative of the outcome of the legal causal enquiry. Finally, Section III demonstrates how the current UK approach to determining causation in certain categories of personal injury litigation could be improved through greater use of epidemiological expert witnesses. The high-profile House of Lords decision in *Gregg v. Scott* (2005) is used as a case study to illustrate the common legal and scientific errors made by UK lawyers in assessing questions of probabilistic causation. The case of *Gregg v. Scott* highlights the problems associated with the UK's tendency to turn to clinicians, rather than epidemiologists, for expert guidance on highly specialised questions of epidemiology and statistical interpretation.

Part I: Judicial Understanding of Epidemiology

The first important case to turn to is *XYZ and others v. Schering Health Care Ltd* (2002). The claimants in this case were a group of women who alleged that they had developed various cardiovascular injuries, falling under the collective description of venous thromboembolism (VTE), after ingesting certain brands of third-generation combined oral contraceptives (COCs) manufactured by the defendant pharmaceutical companies. They sought to establish that these COCs were defective under the provisions of the Consumer Protection Act 1987 and that they should accordingly have been advised of the risks of harm before making their decisions about whether to use the product. The claimants accepted that they were required to prove that the third generation COCs carried a true excess risk of VTE which is more than twice that carried by second generation COCs (i.e. the product that they would presumably have taken in place of third generation COCs had they been aware in advance of the risks of VTE). The trial on this one issue lasted 42 days, involved ten epidemiological expert witnesses and resulted in a dismissal of the claim. In delivering his lengthy judgment and concluding that the evidence indicated, at best, a relative risk of 1.7, the trial judge, Mr. Justice Mackay, was highly critical of several of the claimants' epidemiological experts. Of the epidemiological testimony generally, he described it as:

> unyielding, at times almost rancorous in tone, and with a few honourable exceptions with which I will deal as I go through the issues, devoid of willingness to countenance that there may be two sides to the question. So, science has failed to give women clear advice spoken with one voice (EWHC, 2002, 1420 at paragraph 33).

The fact that the epidemiological experts were able to disagree so strongly and so widely in their interpretations of the results of the various epidemiological studies called upon in evidence did much to tarnish the reputation of epidemiology in Mr. Justice Mackay's view. In attempting to sum up the evidence, he referred to "the potential for almost endless adjustment" of the results of the studies. Taking issue with the metaphor of "an anchor" as used by one of the experts to describe the role of meta-analysis in conflicting observational studies, he commented that "shifting sand" seemed more apt (2002, paragraph 327). His most strident criticism, however, was reserved for two of the claimant's experts, Professor Alexander M. Walker and Professor Klim McPherson.

Addressing first Professor Walker's attempt to refute under cross-examination the defendant's use of Cox regression analysis to demonstrate that there is no enhanced relative risk at all between the two generations of the contraceptive pill, Mr. Justice Mackay delivered the following scathing assessment of Walker's performance:

> At the outset of this exercise I warned him….that my own familiarity with algebra lay in the past and at an elementary level. Quite undeterred Walker proceeded over 8 pages of transcript, aided by several pages of a flip-chart, to go through a series of calculations at some speed which purported to support what he had just said. I considered the matter overnight with the benefit of the transcript. I concluded that I did not understand the evidence and so I thought it right the next morning to say so in open court…. This problem was left with [counsel for the claimants] who later in the trial told me that the Claimants had decided not to persist with this evidence. This episode in the evidence was, I have to say, typical of Professor Walker as a witness. It was done with immense panache and every appearance of authority; it made no concessions to the tribunal and did not constitute, in my opinion, a serious attempt to assist the court ([2002] EWHC 1420 at paragraph 149).

He later described Professor Walker's meta-analysis as a "tortuous, unconvincing and poorly described process" which was "the least impressive of the various attempts to reach overall conclusions" from the various studies presented in evidence (paragraph 316).

As regards Professor McPherson, Mr. Justice Mackay was able to point to at least eight serious errors or incorrect statements in his main report to the court. Describing these errors as amounting to more than mere carelessness, Mr. Justice Mackay concluded that Professor McPherson "did not approach this exercise in a careful or an even handed manner" and stated that as a result he was "not confident in him as an expert witness on whom [he could] rely in this case" (paragraph 330).

A further one of the claimants' experts, Dr. Hershel Jick, who was said to be a veteran pharmacoepidemiologist with a distinguished record of achievement, was described by Mr. Justice Mackay as "at times a testy, flippant and even cantankerous witness" who demonstrated "palpable" contempt for another expert witness who had disagreed with his findings, who voiced criticisms of this other expert which were said to be "almost corrosive in their quality" and who "made a grimace of disgust which spoke volumes" when asked to meet privately with this other expert to try to work out an explanation for the marked differences between their results (paragraph 210).

Having formed the distinct impression that very little of the evidence presented could be relied upon and also having resolved that the defendants' experts were generally far more compelling than those proffered by the claimants, Mr. Justice Mackay's dismissal of the legal claim was clear and decisive. He concluded that the most convincing evidence indicated that there was in fact no increased risk of VTE carried by the third generation COCs as compared to second generation COCs. He further concluded that, in the event that he was wrong about this, the highest risk indicated by any of the "reliable" evidence was only 1.7 and thus significantly below the relative risk of 2, the minimum requirement.

It is a matter of regret that so much contradictory and, it would appear, methodologically problematic, epidemiological evidence was submitted to the court. It is argued here that the *XYZ* debacle demonstrates the need for the introduction into UK civil law of a pretrial admissibility test for scientific evidence which would afford the court an opportunity to evaluate the scientific and legal reliability of the epidemiologic evidence that parties wish to introduce at trial. To protect the reputation of epidemiology as a discipline, it is important that only reliable and relevant epidemiological evidence is relied upon in litigation. Sadly, it is evident from the *Sienkiewicz* case, as will be demonstrated presently, that the *XYZ* litigation has greatly influenced the current judicial view of epidemiology as a kind of pseudoscience based on assumptions and speculations and carrying a false air of authority. The *XZY* decision is described in the recent Supreme Court decision in *Sienkiewicz* as a "remarkable" case and one which contains "a detailed and illuminating discussion of epidemiology" (2011, paragraphs 8, 74).

The next decision of interest is that of the Scottish Court of Session in *McTear v. Imperial Tobacco Limited* (2005). The victim in this case was a smoker who died of lung cancer at the age of 48 and his widow brought a negligence action against the manufacturer of his regular brand of cigarettes. As part of her claim, she was duly required to prove, on the balance of probabilities (the UK equivalent of the standard known in the US as the preponderance of the evidence) that her husband's cancer had been caused by smoking the defendant's cigarettes, in the sense that had it not been for smoking those cigarettes, he would not have developed the disease. Vigorously defending the claim, Imperial Tobacco denied not only the existence of a specific causal connection between Mr. McTear's lung cancer and his smoking habit, but even the existence of a proven causal connection between smoking and lung cancer more generally. It maintained this position even in the face of its admissions that the World Health Organisation, the UK Government and the US Government had accepted for many years that cigarettes can cause lung cancer. The judge, Lord Nimmo Smith, held in favour of Imperial Tobacco on both counts (and indeed on every other count).

For present purposes, it is quite astonishing that Lord Nimmo Smith was not prepared, on the basis of the voluminous medical literature submitted in evidence before him, to draw even a general inference of causation between smoking and lung cancer. His main justification for refusing to accept the epidemiological evidence on this issue was the fact that he had not been "sufficiently instructed by the expert evidence about this discipline" to be able to form his own judgment of the evidence. To some extent, this was not an unreasonable point. Arguably, it was unwise, in hindsight, for the pursuer's legal counsel to have relied almost entirely on published reports in the absence of expert witnesses to speak to the reports in court (and crucially to be cross-examined on these issues). Sections II and III below underscore the importance of having epidemiologists appear as expert witnesses in cases involving epidemiological information so that they can provide expert guidance to the court on how to interpret the information, in terms of its reliability and pertinence to the particular causal issues at stake in individual cases. To that extent, Lord Nimmo Smith's plea for epidemiological evidence to be accompanied by epidemiological expert witnesses is both helpful and reasonable.

As pointed out by Goldberg (2011), however, to the extent that this plea presupposes an entirely passive role on the part of the judge, it must be called into question. It is not acceptable for judges to refuse to even attempt to engage with a set of evidence in the absence of expert witness guidance. As such, it is argued that Lord Nimmo Smith incorrectly held that there was no proven causal connection between smoking and lung cancer. Even without the help of an epidemiological expert witness, the evidence on this issue was clear and overwhelming. Moreover, as commented by Miller (2006, p. 544),

> quite apart from public understanding of the strength of the link between smoking and lung cancer, it is somewhat ironic that a Scottish judge should come to a contrary conclusion at a time when the Scottish Parliament was passing legislation which, to protect public health, would ban smoking in public places.

As regards the issue of individual causation, namely the requirement of proof on the balance of probabilities that smoking was the cause of Mr. McTear's illness, the absence of epidemiological expert witnesses to explain the potential application of the relevant epidemiological studies to the circumstances of Mr. McTear as an individual was arguably fatal to the claim. As the detailed discussion below of *Sienkiewicz* demonstrates, lawyers generally have not had training in and therefore do not understand epidemiology. As a result, they tend to equate epidemiology with the production of so-called "naked statistics." The term "naked statistics" is used by the UK courts to refer to raw statistical data which are not supported by causal inference and which do not directly relate to the specific circumstances of the claim at hand. For good reason, the courts do not attach much probative weight to naked statistics, at least when it comes to establishing causation in law. Where epidemiological evidence is central to a legal claim, it is therefore imperative that epidemiologists are on hand to explain the difference between epidemiology and naked statistics, and to reassure the courts that it is possible not only to independently assess the scientific reliability of an epidemiological study and to assess its specific relevance (or lack thereof) to the individual causal issues at stake, but also to use various techniques, such as Bayes' Theorem, to refine general statistical chances into personal chances, tailored to the characteristics of the victim in question (Goldberg, 2011).

The next decision of particular interest here is that of the Court of Appeal in *Novartis Grimsby Limited v. Cookson* (2007). The victim in this case started working in the dyestuffs industry in 1964, and during the course of his employment, but in particular prior to 1980, he was exposed to carcinogenic amines. In 2001, he was diagnosed with bladder cancer. He subsequently sued his employer in negligence, alleging that the cancer had been caused by the employer's failure to adequately protect him from exposure to amines. In defending the claim, the employer argued that the bladder cancer had most likely been caused by the victim's own smoking habit. The victim had smoked between 10 and 20 cigarettes a day for about 20 years before giving up the habit completely in about 1980. It was accepted by both parties that cigarette smoke contains amines and that the amines from both sources act on the body in the same way. It was further accepted that the two forms of exposure would have had at least an additive, if not synergistic, effect. The dispute lay in the relative potency of the two sources. Legal counsel for the victim sought to argue that the risks of bladder cancer associated with the occupational exposure were much higher than those associated with the smoking, while legal counsel for the employer sought to argue the contrary.

The matter fell to be determined by the expert witness evidence. The victim's team relied upon a clinician, a consulting urologist who, having reviewed the published work on the causes of bladder cancer, concluded that the occupational exposure was the major contributing factor. He assessed the contribution of the occupational exposure at between 70 and 75 % and the contribution of the smoking at between 25 and 30 %. The employer's team relied primarily upon the evidence of an epidemiologist with an extensive list of publications on the causes of bladder cancer. He considered that the levels of occupational exposure were so low that the exposure to amines in the cigarette smoke had to be regarded as the main cause. At first instance, the judge had preferred the evidence of the clinician over that of the epidemiologist and had found in favour of the victim. On appeal to the Court of Appeal, counsel for the defendant argued that the epidemiologist was the real expert on the issues and that as such, his evidence should have been preferred. Not only was the clinician's opinion pure assertion, unsupported by the published literature, but it also went beyond his expertise as a clinician. The Court of Appeal disagreed. To quote Lady Justice Smith:

> The proposition that a clinician is not capable of fully understanding the published epidemiological literature on the causation of a condition within his own speciality seems unsustainable and would, I think, surprise many clinicians and epidemiologists (2007, paragraph 57).

As will be elaborated upon below, Lady Justice Smith's comment is indicative of a general judicial belief that epidemiology is a very simple and unsophisticated branch of science and that clinicians are reliable experts on all matters pertaining to medical science.

The last significant point to make about the Court of Appeal decision in *Novartis* is that it endorsed the application of a "doubling of the risk" test of causation. Relying on the clinician's apparent "guesstimate" to the effect that occupational exposure to amines accounted for 70–75 % of the total risk of the victim's bladder cancer, with smoking accounting for the remaining 20–25 %, the Court concluded that occupational exposure had more than doubled the risk of harm due to smoking. In the view of Lady Justice Smith, these figures also satisfied the orthodox "but for" test for causation:

> The natural inference to draw from the finding of fact that the occupational exposure was 70 % of the total is that, if it had not been for the occupational exposure, the [victim] would not have developed bladder cancer. In terms of risk, if occupational exposure more than doubles the risk due to smoking, it must as a matter of logic, be probable that the disease was caused by the former (at paragraph 74).

Such conclusions on causation are highly contestable. Serious concerns must be raised about both the reliability of the crucial figures of 70–75 % and 25–30 % and the soundness of the assumption that there were no other significant causal factors at play. Moreover, it is simply not true to say that bare statistical evidence to the effect that the risk of harm associated with exposure A is more than twice as high as the risk associated with exposure B leads *inexorably* to the conclusion that, as a matter of fact, an individual instantiation of harm was *probably* caused by A. It is important to note here that statistical evidence cannot *automatically* determine the question of causation in law. (The problematic nature of the casual reasoning adopted by the Court of Appeal in *Novartis* is discussed in detail in Sections II and III below.)

To meet the balance of probabilities standard of proof which applies to the test for causation in tort law, the court must hold a minimum degree of belief in the evidence indicating a causal connection. Contrary to common judicial belief, the numerical value associated with the piece of evidence indicating a causal connection, e.g. the relationship between exposure to a specific substance and the alleged adverse health outcome, does not correlate in any way with the separate belief value. In weighing up the probative value of a piece of statistical evidence which indicates, for example, a 90 % probability that X caused Y, the court should look at much more than just the value of 90 % in determining whether it is persuaded overall that it is at least more likely than not that X actually did cause Y. Of crucial importance will be any information which speaks to the reliability (or unreliability) of the study that produced the result of 90 %. The statistical evidence will also have to be weighed up against what Wright would describe as any "particularistic" evidence that has been submitted to the court, such as eyewitness testimony to the effect that Y was actually caused by Z (Wright, 2008)

This brings us to the most recent case of interest, and arguably the most important, that of the Supreme Court in *Sienkiewicz v. Greif* (2011). The claim in *Sienkiewicz* concerned liability in negligence for occupational exposure to asbestos. The victim in question had developed and subsequently died from mesothelioma; her estate sought to establish that the disease had been caused by her former employer's failure to adequately protect her from asbestos in the workplace. The fault of the employer in exposing the victim to asbestos was not in dispute. Rather, the problem for the court was the fact that the victim had also been exposed to high levels of asbestos in the general atmosphere of the area in which she lived, namely, Ellesmere Port in Cheshire. It was clear on the evidence presented that, by comparison with the degree of environmental exposure to asbestos, the level of occupational exposure was very light.

Relying on the fact that it could not be shown on the evidence that the victim's mesothelioma was due to the occupational exposure rather than the environmental exposure, the defendant employer argued that the claim should fail for lack of causation in law. The Supreme Court disagreed. Imposing liability on the employer for the entirety of the harm sustained by the victim, the Supreme Court held that causation could be inferred from the fact that the occupational exposure had "materially contributed to the risk of the harm." This "material contribution to the risk of harm" test is an exceptional test reserved for so-called "evidentiary gap" cases, that is, cases in which, as a direct result of gaps in scientific knowledge, it is not possible to prove causation on orthodox grounds (*Barker v. Corus (UK) plc*, 2006; *Fairchild v. Glenhaven Funeral Services Ltd*, 2002; Steele & Ibbetson, 2011). Coming from the highest court in the land, *Sienkiewicz* confirms the commitment of the UK judiciary to the compensation principle in mesothelioma cases and its willingness to side-step the traditional rules of causation in pursuit of this public-policy-based objective.

The ruling in *Sienkiewicz* raises numerous issues of great interest to tort lawyers. For present purposes however, the significance of the decision lies in fact that it represents the highest judicial pronouncement on the issue of using epidemiology to establish causation in personal injury litigation. The Supreme Court discussed epidemiology at some length in this case. Unfortunately, the strong steer that it ultimately gave is that, as a legal tool, epidemiological evidence is both generally unhelpful and unreliable. The clear signal given to lower courts and to personal injury lawyers who may encounter or contemplate relying upon epidemiological evidence is to treat such evidence with extreme caution, and to refrain from using it as a basis for determining causation.

The lead speech in *Sienkiewicz* was delivered by Lord Phillips, who at the time was President of the Supreme Court. As such, his views are widely influential. His basic conclusion is that epidemiological evidence cannot provide a satisfactory basis upon which to make findings of causation in law. In justifying this conclusion, he referred throughout his speech to problems associated with the adequacy and reliability of such evidence. Moreover, he gave the impression that these problems are insurmountable. The following quotation neatly sums up his general attitude towards epidemiology:

> Not only is the adequacy of epidemiological evidence relevant to the weight to be attached to it. So is its reliability.... Deducing causation in relation to mesothelioma on the basis of epidemiological evidence requires a comparison between the statistical relationship between exposure and the incidence of the disease and the experience of the victim who has sustained the disease. A number of factors make this exercise particularly problematic. The first is the difficulty in collating sound epidemiological data. The second is the difficulty of obtaining reliable evidence as to the relevant experience of the victim. The third is uncertainty as to the adequacy of the epidemiological evidence that is available as a guide to causation (paragraph 98).

Lord Kerr goes so far as to suggest that epidemiology lacks credibility as a scientific discipline:

> There is a real danger that so-called "epidemiological evidence" will carry a false air of authority. It is necessary to guard against treating a theory based on assumptions as a workable benchmark against which an estimate of the increase in the risk could be measured (paragraph 206).

Given the time spent by the Supreme Court in *Sienkiewicz* in discussing the legal value of epidemiology, it is perhaps surprising to note that the negligence claim at issue did not actually involve epidemiological evidence. At no point in the proceedings did either party seek to introduce any epidemiological evidence. In addition, none of the specific legal issues raised by the case as pleaded before the Supreme

Court required any direct consideration of epidemiology. The only reason for the Supreme Court to broach the subject was a mistaken belief that epidemiology is intrinsically linked with a doubling of the risk approach to causation in law. The Supreme Court disagreed with a suggestion made by Lady Justice Smith in the Court of Appeal decision in *Sienkiewicz* to the effect that a doubling of the risk test should operate as the default test for causation in so-called "evidential gap" cases. To cast doubt on the doubling of the risk approach, the Supreme Court consequently thought that it was necessary to take issue with epidemiology. As this chapter demonstrates below, the intrinsic link conventionally made by the UK courts between epidemiology and a doubling of the risk approach to causation is not only misconceived, it is just one symptom of a wider problem of judicial ignorance about epidemiology.

When it comes to analysing the sceptical attitude of the Supreme Court in *Sienkiewicz* to epidemiological evidence, it is important to bear in mind that the Court will necessarily have been influenced by the previous negative judicial experiences of epidemiology as discussed above. That discussion has also identified a general judicial lack of understanding of epidemiology as a discipline. From the decision in *Sienkiewicz*, it is possible to pinpoint three specific judicial misconceptions about epidemiology and its application to tort law principles which have operated in a cumulative and distorted fashion: (1) that epidemiology is concerned solely with "naked" statistics; (2) that epidemiologists treat evidence of a doubling of the risk as sufficient proof of causation; and (3) that if accepted in court, epidemiological evidence would have to be regarded as determinative of the outcome of the legal causal enquiry.

Part II: Addressing the Misconceptions

Misconception 1: Epidemiologists Deal Only in "Naked" Statistics

Central to the negative stance on epidemiology adopted by the Supreme Court is the misconceived notion that epidemiology is to be equated with basic statistics. In the first part of his speech, Lord Phillips describes epidemiology as "statistical analysis" (*Sienkiewicz v. Greif*, 2011, paragraph 11). Further on, he explains that epidemiology is "the study of the occurrence and distribution of events (such as disease) over human populations" and states that it "seeks to determine whether statistical associations between these events and the supposed determinants can be demonstrated" (2011, paragraph 80). Crucially, he goes on to state that epidemiology is not concerned with the further question of whether these statistical associations demonstrate an underlying biologically causal relationship. While statistics are certainly an important tool used by epidemiologists, they are no more than a tool and epidemiologists are more than just statisticians. In addition to designing and executing studies to collect relevant data, epidemiologists use various sophisticated techniques for interpreting the data precisely in order to determine whether any indicated statistical associations provide evidence of an underlying biological relationship of cause and effect. What the courts do not appear to realise is that epidemiologists are trained in both statistics and research methodologies, that many also have training in medicine and that the highly specialised techniques that they use for drawing causal inferences from empirical data are informed by all three disciplines.

Also telling in this respect is the discussion in *Sienkiewicz* by both Lord Phillips and Lord Rodger of what they describe as the "epidemiological example" used by Lord Mackay in the famous case of *Hotson v. East Berkshire Area Health Authority* (1987). This example draws on the facts of the House of Lords decision in *McGhee v. National Coal Board* (1973). The causal issue for determination in that case was whether the provision of washing facilities at the end of their shift for employees who had been exposed to brick dust during the course of their employment would have prevented the employee victim in question from developing dermatitis. Lord Mackay hypothesised the following set of figures as applying to the claim in *McGhee*:

> One might, for example, say that it was established that of 100 people working under the same conditions as the pursuer and without facilities for washing at the end of their shift, 70 contracted dermatitis: of 100 people working in the same conditions as the pursuer when washing facilities were provided for them at the end of the shift, 30 contracted dermatitis (1987, p.786).

By presenting this as an epidemiological example, the Supreme Court creates the misleading impression that such bare statistical information represents the sum-total of what epidemiology can provide in the circumstances. In giving his account of his perceived shortcomings of epidemiology as a legal tool, Lord Phillips suggested that a further reason for doubting the results of an epidemiological study is that it would focus on only one specific agent, or a number of specific agents and that it would not take into account "other casual factors operating in conjunction with the agent exposure which is the particular object of the investigation, e.g. the age or genetic susceptibility of the victim" (2011, paragraph 84). In a similar vein, Lord Nimmo Smith in *McTear* suggested that

> group estimates obscure the underlying heterogeneity of the population so that it is entirely possible that other group memberships besides exposure, like genetic profile, socio-economic status, workplace, diet and other exposures make a major contribution to disease occurrence (2005, paragraph 6:180).

As observed by Goldberg (2011), such statements exhibit a lack of awareness of the epidemiological doctrine of confounding. In designing, executing and interpreting the results of a study, any good epidemiologist would automatically consider potential confounders, as well as potential effect modifiers and sources of bias (Rothman, Greenland, & Lash, 2008).

To overcome the current judicial aversion to epidemiology, it is necessary to directly challenge the judicial perception of epidemiology as an unsophisticated branch of science that deals only in the calculation of incidence rates and relative risks.

Misconception 2: Epidemiologists Treat Evidence of a Doubling of the Risk as Proof of Causation

As evidenced by *Sienkiewicz*, the UK courts also mistakenly believe that epidemiologists will make a finding of causation on the sole basis of a relative risk result of just over 2. Taken in conjunction with the belief that epidemiologists deal only in naked statistics, this misconception about the significance of RR>2 serves to cement the judicial view of epidemiology as a pseudo-science.

In the course of pressing his concerns about the reliability and adequacy of epidemiological evidence as a legal tool, Lord Phillips attempted to explain the epidemiologic concept of relative risk or RR. In doing so, he stated that where the RR exceeds 2, the statistical likelihood is that the particular exposure was the cause of the disease. Having just stated that epidemiology is concerned with the question of statistical associations and not with the separate question of whether such associations demonstrate an underlying biological causal relationship, he thereby implies that epidemiologists would not look any further than the statistical likelihood calculated by the RR when formulating their conclusions about causation. Thus, he concludes that RR>2 is a "tenuous basis for concluding that the statistical cause of a disease was also the probable biological cause, or cause in fact" (paragraph 84), with the term "cause in fact" being used in its legal sense.

To be fair to the Supreme Court, the misconception that epidemiologists use RR>2 as proof of causation has been prevalent in legal circles for some time and has been largely unchallenged. It is also the source of the highly suspect legal test for causation known as the "doubles-the-risk" test. As explained by Lord Phillips at the beginning of his speech in *Sienkiewicz*, this test is usually applied to epidemiological evidence. The test functions by attributing causative effect to any factor that more than doubles the risk of a specific outcome compared to the risk that would have otherwise existed.

There are at least two fundamental problems with the doubles-the-risk test in law, one theoretical and the other practical. First, it is based on a misunderstanding of the epidemiological significance of the concept of RR. Epidemiologists do not treat evidence of a doubling of a statistical risk as proof of causation. As explained above, epidemiology involves much more than the basic calculation of incidence rates and epidemiologists do not base any conclusions about causation on RR results alone. Contrary to the impression given by the courts, RR>2 holds no intrinsic significance or value in epidemiology. While RR>2 can sometimes be used as a floor value for deciding whether further epidemiological investigations are warranted into the relationship between a particular agent and a disease outcome, such investigations will often proceed even with a relative risk of less than 2. Furthermore, the RR calculation is just one of many different measurements of disease occurrence used by epidemiologists. When analysing the results of a study, an epidemiologist will employ a variety of complicated mathematical equations, each one designed to measure a specific aspect of disease occurrence.

This leads us to the second problem with the doubles-the-risk test as used in UK tort law, namely that it bears no resemblance in practice to the scientific concept on which it is supposed to be based. RR has been referred to above as a measurement of disease occurrence, and it is important to clarify at this point what it is that RR actually measures. As explained by Broadbent (2011, p. 240), "RR is a measure of how much more common a given condition is among people who are subject to a given exposure than among those who are not." It is a simple ratio which compares the relative frequency, over a specified time period, of the occurrence of a disease between two populations or groups, one group having been exposed to a particular agent and the other not having been so exposed. An RR of 1 means the same proportion of people developed the disease in both groups during the relevant timeframe. An RR of 2 indicates that twice as many people in the exposed group developed the disease compared with those in the unexposed group, and so on. The main point to take from this description of RR is that it is a specific epidemiologic concept with a specific function.

By contrast, tort law's doubles-the-risk test operates in an altogether unscientific and unsystematic fashion. A large part of the problem is a lack of judicial guidance on how the notion of background risk is to be defined for the purposes of the test and also how these risks should be quantified. This has resulted in decisions about causation being based on a series of random calculations of arbitrarily chosen, and crudely quantified, risk factors.

The first application of a doubles-the-risk test in a personal injury context may be traced to *XYZ v. Schering*, discussed above in Section I. While this case is problematic on a number of fronts, its manner of application of the doubles-the-risk test was generally sound. This is because the test was applied to actual epidemiological data about relevant incidence rates, which made the exercise a straightforward one. It is also important to note that the test was not used in *XYZ* to establish causation as such, but rather to determine whether a product was defective for the purposes of the relevant consumer protection legislation. While the notion of defect contains a causal element, in that it requires some kind of plausible link to be shown between the proper use of the product and a harmful outcome, this link is much weaker than that which applies to the requirement of causation in negligence. If the claimants in *XYZ* had been able to show that third generation COCs carried in excess of a two-fold increase in risk of VTE as against second generation COCs, all that they would have succeeded in establishing is that they should have been warned about this risk before deciding whether to take the product. They would still have had to have shown separately that had it not been for the defect they would have avoided the harms complained of.

Unfortunately, the *XZY* decision has subsequently been interpreted as establishing that a doubling of the risk test may be used to establish causation in any case involving probabilistic evidence. The Court of Appeal decision in *Novartis v. Cookson* provides an example of its misuse in this respect. As will be recalled, causation was found to have been established in this case on the basis of expert evidence indicating that there was a 70–75 % chance that the victim's bladder cancer had been caused by occupational exposure to amines and only a 20–25 % chance that it had been caused by cigarette smoke. Section I above questioned the logic behind Lady Justice Smith's reasoning that "if occupational exposure more than doubles-the-risk due to smoking, it must… be probable that the disease was caused by the former" (*Novartis v. Cookson*, 2007, paragraph 74). While evidence indicating that the risk of harm associated with the tortious exposure is at least twice as high as the total combined risk of all other relevant factors may be persuasive, it would not necessarily be conclusive of the causation issue. Bearing in mind the supposed epidemiological basis of the test, serious concern must also be raised with respect to the methods used in this case to quantify the respective risk factors. The expert who provided the estimates was not an epidemiologist and the figures of 70–75 % and 20–25 % appear to have been subjective approximations. No allowance appears to have been made for the possibility of any idiopathic causes.

The approach taken in *Novartis* can be compared with that adopted by the trial judge, Judge Main QC, in *Sienkiewicz*. Although Judge Main QC's decision to apply the doubles-the-risk test to the claim in *Sienkiewicz* was overruled on appeal by both Court of Appeal and the Supreme Court, the overruling related only to the choice of this test over the more victim-friendly "material contribution to the risk of harm" test; no questions were raised about the way in which he applied it to the facts of the claim. It will be recalled that the claim in *Sienkiewicz* involved two potential sources of asbestos exposure, one being occupational and the other being environmental. Applying the doubles-the-risk test, Judge Main QC held that in order to show that the defendant employer had caused the mesothelioma, the victim had to demonstrate that the tortious occupational risk of mesothelioma had more than doubled the risk from the non-tortious environmental exposure. The official case report of the decision indicates that the quantitative assessment of the two sources of exposure was carried out by Judge Main QC personally and without the help of an expert. The case report provides little information about how he did this. The report concluded that the victim's lifetime environmental exposure created a risk of mesothelioma of 24 cases per million, while the cumulative occupational exposure gave rise to a risk of just 4.39 cases per million. Dividing 4.39 by 24, Judge Main QC concluded that the occupational exposure had only increased the risk due to the environment by 18 % and that the claim should fail for lack of causation. On appeal, the victim was successful in establishing causation in accordance with the material increase in the risk of harm test for causation. Relying on the calculations carried out at first instance, both the Court of Appeal and the Supreme Court held that an 18 % increase in risk constituted a sufficiently material increase for this purpose.

It is clear that the relative risks were assessed in very different ways in *Novartis* and *Sienkiewicz*. In *Novartis*, the risk values were presented as personalised probabilities (20–25 % versus 70–75 %) which totalled 100 %, reflecting the fact that the victim had contracted the harm in question. In *Sienkiewicz*, the risk values related instead to abstract, population-level risks (24 cases per million versus 4.39 cases per million). A particular concern with the latter approach is that it fails to emphasise the need for the "background risk" calculation to include *all* of the relevant background risks. Thus, there is a danger that the *Sienkiewicz* approach could be interpreted as establishing that it is sufficient for the purposes of the doubles-the-risk test to measure the tortious risk factor against just one other relevant risk factor. In his unreported decision in *Shortell v. BICAL*, Mr. Justice Mackay opined that where

> the claimant has proved causation….by showing a more than doubled relative risk it is not relevant as between the claimant and the defendant to argue that another agent (tortious or otherwise) may also have contributed to the occurrence of the disease (2008, paragraph 51).

Fortunately, the Supreme Court in *Sienkiewicz* expressed strong reservations about using a doubling of the risk approach as a legal test for causation. Although its reservations in this respect relate to its general scepticism of epidemiological methods rather than to any specific concerns about the test in itself, the adoption of any kind of negative stance on the issue is to be welcomed insofar as it will discourage use of the test. It can only be hoped that the doubles-the-risk test will eventually be abandoned entirely.

Misconception 3: If Epidemiological Evidence Is Accepted in Court, It Must Be Treated As Determinative of the Causation Issue

This mistaken belief hinges on the all-too-common error made by the courts (and one which they only make when dealing with statistics) of conflating the substantive and evidential aspects of the test for factual causation and then reducing that conflation to a nonsensical numerical test.

To explain this point, it is necessary to briefly outline the tort law requirement of causation. As explained by Steel and Ibbetson (2011), it consists of two separate parts: (1) the conceptual/substantive part, which requires that the claimant (as the party carrying the burden of proof) establish that there is a necessary connection between the defendant's breach of duty and the pleaded actionable damage (this is what is meant by the term "but for" test); and (2) the evidential part, which requires that the claimant satisfy the substantive part in accordance with the relevant standard of proof, which in tort contexts is the balance of probabilities standard. According to this standard of proof, the claimant need only convince the court that it is at least more likely than not that his/her substantive arguments about causation, when judged against the corresponding arguments put forward by the defendant, represent what actually happened. In other words, in weighing up all the evidence about causation, the court has to be at least slightly more convinced by the claimant's case than the defendant's before the court can find in favour of the claimant. Indeed, the standard *requires* a court to find in favour of the claimant if it is, at the very least, marginally more convinced by the claimant's case than by the defendant's, notwithstanding the fact that it may still harbour serious doubts in this respect.

The problem where statistical evidence is concerned is the common practice of describing the test for causation as requiring a minimum 51 % proof (with everything above 50 % equating with 100 % proof and everything below equating with 0 %)and then mapping this figure of 51+ % directly on to the relevant piece of statistical evidence. Thus, if the claimant were to produce a piece of evidence which indicated that there was a 64 % likelihood that the pleaded harm was caused by the defendant's faulty conduct, this would be taken to mean that the claimant has duly satisfied the test for causation on the basis that 64 % is more than 50 % and that the court would be bound to find in the claimant's favour. This reasoning reflects a misunderstanding of the relationship between causation in epidemiology and causation in the legal context. Reluctant to be tied to the perceived determinative effect of epidemiological evidence (or any form of statistical evidence), the courts look for reasons to dispute the value or relevance of such evidence to the claim at hand.

Part of the problem underlying the tendency to map statistical results directly onto a numerical test for causation is that many lawyers have not had substantial training in mathematical-based reasoning. Lawyers' natural strengths lie instead with words, language, conceptual reasoning and analytical theorising. Barnes (2001) has advocated a helpful conceptual framework to assist lawyers in understanding (1) the distinction between the probability notion associated with the balance of probabilities standard in law and the various probabilities associated with a piece of statistical evidence, and (2) how to interpret the significance of a piece of statistical evidence for the purposes of the legal test for causation. This framework involves three probabilistic categories: fact probabilities, belief probabilities and sampling error probabilities (Barnes, 2001). As explained by Miller (2006), Barnes' framework builds upon a model previously developed by Gold (1986). It is worthy to note that in discussing the value of epidemiological evidence, several members of the Supreme Court in *Sienkiewicz* actually referred to Gold's work. Unfortunately, as their speeches subsequently demonstrated, they failed to integrate into their opinions his central arguments.

Under the Barnes model, the term "fact probability" is used to refer to a piece of probabilistic evidence which speaks to the existence (or non-existence) of a causal connection between the relevant tortious agent, X, and the pleaded damage, Y. A piece of statistical evidence indicating, for example, a 64 % likelihood that Y was caused by X is therefore relevant to the question of whether the "but for" test has been satisfied. As a relatively strong likelihood value, this piece of statistical evidence may be said to speak moderately favour of the existence of a "but for" connection between X and Y.

As stated earlier in this chapter, fact probabilities are never determinative in their own right of the legal causal enquiry, regardless of the strength of the probability value that they indicate. As such, the statistical value of 64 % holds no intrinsic legal significance. This is because the legal weight of the fact probability (the result of 64 %) will depend entirely on the level of confidence that the court holds in it as a piece of evidence about causation. This is where the notions of "belief probability" and "sampling error probability" come in. The term belief probability relates to the overall strength or credibility of the fact probability evidence. In assessing its level of confidence in the fact probability, the court will look at a variety of factors which speak to the credibility not just of the study that produced the fact probability, but also the credibility of the person who carried out the study. For instance, evidence submitted to the court indicating that the author of the study had previously been exposed as having falsified data would significantly reduce the court's confidence in the reliability of the result of 64 %. As regards the quality of the study itself, in determining belief probability, the court would look for information about the quality of the study design and the robustness of its execution. For this purpose, the use of appropriately qualified expert witnesses is essential. Where the fact probability is presented as a piece of epidemiological evidence, the relevant expert witness should be an epidemiologist.

When assessing the scientific robustness of a piece of epidemiological evidence, an epidemiologist would look at factors such as the sample size utilised in the study, the manner in which data were collected and potential sources of bias accounted for, the control of relevant variables, adjustments for confounders and effect modifiers, etc. As an expert witness, the epidemiologist would be able to provide valuable information to the court about the degree of pertinence of the study results to the specific circumstances of the claimant in question. Additional indicators of scientific reliability are the *p*-values or the confidence intervals associated with the risk estimates produced by the relevant studies. While these measurements also speak to the scientific robustness of the study, Barnes advocates placing them under a separate probability category, that of the sampling error probability. These measures are expressed as numerical values and so dealing with them separately reduces the potential for confusion with the other numerical evidence and helps to clarify the nature of the relationship between general belief probabilities and specific sampling error ones.

Put very simply, *p*-values and confidence intervals measure the degree of variation in the results produced by data against the size of the sample of individuals used for the study; they help to assess whether the results produced by the study are due to the unrepresentativeness of the sample rather than a biological association. The higher the *p*-value, for example, the higher the likelihood that the results have been skewed by the atypical nature of the individuals making up the study sample and that they are therefore not reliable. As explained by Miller (2006), medical scientists customarily treat a 5 % ($p < 0.05$ or confidence interval of 95 %) sampling error probability as a standard benchmark of reliability, in the sense that it safely warrants an assumption that any statistical associations indicated by the study are a product of a relationship between the variables being tested rather than happenstance. Overall, a sampling error probability is just one factor that is relevant to determining the court's belief probability in the piece of statistical evidence about cause, that is, the fact probability.

To apply all of this to the legal test for causation, fact probabilities, as pieces of evidence about the existence of a causal connection between X and Y, may be said to relate to the substantive/conceptual element of the legal test for causation, the so-called but for test. Belief probabilities and sampling error probabilities are together relevant to the evidential part of the legal test, that is to the question of whether the balance of probabilities standard of proof has been met. In this respect, the balance of probabilities may be described as referring to the court's overall belief assessment of the case made by the claimant about causation. As explained above, to meet this standard, the court has to be at least marginally more convinced by the claimant's case than the defendant's. In determining its overall belief assessment, the court has to take into account all the evidence. Where epidemiological evidence is involved, it will therefore constitute just one factor to be weighed into the mix. Moreover, it would be entirely possible for a court to accept the epidemiological evidence in support of a causal connection but then to decide that, overall, it is more convinced by evidence disputing the existence of causation.

Since belief values are impossible to quantify in precise terms, in the sense that ordinary human beings cannot differentiate between a 51 % degree of belief and a 58 % degree of belief, it is argued here that we should dispense with the practice of expressing the balance of probabilities standard in numerical terms and describe it instead as requiring the court to decide overall whether it is, at the very least, marginally more convinced by the claimant's submissions than by the defendant's. Such an approach would avoid much of the current confusion about the relationship between scientific probabilities and the legal test for causation.

Part III: Epidemiologists as Expert Witnesses in Personal Injury Litigation

This section demonstrates how the current UK approach to determining questions of probabilistic causation in personal injury litigation could be improved through greater use of epidemiological expert witnesses. The high-profile decision of the House of Lords in *Gregg v. Scott* is used as a case study to demonstrate that the current approach is beset with fundamental scientific and legal errors. It also highlights the common UK practice of turning to clinicians for expert guidance on all aspects of biomedical science, including those aspects which fall outside the field of ordinary clinical medicine. Increased court reliance on epidemiologists as expert witnesses could help the courts to address these problems in two principal ways: (1) by providing the courts with statistical information that is both scientifically robust and pertinent to the causal issues at stake, and (2) by providing the courts with guidance on how to use and interpret such information.

The facts of *Gregg v. Scott* are far from unusual. The claimant, Mr. Gregg, went to see his General Practitioner, Dr. Scott, in November 1994 to ask about a lump which had developed under his left arm. Dr. Scott concluded that the lump was merely a lipoma, a benign collection of fatty tissue, and that no medical action was required. In August 1995, Mr. Gregg went to see a different doctor about the lump and this doctor referred him to a specialist for further investigation. In November 1995, following a biopsy ordered by the specialist, a form of cancer known as non-Hodgkin's lymphoma was diagnosed. By that time, the tumour had enlarged and spread into the left pectoral region causing Mr. Gregg acute pain. There followed during the month of August 1996 six sessions of chemotherapy, a course of radiotherapy and a session of high dose chemotherapy.

In early 1998, Mr. Gregg unfortunately suffered a relapse which was said to give him a very poor prognosis, and he underwent two further courses of chemotherapy which were described as being palliative rather than curative. Against the odds, however, Mr. Gregg's cancer then appeared to go into remission and from mid-1998 to the date of the House of Lords hearing in January 2005, there seemed to have been no further recurrence of the disease. Nevertheless, as set out by the trial judge, the impact of the whole experience on Mr. Gregg had been devastating. He had suffered severe side-effects from the original treatment, particularly the high dose chemotherapy. He continued to feel very ill and he had to give up work. He claimed that since the relapse in 1998, he felt that he was living on borrowed time. Both he and his wife were said to be very anxious and distressed, with Mr. Gregg having become preoccupied with his illness and possible death.

Mr. Gregg brought an action in negligence against Dr. Scott, alleging that he had breached his duty of care in failing to refer him for tests in November 1994, and that this breach of duty had resulted in a 9-month delay in the initiation of treatment. Mr. Gregg initially claimed that Dr. Scott's breach had deprived him of a complete cure, with a cure being defined in this context as disease-free survival for more than 10 years. However, before the initial trial, it was discovered that Mr. Gregg had a rare form of cancer known as ALK negative lymphoma which has a less favourable prognosis than the more common ALK positive variety. Realising that it would be difficult to prove that Mr. Gregg would probably have been cured but for Dr. Scott's breach, Mr. Gregg's legal team decided to advance an alternative claim for damages for the loss of chance of obtaining a more favourable outcome.

Although each side employed one medical expert, and these experts collaborated at one point in the proceedings on a joint report, only one of these experts, a Professor Goldstone (who was described as a consulting haematologist), actually gave oral evidence and it was on the sole basis of his evidence that the claim was decided. This means that before the three separate courts which ultimately heard the case (that is, the High Court, the Court of Appeal and the House of Lords), only one piece of expert evidence was ever relied upon. Professor Goldstone was actually Mr. Gregg's expert, and so it is somewhat surprising that it was his evidence which was to seal Mr. Gregg's fate. At first instance, and on appeal to both the Court of Appeal and House of Lords, Mr. Gregg lost his case.

However, it is important to take account of the fact that there was a change in circumstances in between Professor Goldstone first being instructed by Mr. Gregg's legal team and the date of the trial. In his first report on Mr. Gregg, which was written in July 1999, Professor Goldstone estimated that Mr. Gregg would have had an 84 % chance of being cured had treatment started 9 months earlier, and that as a result of the 9 month delay, his chances had been significantly reduced to below 50 %. After writing the report, however, it seems that his attention was drawn to a paper authored by Falini et al., and published by the American Society of Hematology in 1999. As set out in Lord Justice Latham's judgment in the Court of Appeal, this paper suggested that for prognosis purposes it was necessary to divide this non-Hodgkins lymphoma into the two categories known as ALK positive and ALK negative and that patients falling into the latter category had much lower prospects of recovery. To take account not just of this report, but also of the fact that at this point the claimant had survived for a further 3 years without relapse, Professor Goldstone and the expert witness instructed by Dr. Scott prepared a joint report in which they concluded that the delay in diagnosis resulted in the claimant having a "poorer prognosis" (*Gregg v. Scott*, 2002, paragraph 12). In terms of percentage figures, they indicated that Mr. Gregg would have had a 55 % chance of complete remission after the first course of treatment, but with a 40 % chance of relapse. They suggested that it was "quite possible" that his individual prognosis had been reduced to less than 50 % of what it would have been but for the delay in treatment (*Gregg v. Scott*, 2002, paragraph 13).

In his oral testimony at the time of the trial, Professor Goldstone presented a different set of figures. Working from the figures indicated in the joint report, he subsequently developed a special prognostic module which was said to have been based on the experiences of a cohort of 100 ALK negative patients. Based on this cohort study, Professor Goldstone postulated that only 42 % of patients who might start treatment at the point in disease development at which Mr. Gregg's treatment ought to have commenced would have been cured. As to Mr. Gregg's individual prognosis at the date of the trial, the "naked" statistical likelihood of being cured was said to be no more than 10–15 %. However, it is highly significant that Professor Goldstone attempted to personalise this particular figure by taking into account the fact that Mr. Gregg had by the time of the trial been in remission for 3 years. On this basis he estimated that Mr. Gregg's chances of 10 years survival had increased to 20–30 %.

From Professor Goldstone's evidence, the trial judge Mr. Justice Inglis concluded that even if Mr. Gregg had begun his treatment 9 months sooner, he would only have had at most a 42 % chance of being cured and that, as a result of Dr. Scott's breach of duty, his chances of being cured had been reduced by 17% to 25% (25 % having been selected on the basis that it represented the half-way point between the 20 and 30 % mentioned by Professor Goldstone). Applying these figures to his understanding of the but for test on the balance of probabilities, Mr. Justice Inglis held that Dr. Scott's breach of duty had not deprived Mr. Gregg of a cure because the evidence indicated that even if treatment had begun 9 months earlier, it was more likely than not that Mr. Gregg would still not have been cured. Mr. Justice Inglis understood the balance of probabilities standard to mean that for the claimant to discharge his or her burden of proof, it is only necessary for him or her to prove that there was at least a 51 % statistical likelihood that a specified course of events took place. Applying this directly to the statistical evidence produced by Professor Goldstone, Mr. Justice Inglis concluded that since Mr. Gregg had at best a 42 % chance of achieving complete remission for more than 5 years, and since 42 % is less than the required 51 % minimum, Mr. Gregg never had any chance of being cured. Accordingly, Mr. Justice Inglis concluded, Dr. Scott's negligence could not be said to have changed his outcome. With respect to the alternative pleading put forward, to the effect that Mr. Gregg should be entitled to recover for the loss of the chance of being cured, Mr. Justice Inglis held that on the basis of the decision in *Hotson v. East Berkshire District Health Authority* (1987), there is no recovery under UK tort law for the loss of a chance of a better medical outcome.

The Court of Appeal, by a majority, dismissed an appeal by the claimant against the findings of the trial judge. Significantly, the Court unanimously endorsed Mr. Justice Inglis' assessment of the statistical evidence and his application of the evidence to the question of factual causation as it related to the claim for outcome liability. Before the House of Lords, Mr. Gregg's appeal was based primarily on the loss of chance issue. It appears that by this point he had admitted defeat as to the possibility of holding Dr. Scott liable for the entirety of his current medical state; accordingly, he concentrated on establishing Dr. Scott's liability for at least some harm, i.e. the loss of the 17 % statistical chance of obtaining a better medical outcome. Presumably, Mr. Gregg had been advised by his legal team that the claim for full outcome liability could not be sustained in the face of the statistical evidence presented by Professor Goldstone and the way in which it had been unanimously interpreted by the trial judge and the Court of Appeal.

Unfortunately for Mr. Gregg, the House of Lords rejected his appeal by a three-to-two majority. While Lords Nicholls and Hope dissented, Lord Hoffman, Lord Phillips and Baroness Hale decisively rejected the proposition that a principle of liability for loss of a more favourable health outcome should be introduced into tort law. To recover in negligence for the consequences associated with Dr. Scott's misdiagnosis, Mr. Gregg was accordingly required to prove on the balance of probabilities that the delay in treatment had deprived him of a curative outcome. He had been unable to prove this and so his claim had to fail. Central to this conclusion was the evidence indicating that his chances of survival had never been as good as even and, as such, it could not be said that the doctor's negligence had affected either the course of his illness or the prospects of his survival.

It seems intuitively unfair that Mr. Gregg left the court with nothing, given that the delay in treatment had certainly resulted in some harm. At the very least, the defendant's negligence had resulted in the pain and suffering associated with the spread of the tumour and the side effects of the more aggressive form of treatment that might not otherwise have been needed. His life expectancy would also appear to have been reduced. Nevertheless, in terms of strict legal principle, the decision to dismiss the claim was arguably correct. Mr. Gregg had unfortunately chosen to plead his case at the outset as a claim for deprivation of a cure and thus, as noted by Lord Hope, he had "put all his eggs in one basket" (*Gregg v. Scott*, 2005, paragraph 97). Since he had not specifically pleaded the harm associated with the growth of the tumour, it was simply not within the remit of any of the courts to award damages for such harm.

Although the claim for deprivation of a curative outcome was rightly dismissed, it was not for the reasons put forward by the courts. The simple fact is that Mr. Gregg was not just still alive at the time of the House of Lords decision but that his disease was actually in remission. This state of affairs totally undermined the basis of his main claim, which was that Dr. Scott's negligent behaviour had doomed him to die within 10 years, when otherwise he would have lived. By the time of the appeal hearing in the House of Lords, 9 years had passed and his prospects of recovery looked good. While this ought to have been determinative of the case, it was surprisingly not addressed directly by any of the members of the panel, apart from

Lord Phillips, who nevertheless failed to acknowledge directly its central significance. Instead, the case was decided by reference to the statistical evidence and the fact that Mr. Gregg never had a more than even chance of surviving.

Similar to *Novartis* and *Sienkiewicz*, the legal and scientific errors underlying this flawed reasoning resulted from a tendency to conflate the two separate aspects of the legal test for causation, to reduce this conflation into a faulty numerical test, and to map this numerical test directly on to a statistical value. This is encapsulated in the following extract from the speech of Lord Nicholls:

> The present state of the law is crude to an extent bordering on arbitrariness. It means that a patient with a 60 % chance of recovery reduced to a 40 % prospect by medical negligence can obtain compensation. But he can obtain nothing if his prospects were reduced from 40 % to nil. This is rough justice indeed (*Gregg v. Scott*, 2005, paragraph 46).

As demonstrated in the last section, the numerical value of a piece of statistical evidence holds no intrinsic legal significance. It is merely a piece of evidence which speaks to the existence (or non-existence) of a causal connection between two events. Whether or not the trier of fact is at least marginally convinced by that evidence is a separate question and one which involves a whole host of considerations, just one of which relates to the strength of the statistical association indicated. That a court is never bound by a statistical result of 51+ % to hold that a causal connection has been established is a point that cannot be overemphasised.

The circumstances of *Gregg v. Scott* also provide a good illustration of another point made earlier, which is that statistical evidence will give way in the face of reliable particularistic evidence to the contrary, such as the testimony of an eye witness, or as here, the incontestable fact that someone is still alive when they are supposed to be dead. Again, this serves to emphasise the point that statistical evidence is not automatically determinative of the legal causal enquiry.

Mr. Gregg's state of remission demonstrated that he had beaten all the odds. In addition to the remission being fatal to his negligence claim because it negated his pleaded actionable damage, the fact of his remission also contradicted the statistical evidence provided by Professor Goldstone. Yet Lord Phillips was the only member of the panel to acknowledge this; as far as he was concerned, this served only to cement his general reservations about using statistical evidence as a basis for determining questions of causations in law. The foregoing discussion of *Sienkiewicz* has demonstrated that his reservations in this respect are generally misconceived.

In the context of *Gregg v. Scott*, however, Lord Phillips was entirely correct to express concerns about the specific statistical evidence relied upon in this case, for its scientific reliability and robustness are contestable on multiple grounds. But rather than undermining the legal value of medical statistics, the problematic nature of the evidence in this case serves instead to highlight the fact that medical statistics (biostatistics) constitutes a very specialised branch of biomedical science, that evidence of this nature should be obtained only from appropriately qualified specialists, and that such specialists should be made available as expert witnesses to the court.

The statistical evidence relied upon in *Gregg v. Scott* was not produced by an appropriately qualified expert. Professor Goldstone is a clinician, a haematology special. He has no qualifications in medical statistics. He purported to produce epidemiological data but did so without applying sound epidemiological methodologies. His actual methodology can, at best, be described as crude. He produced the crucial results of 42 and 25 % by manipulating a standard prognostic model to take account of a small cohort study (100 patients) which he seems personally to have carried out. According to the trial judge, the 100 patients included all ages and also people with other unrevealed personal characteristics, one of which being the stage of the disease at diagnosis. It appears that he did not review the relevant literature prior to performing his analyses, but then adjusted his results to take into account the Falini paper that he came across during the course of the litigation. The basis for these adjustments remains unclear, as does the weight that he assigned to the Falini study, which was premised on a sample size of 78 persons. Professor Goldstone's subsequent revisions to his estimates of Mr. Gregg's statistical chances are further indicative of a general lack of scientific rigour. Although he adjusted Mr. Gregg's post-tort statistical chances upwards from 10–15 % to 20–30 % to take into account Mr. Gregg's unexpected survival for 3 years without relapse by the time of the original trial, he did not similarly adjust his pre-tort assessment. Thus, while he personalised the post-tort chances by taking into account new information indicating that Mr. Gregg was an atypical patient who had better than average chances of survival, his based his pre-tort estimate on abstract population level probabilities.

An epidemiologist would have been able to supply the court with methodologically sound statistical information about the survival prospects of ALK negative non-Hodgkins lymphoma patients within the same population grouping as Mr. Gregg in terms of age, gender, race, etc. Crucially, an epidemiological expert witness would also be able to make scientifically robust adjustments to take account of new particularistic information, such as the claimant's unexpectedly entry into remission. It is important to note that in addition to providing evidence grounded in science about a particular claimant's personal chances, an epidemiologist acting as an expert witness would also be able to assess the reliability and pertinence of any other statistical evidence submitted to the court. In *Gregg v. Scott*, an epidemiologist would thus have been able to point out the problems with Professor Goldstone's evidence, thus ensuring that no time was wasted by the court in considering it. In short, reliance on epidemiologists as expert witnesses would increase court confidence in the use of epidemiological evidence.

Conclusion

This chapter has demonstrated that the UK judiciary's current scepticism of epidemiological evidence is founded upon a series of fundamental misconceptions of epidemiology as a discipline. By distinguishing epidemiology from the application of bare statistics, and by explaining that the courts are not automatically bound by an epidemiological result of 51+ % to hold that the causation has been established, it has sought to allay common judicial concerns about epidemiological evidence.

It has further demonstrated that the current judicial approach to determining questions of probabilistic causation is fundamentally flawed and that it could be significantly improved through increased reliance on epidemiology.

It is not suggested here that epidemiology is capable of solving of the law's problems with probabilistic causation. Depending on the substance of the causal issue at stake, and in particular on the disease in question, epidemiology will be more helpful in some cases than in others. This is because some areas of epidemiological research are more developed than others. Nor is it suggested that epidemiological evidence *should* be used on its own to determine questions of causation. The argument being made is that epidemiology can provide the courts with potentially useful pieces of information about causation. In determining causation, the courts must assess the totality of the evidence submitted and the weight to be given to each component thereof. In exceptional cases where epidemiological evidence is the only form of evidence submitted, and it is both strong and pertinent, the court may wish to entertain such evidence as the sole basis for determining causation. While epidemiology can obviously never tell the court what actually happened in an individual case, where tort law claims are concerned, the claimant is not required to prove what actually happened but only what was likely to have happened. In practice, the claimant needs only provide an account of causation that is plausible and at least marginally more convincing than the defendant's and vice versa.

To ensure that epidemiology is used properly as a legal tool, it is essential that epidemiologists are employed as expert witnesses in appropriate cases. In this respect, the UK judiciary needs to move away from the practice of using clinicians for all matters pertaining to biomedical science and to appreciate that medical science is a huge discipline encompassing numerous subdisciplines. The introduction of a pretrial admissibility test for scientific evidence in civil litigation would also help to protect the reputation of epidemiology.

Most importantly of all, personal injury lawyers need to learn more about epidemiology. Similarly, epidemiologists would benefit from learning more about tort law. A basic understanding of the correct tort law principles of causation would encourage epidemiologists to contemplate the potential legal applications of their discipline, to take on the role of expert witness, and to execute this role in an effective manner. Arguably, the greatest lesson to take away from the UK's negative legal experiences of epidemiology is the need to develop interdisciplinary research collaborations. Through such collaborations, lawyers and epidemiologists can learn from each other and work together to improve legal decision-making about causation.

References

Barker v. Corus (UK) plc. (2006). UKHL 20.

Barnes, D. W. (2001). Too many probabilities: Statistical evidence of tort causation. *Law and Contemporary Problems, 64*, 191–212.

Broadbent, A. (2011). Epidemiological evidence in proof of specific causation. *Legal Theory, 17*, 237–278.
Fairchild v. Glenhaven Funeral Services Ltd. (2002). UKHL 22.
Falini, B., Pulford, K., Pucciarini, A., Carbone, A., De Wolf-Peeters, C., Cordell, J., et al. (1999). Lymphomas expressing ALK fusion protein(s) other than NPM-ALK. *Blood, 94*, 3509–3515.
Gold, S. (1986). Causation in toxic torts: Burdens of proof, standards of persuasion and statistical evidence. *Yale Law Journal, 96*, 376–402.
Goldberg, R. (2011). Using scientific evidence to resolve causation problems in product liability: UK, US and French experiences. In R. Goldberg (Ed.), *Perspectives on causation* (pp. 149–178). Oxford and Portland, OR: Hart Publishing.
Gregg v. Scott. (2002). EWCA Civ 1471; (2005). UKHL 2.
Hotson v. East Berkshire Area Health Authority. (1987). A.C. 750.
McGhee v. National Coal Board. (1973). 1 W.L.R. 1.
McTear v. Imperial Tobacco Limited. (2005). CSOH 69.
Miller, C. (2006). Causation in personal injury: Legal or epidemiological common sense. *Legal Studies, 26*, 544–569.
Novartis Grimsby Limited v. Cookson. (2007). EWCA (Civ) 1261.
Rothman, K. J., Greenland, S., & Lash, T. L. (2008). *Modern epidemiology* (3rd ed.). Philadelphia, PA: Lippincott, Williams & Wilkins.
Shortell v. BICAL Construction Ltd. (Liverpool District Registry, 16 May 2008).
Sienkiewicz v. Greif. (2011). UKSC 10.
Steele, S., & Ibbetson, D. (2011). More grief on uncertain causation in tort. *Cambridge Law Journal, 70*(2), 451–468.
Wright, R. W. (2008). Liability for possible wrongs: Causation, statistical probability and the burden of proof. *Loyola Los Angeles Law Review, 41*, 1295–1343.
XYZ v. Schering Health Care Ltd. (2002). EWHC (QB)1420.

Chapter 4
Forensic Epidemiology in the Romanian Legal System

Domnița Oana Bădărău and Beatrice-Gabriela Ioan

Introduction

Epidemiologic findings are only now being utilized by the Romanian judicial system to aid in its determinations of causation in legal cases involving personal injury and occupational and environmental exposures. This chapter examines the issues arising in the civil and criminal contexts in making use of these data. The chapter comprises five sections. The first portion of the chapter describes the development of epidemiology in Romania, which closely parallels the development of medicine. The chapter then explores the use of scientific tools utilized in the Romanian legal system. The third and fourth portions of the chapter provide an analysis of an ongoing and yet unresolved case involving an occupational exposure to lead, the health injuries alleged to have resulted from that exposure, and the implications of that case within the civil and criminal contexts. The chapter concludes with recommendations for the training of lawyers, the judiciary, and epidemiologists.

D.O. Bădărău (✉)
Institute for Biomedical Ethics, University of Basel, Basel, Switzerland
e-mail: dob10@case.edu; domnita.badarau@unibas.ch

B.-Gabriela Ioan
Department of Legal Medicine, Medical Deontology and Bioethics, Gr.T.Popa University of Medicine and Pharmacy of Iasi, Iasi, Romania

Department of Behavioural Sciences, Gr.T.Popa University of Medicine and Pharmacy of Iasi, Iasi, Romania
e-mail: ioanbml@yahoo.com

S. Loue (ed.), *Forensic Epidemiology in the Global Context*,
DOI 10.1007/978-1-4614-6738-0_4,

The Development of Epidemiology in Romania

Epidemiology's historical development in Romania is closely related to medical history in this country. In general, Romanian medicine was poorly developed until the early nineteenth century. The population was characterized by high illiteracy rates and low health education. During plague, cholera, typhus and typhoid fever outbreaks, "folk" methods of healing were generally utilized; these had been passed down from the time of the Roman occupation.

In its beginnings, epidemiology in Romania was concerned exclusively with communicable diseases, one of the main causes of death at that time. For example, the first paper on preventive medicine was written in 1530 by the Romanian physician S. Panschner. Under the title *A small notice-how to protect ourselves during the merciless epidemic—the plague* (*O mică înştiinţare- cum să ne păzim în timpul nemiloasei molime—pesta*), the physician described the preventive methods to be applied in cases of plague. This paper appeared at a time when epidemiology was just being established as a discipline. The scientific basis of the quarantine system as a means of protection against plague and other communicable diseases was established in 1764 by Adam Chenot, considered to be the first Transylvanian epidemiologist.

The nineteenth-century technological and scientific revolution positively influenced the field of preventive medicine in Romania. At that time, Romanian medicine went through considerable transformation following the development of hospitals, the establishment of medical schools, and the education of specialists abroad. The latter played an important role in the development of preventive medicine, especially through the imposition of quarantine in cases of infectious diseases; this activity was coordinated by the *Quarantines Committee (Comitetul carantinelor)*, established in 1830. Subsequently, preventive medicine continued to develop in close relation to curative medicine, being coordinated by the *Physician Commission* (*Comisia doftorilor*) in Wallachia and the *Physician Advice* (*Sfatul doftoricesc*) in Moldavia.

During this period, a number of scientific papers on preventive medicine were written and published in Romanian. These papers contained useful advice and instructions aimed at preventing plague and promoting the necessity and vital importance of vaccination as well as the key role played by a healthy lifestyle, the avoidance of binge eating and heavy drinking, and the practice of physical labor. In 1830, C. Caracas edited the first hygiene and sanitary monograph of Wallachia, entitled "Topography of Wallachia". In 1844, C. Vârnav presented the first Romanian scientific paper on preventive medicine, entitled *The advisor of health and economy* (*Povăţuitorul sănătăţii şi al economiei*).

In 1853 the first Romanian medical law was issued, containing provisions on both preventive and curative medicine. The field of preventive medicine was marked in the second half of the nineteenth century by the activity of two physicians. Iacob Felix, the promoter of modern hygiene in Romania, authored the first Romanian treatise on epidemiology, entitled *Treaty of public hygiene and sanitary police* (*Tratat de igienă publică şi poliţie sanitară*). Aladar Rozsahegy established the foundation of modern epidemiology in Transylvania.

For the first time in the history of wars, during the 1877 Romanian Independence War, the Romanian physician Carol Davila applied antisepsis and asepsis techniques as a means of combating infections and preventing epidemics. Shortly thereafter, in 1884, the first congress of physicians, veterinarians, and pharmacists was held in Bucharest with a focus on various aspects of preventive medicine.

The development of Romanian preventive medicine progressed significantly during the twentieth century. During that period new intervention techniques were developed and applied at the population level, such as immunoprophylaxis, antibiotics prophylaxis, seroepidemiology, and chemical decontamination. During the period from 1913 through 1916, the Romanian physician Ioan Cantacuzino realized the first large-scale epidemiological intervention, a vaccination measure in areas affected by cholera.

Medical epidemiology as a medical discipline was established at the end of the nineteenth and early twentieth centuries (having previously been called "social hygiene"). Its main objective was the study of health status and causes of diseases at the population level. In Romania, higher education in epidemiology was introduced first in Iasi in 1922 under the Department of Hygiene, chaired by M. Ciuc , as a part of medico-social education (Ivan, 1993). Currently, epidemiology in Romania is coordinated by the Romanian Society of Epidemiology. This professional association monitors the implementation of epidemiology activities and preventive medicine's efficiency. The Romanian Society of Epidemiology provides advice and consultation in epidemiologic surveillance and prevention and the combat of communicable and noncommunicable diseases, and also provides legal and organizational support in epidemiology.

As in many other countries, the use of epidemiology in the Romanian judicial setting began to be employed for the purpose of gathering scientific evidence for authorities that was relevant to public policy, victim identification, and determination of the cause of death. The focus of such studies included the causes of road accidents, aviation crashes, sudden death in newborns and infants, and head traumas following car accidents (Ciuchilan, Iov, & Pendefunda, 2011). However, such data are not required as evidence, although forensic examinations and other expert contributions are mentioned in the Penal Code and the Penal Procedure Code as means of determining whether an act falls within the scope of the criminal law. It is very likely that epidemiologic data are used primarily in cases involving car accidents and cases in which the cause of death is difficult to establish. Notably, most such criminal investigations rely heavily on forensic reports and the physical examination of the victim.

Scientific Tools Utilized in the Romanian Judicial System

Built on a hybrid legal system with its foundations in the Roman Empire's ancient law, the Romanian judicial structure is similar to the ones existing in other several European countries. It is incorporated into the civil law, based on norms and not solely relying on precedent and courts' interpretation of the law (Kritzer, 2002). The legitimacy of the regulation system as a whole derives from the Constitution and the statutes, which represent the only source of legitimacy. The primary source of law is the Constitution, whose principles must be enforced, promoted, protected, and embedded in all other legislative acts. It sets the grounds for the functioning of the democratic state, states the power of the people and the relation between the people and the government, reiterates the human rights and values that the state must protect, and delineates and divides the state's powers.

Adopted in 1991 and revised following a national referendum in 2003, the Romanian Constitution consists of seven titles addressing the main principles that drive the entirety of the legal and sociopolitical system (Bondoc, 2001). The text then addresses the fundamental rights, freedoms, and obligations; regulates the state's authority and economy; and establishes the Constitutional Court and the steps and criteria to be met in order to amend the Constitution (Frankowski & Stephan, 1995).

A detail worthy of thoughtful consideration is Article 11 of Romania's Constitution which established the grounds for the application and interpretation of the international law in relation to the national one (Constitution of Romania, 1991). According to this Article, the Romanian State is obligated to implement all regulations to which the state has been bound by signing and ratifying international treaties. Provisions resulting from such treaties must be fulfilled in good faith and in the spirit they were formulated. Paragraph (2) of the same Article states that ratified documents will be given the same legal standing as any national law, thus acknowledging that international provisions are incorporated into the Romanian law. This is of particular importance in the context of joining the European Union (EU) and in dealing with legal disputes for which national provisions are inadequate to bring about a fair ruling. At the same time, legal provisions are embedded in the social environment, its changes, and socioeconomic dynamics. At a national level, legal requirements and protections cannot be updated at a fast pace as to be immediately aligned to new situations that create socio-legal tensions in that particular society. In such cases, appealing to international norms and procedures might be the only guidance for new situations created by technological advances or social dynamics and for which there is no existing national legal framework. This leaves the possibility for a more suitable and feasible solution to bring about justice.

By joining the European Union, new judicial reforms took place in Romania and many laws were passed in order to synchronize the Romanian law with the requirements and necessities of the European community. This requires that the States partially cede their sovereignty to the European Union's institutions which are thus empowered to adopt directives and regulate the areas where they have competency under the European treaties. The importance of referring to the community regulations when discussing the Romanian legal framework arises from the fact that these laws take precedence over national law. The Romanian legislature's regulations mention explicitly in several texts that under certain circumstances, if the international law or treaties ratified by the Romanian State are more favorable in relation to specific rights, the international rules or guidelines will take precedence.

The European Union's regulations, directives, and decisions are binding on national authorities according to the principle of primacy of the community law over the national one and the principle of immediate and direct applicability of the community law. Therefore, all laws that emanate from the European Union's institutions, apart from recommendations and opinions that are nonbinding instruments, must be respected and apply to all member states.

Of classic civil law inspiration, at a national level, the Romanian judicial system consists of legal codes, laws, decrees, governmental ordinances, and ministries' decisions. These represent after the Constitution the main sources of legitimacy in formulating norms and regulating social rights and duties. Characterized by influences of the Roman law and written and codified norms, the judicial regulations within the Romanian law are divided into legal branches and institutions based on the object and method of regulation. As such, criminal law is the principal tool of legal norms in protecting individual rights and liberties, the person, proprieties, and the entire rule of law, as the civil law dispositions regulate the patrimonial and non-patrimonial relations between individuals as civil law subjects. Disputes and claims of rights violations or noncompliance with obligations, as well as guaranteeing the respect for the rule of law and the state order, are settled by courts as follows: the tribunals, the regional courts, courts of appeal, and the Higher Court of Cassation and Justice. Issues surrounding the constitutionality of laws, ordinances, or the interpretation of laws in relation to the Constitution are to be addressed by the Constitutional Court of Romania. In following the judicial procedures for a fair ruling, the codes of procedures are essential and mandatory acts in guiding the legal proceedings and court's decisions.

In the context of using epidemiology in a court setting, it must be said that to the best of the authors' knowledge there is no abundance of litigation in which epidemiologic data have been used in the Romanian courts. Findings of epidemiologic experts have, however, been used both in the criminal and civil settings in the United States for several decades now. Results from epidemiologic studies have guided policy and court decisions and lawyers to find resolutions for claims of injury resulted from exposure to certain agents that have a negative impact on person's well-being (Loue, 2002). The use of epidemiologic data in a judicial setting has, therefore, increased over the years and more court claims rely on experts in establishing the probability, risk, incidence or prevalence of diseases, and injuries in a population and even in an individual. At the same time, such opinions could serve to point out the contrary, that an individual or a population is not affected or that a disease does not manifest itself in a certain population or an individual. Opinions admitted in court and the use of evidence-based epidemiologic data and well-established epidemiologic principles in judicial investigations go beyond the traditional sphere of the science of epidemiology. Such applications fall under the branch of Forensic Epidemiology, a concept introduced by Loue S. more than a decade ago and that has gained recognition in the context of bioterrorism threats (Freeman, Rossignol, & Hand, 2008).

Given all of these considerations in the context of the Romanian judicial system's framework, its weaknesses, fallacies, and slow processes, it is probable that there is no solid corpus of forensic epidemiologic cases. In the next sections of this chapter, we therefore propose to analyze which tools could be employed within the Romanian legal system to judge claims of injury or claims for damages as a result of a disease relying on epidemiologic data and how that inquiry might be accomplished. We propose a case based on actual events that took place in one of Romania's counties and resulted in formal allegations with the Romanian authorities regarding occupational health risks. As the case has not been concluded and there is no final court decision, the applicable legislation will be identified, and the legal procedures that could be employed will be discussed in order to illustrate how the case might be resolved, the probable solutions, the possible sanctions that might be imposed, and the compensation that could be awarded.

Case Study: Lead Occupational Exposure

A group of five employees working at factory X have complained that, since the first half of 2009, as a result of exposure to lead (vapors and oxides of lead, smoke, and combustion gases) their health status has been impaired. More so, they have declared that they were informed of their exposure to lead compounds.

X Factory produces sanitary porcelain and terra-cotta tiles (spare parts for stoves). The technological process of production of these objects includes the glaze, which provides sealing against liquids and gases and contributes to improving the appearance, giving gloss, smoothness, and color.

Icings are made from silica combined with alkali, alkaline-earth, lead oxide, alumina, etc. and applied in thin layers on the surface of ceramic products.

Since 2008, a type of glaze with lead was introduced in the factory X in the technological process for obtaining terra-cotta.

The Plaintiffs

All five plaintiffs are women. Their professional and medical history indicate the aspects detailed below.

AB, 53 years old, has been working since 1978 in the field of terra-cotta production, in the positions of quality controller of terra-cotta, terra-cotta pottery, and lab technician for terra-cotta in the factory X. At the last job, Mrs. AB assisted dosing of raw materials, determined the amount of grease remover in the mass of basis, and participated in loading mill glaze. She worked in a noisy environment, in a prolonged standing position (8 h/day, 5 days/week), in a room with an inefficient ventilation system, wearing a coat as protection equipment. Also, she was exposed to different pollutants: lead, combustion gases and fumes, and dust silicogene.

CD, 48 years old, worked in the factory X for 27 years and 4 months, being employed in the terra-cotta pottery fabrication.

EF, 56 years old, worked in the factory X for 6 years, most of the time in a prolonged standing position, during which time she was occupationally exposed to high temperatures and lead (vapor, oxides of lead, smoke, and combustion gases). Her job consisted of taking the terra-cotta tiles out from the wagons in order to polish them.

GH, 50 years old, worked for 17 years as a ceramist terra-cotta in the factory X. She declared that in November, 2008, she was exposed to frita, a substance used in making sanitary objects.

IJ, 36 years old, worked for 9 years and 6 months in factory X in various positions: laboratory testing of various samples, including glazes; computer production tracking; and surveillance of technological process. She worked in a noisy and poorly ventilated environment, without wearing a protection mask and being exposed to various pollutants, including lead, combustion gases, and silicogene powders. In December 2008, the lead-based glaze for finishing terra-cotta was introduced into the technological process.

The Events

During the first half of 2009, all five plaintiffs began to complain of pain and paresthesis of the legs, marked physical and mental fatigue, and headaches. In August 2009, the plaintiffs were hospitalized in the Occupational Medicine Clinic, where they were diagnosed with chronic professional polyneuropathy as a result of lead exposure. The diagnosis was established based on clinical and laboratory examination, which also excluded other causes of polyneuropathy. Toxicological examination revealed elevated blood and urine lead concentration and increased blood coproporphyrin concentration which were suggestive of increased absorption of lead. Neurophysiological examination revealed peripheral nerve toxic damage, with decreased nerve conduction velocity in internal and external sciatic popliteal nerves. In addition to the results of the clinical and paraclinic examinations, the professional history was suggestive, showing the plaintiffs' exposure to lead in the workplace.

The standard therapy for the elimination of lead from the body could not have been initiated because the necessary substance for this purpose, Edetamin, was not available. On discharge from the Occupational Medicine Clinic, the plaintiffs were advised to change their workplace. Also, under current procedure, the Occupational Medicine Clinic reported all five cases of lead exposure to the Public Health Office—Occupational Medicine Department by filling in the form BP1 and noting the diagnosis: "Chronic occupational toxic polyneuropathy," caused by the exposure to lead oxides.

In turn, in September 2009, the Public Health Direction—Occupational Health Department (OHD) conducted an etiological investigation in the former workplace of the plaintiffs (factory X), concluding that the polyneuropathy presented by the plaintiffs is an occupational disease due to exposure to lead oxides, this conclusion being recorded in the Declaration of Occupational Disease Case Sheet (BP2). Following this investigation, it was concluded that the manager of the factory bore responsibility for the occurrence of these events, in accordance with Law 319 of 14/07/2006 (Law 319 on Security and Occupational Health, 2006) on safety and occupational health and Government Decision No. 1218 of 2006, which establishes the minimum standards for safety and occupational health to protect workers from risks related to chemical agents. Under these regulations, "the employer shall take necessary measures to: ensure the workers safety and health protection, and prevention of occupational risks" [Law 319/2006, art. 7 (1) and (2)]. Also, "the employer must ensure that the risk to health and safety of the workers, induced by a hazardous chemical agent is removed or minimized. Respecting the limit values for occupational exposure to chemical agents in workplace [...] and the tolerable biological limit values for workers [...], while maintaining the concentrations of chemical agents at the lowest possible level is mandatory" [Government Decision 1218/2006, Article 11 (2)].

Following these investigations at the factory, it was recommended to the plaintiffs that they change their workplace in order to avoid exposure to toxic substances (lead), combustion gases and smoke, unfavorable microclimate, and excessive physical effort. Repeated medical examinations of the plaintiffs during 2010 and 2011 indicated that although they had changed their workplace, the chronic sensory–motor toxic polyneuropathy and the distal algoparestezic syndrome still persisted.

In accordance with Articles 116, 119 and 203 of the Romanian Penal Procedure Code (Penal Procedure Code of Romania, 2008) to establish the existence of the facts of which the plaintiffs complained, the legal consequences, and their legal classification[1], the police asked for a forensic expert in order to establish whether there was a causal link between the plaintiffs' illness and their exposure to lead at the workplace; the exposure to lead affected the plaintiffs' health or endangered their lives; the victims might recover or suffer from sequelae; and the plaintiffs' work capacity was affected, to what extent, and for how long. According to the procedures enunciated for obtaining forensic expertise, all of the plaintiffs' medical records were reviewed and the plaintiffs were examined again at the Occupational Medicine Clinic and at the Work Capacity Expertise Department.

Following the corroboration of medical data, history, and investigation data, the forensic expert concluded that the entire clinical evolution of the cases suggested that the chronic sensory–motor polyneuropathy was the consequence of long-term exposure to lead-based compounds used in the glazing of terra-cotta. The plaintiffs have not been diagnosed with lead poisoning (which is manifested by multiple syndromes: digestive, anemia, pseudorheumatismal, neurological, renal, etc.), but with peripheral neurological toxic damage (polyneuropathy), which is the result of occupational exposure to lead compounds (oxides, steam) used in the technological process of glazing terra-cotta. It was found that the plaintiffs' diagnosed occupational disease did not affect their work capacity. However, it was recommended that they work in an environment without any toxic exposure.

Allegations of Lead Poisoning: A Legal Matter?

As related by the case study above (which is referred to here as the Factory Case), five plant workers in Romania filled a complaint with the local police authorities claiming that, beginning in mid-2009, they experienced health problems following lead exposure. Their complaint specified that the intoxication that lead to their health deterioration occurred at the workplace as a result of continuous and long-term exposure to vapors, gases, smoke, and lead oxides. The factory where they were employed produced porcelain and terra-cotta bathroom items. Within the production process smelting was used to isolate the final products from liquids and gases and give them a smoother, brighter look and color. The glazing material contains different oxides, including lead oxides, and is applied on ceramics in several thin layers. Beginning in 2008, the factory began to use lead smelting in the production processes and within less than 2 years several workers allegedly experienced a worsening of their health condition.

The plaintiffs also pointed out in their complaint that they were not informed about exposure to lead agents as part of their occupational duties. Following this complaint a forensic investigation was set in motion with the aims of establishing:

1. Whether there is a direct causal relationship between the poor health outcomes that the plaintiffs claimed and workplace lead exposure
2. Whether the lead exposure impacted the workers' health or represented a danger to their lives
3. Whether the diagnosed health conditions are curable, whether the workers will need long-term medical care, whether their health suffered irreversible effects, and the nature of these effects, if any
4. Whether the lead intoxication resulted in such a deterioration of the workers' health that their work capacities had been compromised, for how long, and to what degree.

Legal Steps and Epidemiology in the Romanian Court

Once a complaint is filed with the appropriate judicial authorities, an investigative action or process is set into motion, with the aims of fully and timely establishing the acts that were committed and whether they are punishable under the Penal Code, Articles 1, 2, and 6 (Penal Code, 2008). This process is intended to determine by whom and against whom the acts were committed and what consequences resulted from those acts and to gather evidence for a written charge. In this case, the plaintiffs are the alleged victims working in the factory; defendant is the factory, a private entity, and the employer, i.e., those against whom criminal charges may be brought. (A criminal charge could also be brought against an individual who is an employer.) During a criminal investigation evidence is collected and a case is built in order to bring it to court and seek an appropriate sanction, following the principle of proportionality (Penal Procedure Code of Romania, 2008).

According to Title III Evidence and Means of Evidence, Section IX of the Romanian Penal Procedure Code, Articles 116, 119, and 203 (Penal Procedure Code of Romania, 2008), for this case study a first step in establishing the existence, nature, and repercussions of acts that allegedly caused occupational health issues is to proceed with an expert[2]. In the case study, a medical forensic investigation was ordered by the criminal investigation body and the forensic physicians subpoenaed all of the plaintiffs' medical records. Given the nature of the relationship between the plaintiffs as employees and the defendant, as employer, and that the damages or suffered injuries allegedly took place during working hours and during the course of fulfilling employment duties, the records were sent for analysis to the Public Health Office—Occupational Medicine Department and to the Work Capacity Expertise Department.

Once put into motion, the investigation will continue throughout the judicial process and all necessary documents will be drawn up ex officio, unless otherwise specified by law. If the acts or deeds fall under the criminal law, then a criminal accusation will be formulated. This will give way to a criminal action. However, it is noteworthy to mention that the investigation will continue, even during the course of the trial. According to the Code's stipulations, once the five workers have addressed the authorities and all criteria have been met, the criminal investigation will start. The criminal procedures stipulate that the alleged perpetrator will be notified of the complaint as well as the acts that are under criminal investigation and their judicial status, thus providing the basis for the defendant to seek assistance during the criminal process and the trial itself.

At the same time, based on the specific circumstances in which the alleged health problems occurred, at the workplace, and the involvement of the specific state authorities, the Occupational Medicine Office and the Office for Work Capacities Expertise, it is determined that the appropriate labor laws would apply. As mentioned above, once the complaint reaches the authorities, the investigation takes its course and all agencies that have jurisdiction over the matter would be involved. As a result, in this case, it would be the judicial institutions' obligation to determine if the acts fall under the Penal Code and if and to what extent the labor law was violated. If the workers were to decide to withdraw their complaint or there were an amicable settlement between the parties, according to the Penal Code article 10(f) (Penal Code, 2008), the criminal action would not proceed or, if it had begun, it would have to be stopped. The same stopping effect would be produced if the complaint were to be withdrawn or if the parties were to settle during the trial.

With respect to the case under discussion, the complaint was not withdrawn and the judicial investigation proceeded. All medical records were subject to a forensic medical analysis that reconstructed the medical and professional health history of all five workers. Further investigation required that the five female workers be admitted to a Labor Clinic where a definite diagnosis of chronic polyneuropathy in the context of occupational exposure to lead agents was made. It was found that the illness had affected their peripheral sensory–motor function, causing physical and psychological asteny (loss of strength) and headaches. Following this diagnosis, the Clinic notified the Public Health Agency's Labor Bureau, which in turn proceeded with an investigation at the factory's location where the workers were employed.

Upon concluding the Public Health Office's etiological investigation, it was determined that the polyneuropathy was caused by the working environment and that the factory was responsible for the occupational exposure to toxins. The report's conclusion stated that the illness was a direct consequence of exposure to chemical agents containing lead that are employed in smelting terra-cotta products, which were present during the site inspection. These conclusions pointed to a clear violation of Articles 6(1), 39(f) and (i), and 40(2), (a) to (c) of the Romanian Labor Code regarding adequate working conditions, labor security, and social and health protection (Labour Code, 2003). Articles 39(f) and 39(i) of the Labor Code expressly provide for employees' rights to security and occupational health, as well as the right to take part in establishing and improving the working environment. These rights reflect the equivalent obligations for the employer to inform the employees about the working conditions, to ensure proper working spaces, and to respect and grant employees all the rights that they are entitled to according to the law and to the individual or collective work contracts (Labour Code, 2003).

Following the etiological investigation, it was recommended that the victims of occupational exposure to toxic agents change their place of employment and avoid any exposure to toxins, even if within the allowed health levels. The female workers' labor capacity was not completely compromised, but as shown in annual health checkups, the lead levels in the blood were above normal and the sensorimotor polyneuropathy was still present, despite the fact that they were no longer working in a toxic environment.

Based on the forensic investigation and the authorities' reports there are several points to consider. First, it was established that the five female workers who filed the complaint experienced health problems due to the working environment and that these health issues persisted even after changing the working environment. Second, reports concluded that the working conditions were toxic and the employer did not take steps to ensure safe and proper working spaces. This is violative of the Labor Code and other legislative acts regulating the safety and wellbeing in the workplace (Law 319 on Security and Occupational Health, 2006).

In these circumstances, civil claims and possibly criminal charges can be formulated. In order to pursue with a trial, the criminal investigation must conclude that the factory as an entity with legal personhood or the employer or the managerial staff is guilty of acts that fall under the Penal Code. Therefore, charges of one or more offences against persons must be brought and proven in court.

Under Romanian law, damages can be claimed in the civil court as well, if the workers should decide to ask for compensation to pay for their health care costs, for financial remuneration for the injuries they suffered, for the need to change employment, and/or for additional physical and psychological distress due to illness. The plaintiffs can file a civil action contemporaneously with the criminal complaint and as part of the same complaint; both the civil claim and the criminal complaint would then be heard by the same judge. The joinder of both the civil complaint and the criminal complaint in the same action allows the plaintiffs to avoid payment of a "tax" that would otherwise be charged if they were to file the civil claim independently from the criminal complaint (Penal Procedure Code of Romania, 2008). It is important to stress that the two actions will be pursued in parallel within the same trial and the damage claims do not take precedence over the criminal accusations. However, if the plaintiffs did not address the civil complaint to the penal court during the criminal trial, such a complaint can be pursued separately in the civil court.

Based on the complaint of worsening health status due to exposure to a toxic working environment, the judicial authorities would have to proceed in establishing if there is a criminal offence. In the case of this factory, the purpose of a criminal investigation would be to determine whether actions representing offences led to the lead exposure, if the exposure was the cause of the health problems, and the extent to which that exposure endangered a person's health, well-being, and life. These have to be established in court and the etiological and forensic conclusions must be admitted and defended in court. Additionally, in court it must be determined whether the exposure was caused by accident, whether it could have or could not have been prevented, whether it was caused by the employer's neglect due to noncompliance with labor law requirements regarding safety in the workplace, or whether the exposure was a direct result of the factory's or a private party's actions.

Title II of the Penal Code regulates offences against persons. Therefore, if a criminal wrongdoing were to be found in this case, it should fall under Chapter 1 Offences against life, physical integrity, and health (Penal Code, 2008). In order to qualify as an offence under this chapter, the exposure must be proven to have resulted in harm to the workers' physical integrity or health. Article 181 (Penal Code, 2008) states that acts resulting in bodily harm or a worsening of a person's health which requires up to 60 days of hospitalization are criminally punishable by imprisonment from 6 months to 5 years. The criminal action is initiated upon a prior complaint of the injured persons. According to the medical records from the Labor Health Clinic where the five workers were admitted, this criterion was met in this case. All five injured persons were admitted for medical and forensic tests and also for treatment to reduce the blood toxicity levels, resulting in several days of hospitalization. A criminal action could possibly start at this point if the parties do not reach an agreement, through which criminal liability would be eliminated.

Based on the regular medical checkups which indicate that sensorimotor polyneuropathy is still present, the offences against the five injured parties could be prosecuted under Article 182 of the Penal Code. According to this Article, whenever the actions against a person result in a need for medical care for more than 60 days or produce significant consequences, such as the loss of one sense, the punishment should be 2–7 years of imprisonment (Penal Code, 2008). The medical records show that even after the workers changed their place of employment, the sensorimotor polyneuropathy persisted. It could possibly be argued that a permanent physical disability occurred, thus establishing the basis for the offence to be tried under Article 182. Given that the five victims suffered long-term peripheral nerve toxic damage, as attested to by the Occupational Medicine Clinic and the conclusions of the Public Health's etiologic report, the prison punishment could be raised up to 10 years.

At the same time, the degree of guilt should be determined. If it can be established that the offence against the workers' health regulated by Article 181 (Penal Code, 2008) resulted from negligence, then the punishment would be imprisonment from 1 to 3 months or a fine, according to Article 184(1) of the Penal Code (2008). However, the court would consider that the actions led to adverse health consequences for the victims over time and could place the offence under Article 184(2), establishing a punishment of 3 months to 2 years in prison or a fine. To this will add the fact that the offence was the result of noncompliance with legal provisions, i.e., the Labor Code and other regulations regarding security and occupational health. Under these circumstances, Article 184(3) mandates imprisonment from 3 months up to 2 years or a fine (Penal Code, 2008). At the same time, if the offence caused a permanent physical or psychological disability, according to Article 184(4) the imprisonment period is from 6 months up to 3 years (Penal Code, 2008). For offences that fall under Articles 184(1) and 184(3), the criminal investigation will be put into motion following the complaint of the victim; whenever the reconciliation of the parties occurs, if it should, the criminal liability is removed (Penal Code, 2008).

Collecting Epidemiologic Evidence

In order to determine the applicable judicial status of the actions, evidence must be collected in the criminal investigative process. The source, type, and collection methods of any evidence are relevant for court admissibility and in supporting the criminal charges. Criminal acts are tried and evidence is brought to the first instance court, called *judecatoria*. All existing evidence can be brought to this court, including witnesses, written testimony, forensic reports, medical records, and other bodies' official expert reports, according to the terms and conditions stated under Title III Evidence and Means of Evidence of the Romanian Penal Procedure Code (Civil Procedure Code, 2009).

The Romanian Penal Procedure Code specifies that in order to solve a case and find the truth, both the investigative bodies and the courts are under an obligation to pursue all possible leads and clarify all elements of the alleged crimes, based on evidence. Under the same Code, the evidence is defined as being any fact that brings about new knowledge relating to the commission or non-commission of a crime, the alleged perpetrator, and the context in which the crime was committed.

Therefore, under the Romanian Penal Procedure Code, the plaintiffs' complaint will be considered evidence and the defendant will be given an opportunity to declare, clarifying the complaint's points, contradicting them, and formulating his or her defense. This evidence will be supplemented by other findings gathered by the investigative body, as well as by the medical-legal and forensic records, the plaintiffs' medical charts, the Occupational Health Agency's report, and the etiological investigation. Article 64 of the Penal Procedure Code allows for technical and scientific findings to be utilized as evidence in court, together with medical-legal findings, expertise, and other probative means (Penal Procedure Code of Romania, 2008).

All administered evidentiary responsibilities lie with the investigative body and the courts, these being the legal authorities that can investigate, order expert examination and testimony, identify witnesses, and call for physical search. In the case under discussion, the local police received and completed the complaint and then ordered the medical and forensic investigation. The court would then judge which evidence is admissible in court based on how this evidence was collected, according to regulations and by using legal means. Article 67 of the Penal Procedure Code stipulates that evidence cannot be rejected if it is conclusive and with proven utility in the trial; a decision relating to the (in)admissibility of the proffered evidence must be justified.

In the Romanian courts, written evidence is permissible as long as the contents reveal both the alleged criminal acts (Civil Procedure Code, 2009) and the nature and circumstances in which these took place and also serve the purpose of establishing justice. As such, the Occupational Medicine Clinic diagnosis sheets, the medical records, and the epidemiologic records would qualify as written evidence. These medical investigations were carried out at the investigative body's request and meet the admissibility criteria. Furthermore, it can be assumed that the reports were concluded based on solid scientific medical data, following toxicological tests and neurophysiological and paraclinic examinations. These were corroborated with the plaintiffs' medical and professional history that supports the diagnosis of chronic polyneuropathy due to lead exposure. Additionally, a workplace inspection and subsequent etiological investigation were mandated by the OHD under the Public Health Agency. The conclusions of the investigations were registered in the Declaration of Occupational Disease Case Sheet (BP2), which would be added to the written court evidence. The OHD report showed a direct causal link between the presence of lead agents at the workplace and the workers' lead exposure, which led to the elevated blood and urine lead concentrations causing peripheral nerve damage due to toxicity.

It is important to mention that under Romanian criminal law, the defendant benefits from a presumption of innocence. In presenting the defense, he or she may establish the inconsistency of the evidence claiming his or her guilt. Therefore the task of the public attorney is to build a strong case, based on solid evidence. In this case, this refers to the conclusiveness and reliability of the medical and forensic expertise. In turn, the medical records, forensic reports, and experts' conclusions rely on scientific knowledge and epidemiologic data. These data should provide evidence that the workers became ill due to lead exposure and that they were exposed to this chemical at the workplace during working hours.

The epidemiologic data must establish causation. These data would thus be employed in the court and utilized as evidence to support the criminal charges. Therefore, the specificity of the cause, i.e., the lead exposure, must lead to the specificity of the effect (Loue, 2002), i.e., the chronic polyneuropathy diagnosis resulting in the occupational illness. However, following this pure deterministic reasoning, it will imply that the prosecution has to prove that the lead exposure is the only cause for the workers' health issues and at the same time that the consequences stated in the Occupational Medicine Clinic's report, i.e., the chronic occupational toxic polyneuropathy and the persistence of the distal algoparestezic syndrome, are the only effects produced by the causal factor within the plant. From the medical history records there is information that several of the workers used other chemicals during work or were exposed to different toxic agents, not only lead, and that they rotated positions within the factory. Reliance on pure determinism would be very unlikely to result in a satisfactory sentence, given these considerations.

The Penal Code indicates that evidence should be admitted as solid when the data and the reports brought establish in a reasonable manner that the person under criminal investigation is the perpetrator of the criminal acts of which he or she is accused. Section IX of the Criminal Code makes reference to technical, scientific, and forensic or medical-legal certification, articles that would apply to the epidemiologic data, and the forensic reports issued in this case. The evidence resulting from the etiological investigation and the medical exams must both be scientifically sound and bear sufficient validity in order for their conclusions to be accepted in court. In constructing a rigorous accusation against the defendant, physical evidence must be subjected to a technical and science-based analysis conducted by certified and recognized institutions or by specialists in the field, such as epidemiologists, physicians, and forensic experts.

A purely deterministic approach will not be sufficient to obtain a conviction whenever the defendant challenges the causation criteria and points out the limitations of the evidence according to these criteria. The prosecution must not only prove that the lead exposure at workplace is the cause of the workers' health issues. He or she must also present sufficient evidence that addresses the multifactorial etiology of the disease. Therefore, a modified deterministic model would permit the identification of several components of the specific cause. In the case of this factory, the medical diagnosis will be corroborated with the etiological examination, the medical history, and all employment records. Statistical analysis must consider all the necessary elements to assess the risk of disease as it relates to lead exposure during the smelting processes which is the hypothesized causal factor.

Both the etiological investigation and the experts' testimony in court or deposition must be based on solid scientific literature and data. Lead has been long reported as one of the most significant toxins causing occupational poisoning, being heavily used in the production industry (Fu & Boffetta, 1995). Research on the epidemiology of lead intoxication in the workplace has been for many decades primarily focused on cohort studies to examine the possibility of a link between the toxic exposure and cancer (Fu & Boffetta, 1995). As reported by Fu and Boffetta in 1995, occupational intoxication with lead is typical for workers in smelting and refining, the latter presenting higher risks as a result of the generation of high concentrations of lead fumes. Their review showed that death following a cancer diagnosis was a common phenomenon among workers employed in processes using lead (Fu & Boffetta, 1995). This allowed for a positive hypothesis to be formulated, linking cancer and lead exposure, though the reviewed studies had limitations of their own.

The Centers for Disease Control and Prevention's (CDC) 2009 *Report on Environmental Chemicals* mentions smelting processes as one of the sources of occupational intoxication with lead. After being introduced in the body, usually by inhaling fumes, lead particulates deposit at the skeletal level. The *Report* mentions that exposure to significant lead agents can lead to anemia and encephalopathy. For adults who come into contact with the toxin and become lead intoxicated, it is very likely that their neurocognitive functions will be affected, according to the same report (Centers for Disease Control and Prevention, 2009). In the factory case, the literature review and the CDC's report can serve as resources for establishing an argument and sustaining an expert's opinion that the lead exposure caused the workers' health problems. These workers have been employed in the smelting industry, have been exposed to lead fumes for prolonged periods of time, have suffered from anemia, and have developed peripheral neurological toxic damage.

At the same time, the 2009 CDC *Report* states that the standard testing method for lead levels in the body is by blood analysis, as this shows both recently accumulated lead levels in the blood as well as the long-term accumulation at the level of the bones. Lead levels in the blood refer to a reference value that has been established following biomonitoring studies. It thus provides the necessary guidance to physicians and public health institutions, including occupational health agencies, to determine whether persons have been exposed to lead and to what degree in comparison with the baseline (Centers for Disease Control and Prevention, 2009). Although developed countries maintain safety levels and standards in place for handling exposure to lead while protecting workers, these limits for occupational safety might not have been established or are not being enforced in countries currently experiencing industrialization (Craft et al., 2006). This information could potentially validate the forensic examination and medical and forensic analysis that stood as the basis of the medical and forensic report in the Factory Case.

Indeed, in the Factory Case, in order to clarify the claims of health deterioration due to the unhealthy medical environment, the police ordered a forensic examination and a medical assessment of the five workers. This was done in accordance with Article 112 of the Penal Procedure Code (Penal Procedure Code of Romania, 2008). As mentioned before, due to the special relation between the plaintiffs and the defendant, the technical and scientific examinations were carried out by specialists and experts belonging to the OHD, a state institution (Penal Procedure Code of Romania, 2008).

A particularity of the technical or scientific examination, according to Article 113 of the Penal Procedure Code, is that whether the examination is ordered by the investigation body ex officio or upon request, the focus of the examination, the questions to be answered, and the time frame in which the examination is to be carried are mandated by the body itself (Penal Procedure Code of Romania, 2008). This aspect is of particular interest in the use of scientific data as evidence in the criminal court. As pointed out by Loue (2002), there are controversies regarding the degree of confidence attributed to the epidemiologic data and the issue of objectivity. The regulations set by the Romanian criminal law add to these criticisms and fears of rushing for evidence or certainty. Science and law both aim to discover the truth, but there are two different perspectives and completely opposite tools employed for this search. Scientific research does not stop and results are always questioned and are subject to further study. Therefore, although at a specific moment during a court trial, the scientific evidence may suggest claim with a relatively high degree of certainty that a specified phenomenon was caused by the direct action of a particular agent, this might be refuted scientifically in the following months or even years. However, the criminal trial seeks to establish the truth in a timely manner so as to unburden the victim and the alleged perpetrator and bring about justice. It can be a latent conflict between the two goals and in the way evidence is presented or interpreted by scientists and how it is interpreted and accepted in court (Loue, 2002). Nevertheless, the consequences can be tremendous if the evidence is accepted as an absolute truth or rejected in its entirety due to a weak link between the specified exposure and the alleged outcome, only to have those scientific findings refuted in the future.

Another source of evidence that is admitted in court according to Article 114 of the Penal Procedure Code is the forensic and medical examination. The forensic report is ordered by the investigative body; in the Factory Case it includes the physical examination of the alleged victim's body, a toxicological analysis, blood and urine samples, and other tests. Article 115 of the same Code regulates the manner in which these examinations are recorded and the requirement of a written report (Penal Procedure Code of Romania, 2008). The examination's conclusions are recorded in a report which can be reviewed either ex officio or upon one of the trial parties' request if there is a suspicion that the report is not complete or that it is inaccurate. Altogether with the review, a new examination could take place if considered necessary and ordered by a judge and new elements might be investigated and added during this review process.

The forensic examination and other required analyses are to be conducted by official qualified professionals, unless there are extraordinary circumstances or the official experts consider the participation of external experts necessary. The experts will answer the questions posed by the investigative body, taking into account the observations and additional questions demanded by either party in the trial (Penal Procedure Code of Romania, 2008).

Under the Romanian Penal Code, whenever the defendant is a legal person (company) who committed criminal acts in order to carry out or complete the entity's commercial activities or to promote its interests, then that entity will suffer the consequences of the criminal law. According to the same Code, though the legal person (company) will face legal consequences for criminal acts, this does not imply that the person or persons who contributed in whatever way to the same acts will not be brought to justice as well. The penalties applied to legal persons are the main or principal ones, consisting of both a fine and complementary damages. The main penalty's amount value depends on the severity of the committed crime. At the same time, the complementary penalties can result in the dissolution of the legal person or the suspension of that entity's activity for a period of up to 1 year or the suspension of the activity in relation to which the criminal act was committed for a period of up to 3 years. The court can also choose to close several of the legal person's branches or operation sites, restrict its participation in public sales or trade, and/or publish the criminal sentence.

Conclusions

The Factory Case can potentially be the focus of a criminal trial under Romanian legislation, as long as all the elements specified by the legislation in place are met: there is an act that falls under the criminal law, there is a complaint, and the plaintiffs do not withdraw it. At the same time, from the case description and the alleged criminal acts and the harm suffered by the victims, it is implicit that a forensic examination and the following reports are the basis of the criminal investigation once the complaint has been filed. Epidemiologic data and thus the use of epidemiology in the forensic and then the judicial setting are essential in drawing the forensic examination's conclusions.

Under Romanian criminal law, both experts' opinions and written expertise are allowed as evidence in court, as well as witnesses' testimony. However, Article 54 of the Penal Procedure Code (Penal Procedure Code of Romania, 2008) clearly establishes a demarcation between the two positions in a trial: the expert and the witness. There are several incompatibilities with the two positions in the trial and Article 54 states that an expert cannot be at the same time a witness in the same case. An important disposition within the Code refers to the priority of the witness quality during the trial. As long as an expert has a personal interest or connection with the trial case or has been a witness to the acts at trial, his or her opinion will not be admitted in court.

The scientific validity of the data, the expert's opinions, and the arguments made before the judge have an impact not only on the criminal investigation but also on a trial for civil damages. In parallel with the criminal trial, the victims can pursue a civil action demanding compensation for material damages or moral wrongs (Civil Code, 2009). As Freeman and colleagues (2008) noted in their review of common forensic uses of probabilistic determinations, the accuracy and appropriate means of presenting forensic testimony are essential to the avoidance of injustices, underscoring the need for a probability standardization in forensic medicine. This applies also to the present study case. Sufficient data, medical records, employment history, etiology examination, already published data, and public health research on lead exposure are all to be considered. Nevertheless, under Romanian criminal law, these investigations are mandated by the judicial investigation body and conducted usually by affiliated institutes, which can create bias. Given that these institutions are state funded, they may sometimes lack resources, such as highly sophisticated technology for the analysis of blood and urine samples, which can create a bias. An alternative to this and a way to confirm the examination's conclusion is to have another parallel examination or an additional external expert providing support. Both of these means of correction are available under the Penal Procedure Code.

Forensic epidemiology is an almost unknown judicial tool in Romania. However, as shown by the extensive legal analysis above, Romanian legislation provides the appropriate framework for admitting reliable epidemiologic data in civil and criminal trials. Use of epidemiologic data in the Romanian legal context will require extensive training of both attorneys and members of the judiciary in epidemiologic concepts, and of epidemiologists in the nature of legal proceedings.

Notes

1. According to Article 116, "to clarify facts or circumstances of the case, to find for the truth, the knowledge of an expert is necessary, the prosecutor or the court orders an expertise, on request or on its own."
2. Article 119 provides that if forensic experts and official experts in the specialty concerned exist, other experts cannot be appointed "unless special circumstances would require this." This Article also stipulates that "when expertise is to be conducted by a forensic medicine service [...], the prosecutor or the court will ask them to perform the expert service. When the forensic medicine service [...] considers that it is necessary for experts in other fields to be involved, their assistance or opinion can be required."

   Article 203 regulates the way in which the forensic expertise can be required, i.e., by ordinance or motivated resolution. Also, this article stipulates the data that an ordinance or a motivated resolution must contain: "the date and place of preparation, name, surname and position of the person making it, the felony to which it refers, the object of the act, its legal basis, the signature of the person who completed it" (Romanian Criminal Procedure Code).

References

Bondoc, L. (2001). European integration and constitutional law. European Commission for Democracy through Law; Lucian Bondoc. Counsellor, Ministry of Foreign Affairs, European integration and constitutional law: The situation in Romania. in Collection. Science and technique of democracy, No. 30, Council of Europe Publishing, F-67075 Strasbourg Cedex, ISBN 92-879-4730-2, October 2001.

Centers for Disease Control and Prevention. (2009). *Fourth national report on human exposure to environmental chemicals*. Atlanta, GA: Author.

Ciuchilan, E., Iov, T., & Pendefunda, L. (2011). Epidemiology in traffic accidents. *Romanian Neurosurgery, XVIII*(3), 356–361.

Civil Code. (2009). The Parliament of Romania, Law No. 287/2009. Republished in *Romanian Official Gazette* No. 5-5/2011, Romania.

Civil Procedure Code. (2009). The Parliament of Romania, Law No. 57/2008. Republished in *Romanian Official Gazette* 2008, Romania.

Constitution of Romania. (1991). *Romanian Official Gazette* No. 233/1991. Part I, amended by the law published in the *Romanian Official Gazette* No. 669/2003.

Craft, E. S., Donnelly, K. C., Neamtiu, I., McCarty, K. M., Bruce, E., Surkova, I., et al. (2006). Prioritizing environmental issues around the world: Opinions from an international Central and Eastern European environmental health conference. *Environmental Health Perspectives, 114*(12), 1813–1817.

Frankowski, S., & Stephan, P. B., III. (1995). *Legal reform in post-communist Europe: The view from within*. Dordrecht, Netherlands: Martinius Nijhoff Publishers.

Freeman, M. D., Rossignol, A. M., & Hand, M. L. (2008). Forensic epidemiology: A systematic approach to probabilistic determinations in disputed matters. *Journal of Forensic and Legal Medicine, 15*(5), 281–290. doi:10.1016/j.jflm.2007.12.009.

Fu, H., & Boffetta, P. (1995). Cancer and occupational exposure to inorganic lead compounds: A meta-analysis of published data. *Occupational and Environmental Medicine, 52*(2), 73–81.

Ivan, A. (1993). *Medicina omului sănătos [Medicine of the healthy person]*. Bucharest, Romania: Editura Medical .

Kritzer, H. M. (2002). *Legal systems of the world: A political, social, and cultural encyclopedia*. Santa Barbara, CA: ABC-CLIO, Inc.

Labour Code. (2003). The Parliament of Romania, Law No. 53/2003, *Romanian Official Gazette* No. 72/Feb 2003. Republished *Official Gazette* No. 345/May 2011, Romania.

Law 319/2006 on Security and occupational health. The Parliament of Romania. *Romanian Official Gazette* No.646/2006, Romania.

Loue, S. (2002). *Case studies in forensic epidemiology*. New York: Kluwer Academic/Plenum Publishers.

Penal Code. (2008). The Parliament of Romania, Law No. 58/2008, Government Emergency Ordinance 198/2008 C.F.R., Romania.

Penal Procedure Code of Romania. (2008). The Parliament of Romania, Governmental Emergency Ordinance No. 121/2011 C.F.R., Official Gazette No. 145-146/1968, Romania.

Chapter 5
Forensic Epidemiology and Environmental Justice

Sana Loue

Introduction

The impact of environmental policies and practices lies far beyond the borders of the country in which these decisions are made. As an example, tons of toxic waste were shipped illegally from Great Britain to sites in Ghana and Nigeria, where young children would then forage in the waste dumps for raw metals that they could exchange for urgently needed cash to survive (Anon, 2009). The Dutch-registered company Trafigura was found to have illegally dumped toxic waste in Abidjan in Côte d'Ivoire (Anon, 2010; Beckford & Watt, 2009; Simons, 2011). In July 2009, 1,400 metric tons of household garbage labeled as clean plastic for recycling was shipped illegally from Great Britain to Brazil (Rosenthal, 2009). It has been estimated that by 2007, 20 million containers of paper, plastic, and metal waste were being shipped on an annual basis to developing countries from Europe, whether legally or illegally (Rosenthal, 2009). A 2004 investigation in the Netherlands concluded that significant quantities of waste from electrical and electronic equipment (WEEE) originating in Germany, the Netherlands, the UK, and France were being illegally exported to developing countries (Greenpeace, 2008). Rotterdam has earned the dubious title of "Europe's main external garbage chute" because of its role as a gateway for the transport of garbage originating in European nations to China, Indonesia, India, and countries of Africa (Rosenthal, 2009). And this problem is not confined to European companies. An investigation conducted by the US Government Accountability Office found that at least 43 recyclers were willing to export toxic e-waste to would-be buyers in Hong Kong, India, Pakistan, Singapore, and Vietnam, in direct violation of US law (Biello, 2008).

S. Loue (✉)
Department of Bioethics, Case Western Reserve University,
Cleveland, OH, USA
e-mail: sana.loue@case.edu

S. Loue (ed.), *Forensic Epidemiology in the Global Context*,
DOI 10.1007/978-1-4614-6738-0_5, © Springer Science+Business Media New York 2013

The export of this toxic waste to distant locales presents more than aesthetic issues. Significant health risks may be associated with such practices. Trafigura's illegal dumping of toxic waste in the Côte d'Ivoire resulted in the deaths of at least 16 people and injury and illness of at least 108,000 individuals who were exposed to the chemicals (Beckford & Watt, 2009; Simons, 2011). The contamination of underground and surface water with chemicals from industrial, agricultural, and commercial waste has been linked to various cancers, including cancer of the bladder, lung, stomach, kidney, colon, and rectum; leukemia; non-Hodgkin's lymphoma (Cohn, Klotz, Bove, Berkowitz, & Fagliano, 1994; Comba et al., 2006; DeKraay, 1978; Fagliano, Berry, Bove, & Burke, 1990; Griffith, Duncan, Riggan, & Pellom, 1989; Mallin, 1990; Najem, Louria, Lavenhar, & Feiuerman, 1985); and congenital malformations (Comba et al., 2006).

Additional environmental and health issues are raised in the context of industrial development in developing and poorer countries by corporations of developed countries. As one researcher noted, "The labor-intensive and most polluting aspects of industrial productions are increasingly carried out in poor nations that have little or no occupational or toxic waste protection in place" (Nickens, 1990). One such example is provided by Texaco's oil extraction in the Amazon basin of Ecuador which, as research findings suggest, has led to significant adverse health effects (Hurtig & San Sebastián, 2004; San Sebastián, Armstrong, Córdoba, & Stephens, 2001; San Sebastián, Armstrong, & Stephens, 2002).

This apparent inequity in the distribution of health risks from industrial activities, whether through the exportation and dumping of toxic waste from developed countries to poorer nations or through the exploitation of a poorer country's natural resources to the detriment of its environment and the health of its citizens, exemplifies what has been termed environmental injustice. Environmental injustice or inequality refers to situations "in which a specific social group is disproportionately affected by environmental hazards" (Brulle & Pellow, 2006, p. 104). The converse, environmental justice, is the

> fair treatment and meaningful involvement of all people regardless of race, color, national origin, or income with respect to the development, implementation, and enforcement of environmental laws, regulations, and policies. Fair treatment means that no population, due to policy or economic disempowerment, is forced to bear a disproportionate share of the negative human health or environmental impacts of pollution or environmental consequences resulting from industrial, municipal, and commercial operation or the execution of federal, state, local and tribal program and policies (Institute of Medicine, 1999, p. 1)

Once conceived of as an issue at the local or national level, it has become increasingly clear as illustrated by the above examples that environmental justice and injustice are issues of global concern. Various scholars have explained the process by which this occurs as follows:

> The power to determine the course of technological development has become concentrated in private corporations that control and direct much of society's research and development. Driven by the need to maximize profits, corporations in turn continue to develop new technologies that produce unforeseen risks for the entire society. This process breaks down the ability of the society to ensure the safety of its citizens from the production of industrial

hazards, creating a "risk society" in which the politics of distribution of the fruits of economic production is overlaid with the politics of the distribution of environmental pollution, producing environmental injustice (Brulle & Pellow, 2006, pp. 108–109; see also Beck, 1986, 1995).

This chapter focuses on the case of Texaco's oil extraction in the Amazon basin of Ecuador in order to illustrate the interplay between forensic epidemiology and environmental (in)justice.[1] Because the origins of environmental injustice can only be understood within the larger context in which it occurs, the case study begins with a description of the demographic, environmental, political, and economic context in which Texaco's oil extraction occurred. The chapter then discusses the legal proceedings that occurred as a result of Texaco's activities and the role that epidemiology played in those proceedings.

Texaco and Oil Extraction in Ecuador's Amazon Basin

The Exploration, Its Environs, and Its Aftermath

Ecuador's Amazon basin, known as the Oriente, consists of approximately 32 million acres of tropical rainforest, accounting for almost one-half of the country's geographic area (Centro de Derechos Económicos y Sociales, 2006). The region is home to nine indigenous nationalities, consisting of an estimated 200,000 individuals, or 3.5 % of Ecuador's indigenous population (Centro de Derechos Económicos y Sociales, 2006). The region is known as one of the most biodiverse in the world (Finer, Vijay, Ponce, Jenkins, & Kahn, 2009). Ecuador's indigenous populations, including residents in the Amazon basin, have historically been excluded from the country's political and economic spheres and considerations (Sawyer, 2004), resulting in increasing rates of poverty among more than three-quarters of this population (Hall & Patrinos, 2005). As of 2001, the richest fifth of Ecuador's population held 64 % of the nation's wealth, while the poorest fifth, which included indigenous communities, held only 1.7 % (World Bank, 2003).

It appears that the populations of the Oriente were relatively isolated from the outside world, with the exception of periods of contact instigated by companies seeking rubber in the late 1800s and early 1900s, early oil exploration during the 1940s, and missionary efforts beginning in the 1950s (Finer et al., 2009). More intensive oil exploration efforts began in the 1970s, following the 1964 award by Ecuador of the oil concession to Texaco (Kimerling, 2006a).

Additionally, the Ecuadorian Government during the 1970s and 1980s offered incentives, such as land titles, to settlers of the Amazon region who would clear the land for crops or raise livestock. These colonization efforts constituted one facet of government efforts to integrate the indigenous communities into the national culture (Kimerling, 2006a). These efforts at colonization were unwelcomed by the indigenous communities, who viewed the integration policy as a threat to their physical and cultural survival (Whitten, 1976). One anthropologist described these assimilation/colonization efforts as "cultural obliteration and assimilation into a lower class serf-like existence" (Whitten, 1976, pp. 3–4) that was

> systematic, large scale, and planned, as well as random, local, and unintended. Illustrations of ethnocidal policies include monolingual education in Spanish, proselytization by Catholics and Protestants, courses in social organization aimed at altering family, kinship, and other bases of social cooperation and competition launched by government, church, and Peace Corps Volunteers, and the steady encapsulation of natives on eroding territories, without infrastructural support. Even in the area of medicine it is difficult for a native person to buy a physician's services without being treated to a lecture about the evils of *chica*—manioc gruel, with low alcohol content—drinking (Whitten, 1976, p. 24).

Texaco carried out its operations until the expiration of its contract in 1992. By that time, it had enlarged its operations to include multiple provinces within the Oriente. Government concerns over the growing depletion of the nonrenewable oil reserves that fueled its economy and continuing pressure mounted by international oil companies contributed to the government's willingness to modify laws and contracts to favor the interests of the oil companies (Kimerling, 2006b). Proponents of oil production in Ecuador have argued that the country's infrastructure has improved significantly due to the increased financial resources available (Widener, 2007). By 1977, the government income had quadrupled as the result of oil production (Martz, 1987). Petrodollars contributed to the construction and maintenance of roads, bridges, schools, and health care centers. Well-paid employment in the oil industry became available to Ecuadorians of various skill levels. Others, however, have refuted these arguments, emphasizing instead the government's neglect of agricultural production attributable to its long-term dependence on this one commodity (Karl, 1997, 1999).

During the period of its operations, Texaco constructed 340 wells and 1,000 open-air waste pits, and is alleged to have dumped 18 billion gallons of toxic wastewater into the surface and subsurface waters and soils of Ecuador's Amazon (Powers & Quarles, 2006), waters that the indigenous people relied upon for drinking, cooking, and bathing (Herbert, 2005; Powers & Quarles, 2006). Approximately 3.2 million gallons of toxic wastewater were produced daily and, without either treatment or monitoring, were dumped into open-air earthen waste pits (Kimerling, 2008). It is of note that this practice has been prohibited in the United States since 1979 pursuant to regulations promulgated under the Clean Water Act (40 C.F.R. § 435.32). Estimates suggest that the company saved $42 billion through the use of substandard extraction and production methods (Bejarano, 2005).

Texaco's operations dispossessed the Amazonian populations of their land, forcing them to resettle elsewhere, and brought more than 250,000 settlers to the region (Kimerling, 2006a). Once isolated from the outside world, these indigenous communities were now connected to it by the 500 km of road that Texaco had paved deep into the territory (Finer et al., 2009; Kimerling, 2006a). These roads led directly to fragmentation, soil erosion, vehicle–wildlife collisions, and noise (Canaday & Rivadeneyra, 2001) and indirectly to increased rates of deforestation, overhunting, and transformation of subsistence hunters into purveyors of the illegal trade in vulnerable wildlife (Franzen, 2006; Suárez et al., 2009). One scholar described in graphic detail the lengths to which Texaco went to carry out its operations and the devastating consequences for one indigenous community:

> Texaco collaborated with Ecuador and evangelical Christian missionaries from the U.S.-based Summer Institute of Linguistics/Wycliffe Bible Translators to pressure and trick Huaorani clans into leaving the areas where Texaco wanted to work, pacify the Huaorani, and exterminate their culture and way of life. Using aircraft supplied by the company, missionaries contacted and physically removed some 200 Huaorani from the path of the oil crews, and took them to live in a distant Christian settlement located in the western edge of Huaorani territory .... When groups of Huaorani left the Christian settlements to return to the land of their ancestors, it was not the same as before. The rainforest that was their home and source of life had been invaded and degraded by outsiders while they were away (Kimerling, 2008, pp. 221–222).

Significant adverse physical health effects have also resulted from exposure associated with oil production and transport. Exposure due to spills, leaks, dumping, and gas by-product burn off is possible at every stage of the production process, including exploration, extraction, refining, and transport (Widener, 2007). In addition to skin rashes suffered by children who reside near the oil production sites (Drost, 2005), researchers have found an association between exposure resulting from the inhalation, ingestion, and absorption of petroleum-based products and increased incidence rates of childhood leukemia (Hurtig & San Sebastián, 2004); cancer of the stomach, rectum, skin, kidney, larynx, and liver among men (Hurtig & San Sebastián, 2002; San Sebastián et al., 2001); cancer of the cervix and lymph nodes among women (Hurtig & San Sebastián, 2002); and spontaneous abortion among pregnant women (San Sebastián et al., 2002).

It is unclear whether and to what extent the loss of the indigenous people's traditional way of life and livelihood may have led to adverse psychological effects; it appears that the possibility of such an outcome has not been the focus of systematic research to date. However, published studies relating to such losses among Native Americans in the United States (Brave Heart, 1998; Brave Heart & DeBruyn, 1998; Evans-Campbell, 2008; Sotero, 2006; Whitbeck, Adams, Hoyt, & Chen, 2004), Aboriginal populations in Canada (Menzies, 2009, 2010), Japanese internees in the United States during World War II (Nagata & Cheng, 2003), African American slaves and their children (Gump, 2010; Leary, 2005); and Holocaust survivors and their children (Baranowsky, Yiung, Johnson-Douglas, Williams-Keeler, & McCarrey, 1998; Kellermann, 2001; Wiseman, Metzl, & Barber, 2006; Yehuda, Halligan, & Grossman, 2001) suggest that events similar to those experienced by the Huaorani may be associated with multigenerational trauma.[2]

Texaco relinquished its operations to Ecuador's state-run oil company, Petroecuador, and merged in 2001 with Chevron to become ChevronTexaco (Kimerling, 2006a). The company later changed its name to Chevron in 2008. It has been speculated that the poor publicity associated with Texaco prompted this name change (Widener, 2007). Chevron assumed responsibility for all of Texaco's activities in Ecuador. On balance, it appears that

> [d]espite three decades of oil extraction, the majority of Ecuadorian communities remain indigent with limited economic opportunities and limited infusion of oil wealth back into the surrounding communities (Widener, 2007, p. 93, Fig. 2).

Legal Battles

The history of legal proceedings against Texaco, now Chevron, for harms alleged to have resulted from its oil-producing activities in Ecuador's Amazon is long and complex, involving multiple lawsuits against Texaco by multiple plaintiffs filed in the United States and in Ecuador; actions by the president of Ecuador and international groups; and lawsuits and counterclaims filed by Chevron against Ecuador and the attorneys for the plaintiffs. The ongoing legal battles have been described as "one of the nastiest legal contests in memory, a spectacle almost as ugly as the pollution that prompted it" (Keefe, 2012).[3] Shareholders have raised concerns regarding the extent of Chevron's liability exposure due to these protracted proceedings (Hinton, 2012). Additionally, Chevron has earned the dubious title of "Rainforest Jekyll and Hyde" due to its consistent denial of liability for the rainforest contamination on the one hand, and on the other, its presentation of conservation awards to those preserving the environment (Herbert, 2005). Table 5.1 below provides an outline of the legal filings, court decisions, and other legal proceedings. (For a full analysis of court decisions, see Kimerling, 2006b, 2008.) Although transnational advocacy networks (TANs) have played an important role in exposing the consequences to the environment of the oil industry activities in supporting the litigation and in lobbying shareholders for change to corporate policy, their strategies are not addressed here. Readers are referred to McAteer and Pulver (2009) for a review of TANs' participation.

As indicated by this brief summary of the legal proceedings in this case, questions related to epidemiologic findings and to their use in litigation have now been presented to courts both in the United States and Ecuador. New York courts have refused to consider these issues, holding that they are more appropriately considered in Ecuadorian courts. Chevron has challenged the scientific validity of the epidemiologic findings presented in the Ecuadorian courts, essentially arguing that they are the product of fraud and collusion between the court-appointed expert and the plaintiffs' attorney. According to one reporter, even the plaintiffs' lawyer referred to the scientific evidence as "just a bunch of smoke and mirrors and bullshit" (Keefe, 2012).

Assuming for the purpose of this discussion that fraud is not involved, questions relating to the validity of the epidemiologic findings and the weight to be attributed to them remain. The resolution of such issues ultimately depends upon a policy determination, responsibility for which rests variously with the court, the legislature, and/or a regulatory agency, depending upon the legal processes within a particular jurisdiction. The resolution of the ongoing legal battle appears at the present time to hinge on the determination of one primary epidemiologic issue and one major legal issue: Must epidemiologic causality be definitively established as a prerequisite to action which, in the case of TexacoChevron litigation, would entail additional environmental cleanup and compensation to those who have suffered associated adverse health effects? Did the release from Ecuador of claims against Texaco include future claims by unknown third parties, thereby absolving Texaco and its corporate successors from any additional liability? The epidemiologic issue is addressed below; an analysis of the legal issue would require access to the original agreement as well as additional materials and is beyond the scope of this chapter.

Table 5.1 Outline of legal proceedings in connection with claims for alleged harms due to Texaco activities in Ecuador, 1993–2012

Date	Event
1993	Nov. 3: A class action lawsuit on behalf of 30,000 individuals in Ecuador is filed in New York against Texaco from harms alleged to have been caused by its oil operations. *Aguinda v. Texaco*. The lawsuit seeks damages under theories of negligence, private and public nuisance, trespass, civil conspiracy, and violation of the Alien Tort Claims Act.[a]
	Texaco moves to dismiss *Aguinda* for failure to join Ecuador as a defendant and on the grounds of international comity and *forum non conveniens*.[b]
1994	District court for the Southern District of Texas dismisses a case similar to that of *Aguinda,* in favor of it being pursued in Ecuador. *Sequihua v. Texaco Inc*., 847 F. Supp. 61 (S.D. Tex. 1994).
	Dec. 28: A lawsuit is filed by 25,000 residents living in Peru downstream from Oriente. *Jota v. Texaco*, Docket No. 94 Civ. 9266 (S.D.N.Y.).
	1994–1995: Remediation contract is signed by Texaco and the Republic of Ecuador under which Texaco would perform limited environmental remediation, pay Ecuador for socioeconomic compensation projects, and negotiate contributions to public works of four municipal governments of towns that came into existence around the oil company's operations. Ecuador agrees to release the company from all claims, obligations, and liability to Ecuador and the national oil company Petroecuador that are related to contamination from the operations. No dollar amount is specified; Texaco alleges that it spent $40 million.
1996	Nov. 12: Class action *Aguinda v. Texaco* is dismissed by federal district court on grounds that plaintiffs failed to include Petroecuador and the Government of Ecuador as defendants, both of which are not subject to suit in the United States, and *forum non conveniens*. *Aguinda v. Texaco*, 945 F. Supp. 625 (S.D.N.Y. 1996).
1997	Plaintiffs move for reconsideration of dismissal.
	The Republic of Ecuador files a motion to intervene on behalf of plaintiffs.
	The district court denies plaintiffs' motion. 175 F.R.D. 50 (S.D.N.Y. 1997).
	Aug. 12: The district court denies Ecuador's motion to intervene.
1998	The Second Circuit Court of Appeals vacates the dismissal of *Jota* and remands for reconsideration, ruling that a *forum non conveniens* dismissal is inappropriate absent a commitment from Texaco to submit to the jurisdiction of Ecuadorian courts. 157 F.3d 153 (2d Cir. 1998).
	Texaco consents to jurisdiction in Ecuador as to *Aguinda* plaintiffs and in Peru or Ecuador as to *Jota* plaintiffs. Texaco agrees to a stipulation to waive statute of limitations defenses[c] that matured during the period of time between the filing of the complaint and 60 days after the dismissal of the action by the district court.
	Texaco moves again to dismiss based on *forum non conveniens*.
2000	Jan. 31: Judge Rakoff, who is presiding over *Aguinda* litigation, orders investigation into independence and impartiality of Ecuadorian judicial system.
	Plaintiffs in *Aguinda* move to disqualify Judge Rakoff because of his attendance at an all-expense paid trip to a Montana resort, funded by the Foundation for Research in Economics and the Environment (FREE), which receives support from Texaco. An executive of Texaco is a keynote speaker at the conference.
	The motion to disqualify Judge Rakoff is denied. *Aguinda v. Texaco*, 139 F. Supp. 2d 438 (S.D.N.Y. 2000).

(continued)

Table 5.1 (continued)

Date	Event
2001	The Court of Appeals denies plaintiffs' petition for a writ of mandamus[d] to disqualify Judge Rakoff. *In re Aguinda*, 241 F.3d 194 (2d Cir. 2001).
	May 30: The district court grants Texaco's motion to dismiss *Aguinda* and *Jota* complaints, holding that "[t]hese cases have everything to do with Ecuador and nothing to do with the United States. 142 F. Supp. 2d 537, 554 (S.D.N.Y. 2011).
2002	Aug. 16: Court of Appeals for the Second Circuit affirms dismissal of *Aguinda v. Texaco* on grounds of *forum non conveniens*, on the condition that Texaco agrees to litigate the issues in Ecuador. 303 F.2d 470 (2d Cir. 2002).
2003	May 7: A lawsuit is filed in Ecuador against Texaco by 48 plaintiffs, including 46 from the *Aguinda* litigation. *Aguinda v. ChevronTexaco Corp.*, Super. Ct. of Nueva Loja, Lago Agrio, Province of Sucumbios. The lawsuit seeks damages, cleanup of polluted areas, a determination of the costs of comprehensive environmental remediation, and an order directing ChevronTexaco to pay the full amount to the Amazon Defense Front (Frente de le Defensa Amazonia; "la Frente"), a local nongovernmental organization (NGO) founded in 1994 by settlers (colonists) to the Amazon. The NGO did not consult members of some of the indigenous groups affected by Texaco activities and did not request compensation for affected residents.
	July 30: A second lawsuit is filed against ChevronTexaco and Texaco Petroleum, Texaco's Ecuadorian subsidiary, in Ecuador. Plaintiffs Complaint to the President of the Supreme Court of Justice of Tena, Moi Vicente Enomenga Mantohue v. ChevronTexaco Corp. and Texaco Petroleum Co. [*Tena* case].
	The Ecuadorian court refuses to accept the Tena complaint filed by Kichwa and Huaorani because complaint is not translated into English and Texaco is in the United States and because the lands owned by the plaintiff communities that were affected by Texaco are situated, in part, outside of the provinces in which the court was located. Plaintiffs appeal to the plenary of the court.
	Oct. 29: The plenary of the court dismisses the *Tena* case. H. Superior Court of Justice of Tena, Civ.Lawsuit No. 714–2003 (Oct. 29, 2003).
2004	ChevronTexaco Corp. and Texaco Petroleum initiate an arbitration proceeding in New York against Petroecuador, claiming indemnification for their costs and expenses incurred in connection with the litigation in Ecuador, including any final judgment against ChevronTexaco in Ecuador. ChevronTexaco, Press release, ChevronTexaco and Texaco Petroleum Company File Arbitration Claim to Enforce Petroecuador's Obligations Under Joint Operation Agreement: Claim Asserts Petroecuador Required to Pay All Costs Associated with Lawsuit Against ChevronTexaco in Ecuador (June 15, 2004).
	Ecuador and Petroecuador file lawsuit against ChevronTexaco, Texaco Petroleum, and American Arbitration Association in New York State Supreme Court to stay the arbitration, based on the claim that they had never agreed to arbitrate disputes with Texaco.
	ChevronTexaco and Texaco Petroleum move to remove case to federal court. Federal court dismisses the lawsuit against the American Arbitration Association and permits Ecuador and Petroecuador to file an amended complaint.
	ChevronTexaco and Texaco Petroleum file counterclaim against Ecuador and Petroecuador for breach of contract and failure to indemnify an implied agent.
2005	The Republic of Ecuador and Petroecuador sue to stay the arbitration. *Republic of Ecuador v. ChevronTexaco Corp.*, 376 F. Supp. 2d 334 (S.D.N.Y. 2005). The court stays the arbitration temporarily.

2006	A new Supreme Court sends the *Tena* case back, admonishing the original court for its irresponsible and unlawful disobedience of its duty.
	April: New York court denies motion by Ecuador and Petroecuador to dismiss counterclaim by ChevronTexaco and Texaco Petroleum, which claims that the Lago Agrio claims are barred by the releases granted to ChevronTexaco by Ecuador under the 1995 Remediation Contract and subsequent 1998 Final Act that certifies that Texaco Petroleum had fulfilled its obligations under the remediation contract. Ecuador argues that it did not own or release the rights or claims of third parties to environmental remediation. *Republic of Ecuador v. ChevronTexaco*, 426 F. Supp. 2d 334 (S.D.N.Y. 2006).
	Doe v. Texaco is filed in the US district court in San Francisco with nine named plaintiffs, all colonists in the Oriente, for violation of the California Unfair Competition Law and unjust enrichment. The complaint is dismissed for failure to state a claim. An amended complaint will later be filed as *Gonzales et al. v. Texaco.*
	April 25: An amended complaint is filed in *Gonzales et al. v. Texaco*, No. C 06–0280 WHA, N.D. Cal., alleging that plaintiffs' cancer/leukemia was attributable to Texaco's activities in Ecuador.
	May 1: 4 Ecuadorian citizens petition the Organization of American States Inter-American Commission on Human Rights (IACHR) for precautionary measures to protect Tagaeri and Taromenane, a group of Huaorani living in the Intangible Zone, a 758,051-hectare conservation area. The petition seeks protection of the territory they inhabit and of their life and integrity. Petición a favor de los pueblos indigenas Tagaeri y Taromenane (May 1, 2006). Retrieved from http://ciudadanoporlademocracia.org.
	May 11: IACHR calls on the Government of Ecuador to adopt Precautionary Measures to protect the lives and personal integrity of Tagaeri and Taromenane.
	July 20: Amended complaint is filed in *Gonzalez v. Texaco.*
	Oct. 12: 118 representatives from 28 Huaorani and Lower Napo Kichwa communities file a motion to intervene[e] in *Republic of Ecuador v. ChevronTexaco*, seeking damages and equitable relief (remediation, restoration, medical monitoring) and three claims under international law including discrimination, the ethnocide of the Huaorani, and the violation of the Huaorani's right to culture.
	Nov.: Court denies motion to intervene in *Republic of Ecuador v. ChevronTexaco.*
2007	Jan.: President Alfredo Palacio of Ecuador signs a decree establishing boundaries of the Intangible Zone.
	April: The Ecuadorian Government begins an initiative to design a policy specifying that the territories of uncontacted indigenous people are off limits to extractive activities.
	Aug. 3: The US district court for the Northern District of California grants Texaco's motion for summary judgment[f] in *Gonzalez v. Texaco*, finding that the cancer and leukemia alleged by two plaintiffs to have resulted from Texaco's activities are in fact nonexistent. *Gonzalez v. Texaco*, Order Granting Motions for Summary Judgment and Terminating Sanctions, No. C 06–02820 WHA, N.D. Cal.
	Oct. 16: The US district court for the Northern District of California imposes monetary sanctions against attorneys for the plaintiffs in *Gonzalez et al. v. Texaco*, finding that the attorneys knew or should have known that the claims of various plaintiffs were bogus and nevertheless proceeded to file lawsuits on their behalf. No. 006–02820 WHA, Rule 11 Sanction and Award of Attorney's Fees and expenses and Judgment Lien.
	Nov. 15: The court issues its Final Order granting Texaco's motion for summary judgment against plaintiffs Cadena and Zambrano in *Gonzalez v. Texaco*, because claims were filed after California's 2-year statute of limitations had elapsed. The court declines to apply Ecuador's 4-year statute of limitations.
	New York court grants motion for summary judgment of Republic of Ecuador and Petroecuador for permanent injunction staying Chevron from continuing arbitration in New York, finding that Ecuador and Petroecuador had never agreed to submit to arbitration.

(continued)

Table 5.1 (continued)

Date	Event
2008	A new Ecuadorian constitution approved by voters forbids any extractive activity within territories of indigenous people living in voluntary isolation. The provision includes an exception allowing oil drilling to proceed upon the petition of the president and a declaration by Congress that it is in the national interest. Congress may call for a national referendum if it deems it necessary.
	Nov. 26: The court-appointed independent environmental damages expert Richard Cabrera, a geological engineer, delivers a report that recommends finding Chevron responsible for $27 billion in damages. Chevron denounces the report, alleging bias, error, and fabrication. Plaintiffs commission peer review of the report from an environmental consulting firm in Boulder, Colorado. The firm, which has done work for the US Government, endorses the report, characterizing it as both sound and reasonable.
2011	Jan. 31: Chevron sues plaintiffs' attorney and other members of their legal team, alleging participation in a racketeering conspiracy (RICO) and collusion for the purpose of extortion.
	Feb. 14: Ecuadorian court awards plaintiffs $18.2 billion against Chevron. Chevron refuses to pay and files appeal in Ecuador claiming attorney fraud and judicial corruption. Judge Kaplan in NY issues temporary order prohibiting enforcement of Ecuadorian verdict.
	Mar. 7: The US federal district court for the Southern District of New York grants a preliminary injunction, enjoining the Ecuadorian plaintiffs from seeking recognition or enforcement of the Ecuadorian judgment anywhere in the world outside of Ecuador.
	Chevron appeals judgment of the Ecuadorian court.
	Sept.: The US Court of Appeals for the Second Circuit overturns the lower court decision barring plaintiffs from attaching Chevron assets outside of Ecuador.
2012	Jan.: Ecuadorian appeals court affirms judgment against Chevron. NY federal judge denies Chevron's attempt to seize Ecuadorian assets ahead of trial on conspiracy (RICO) and fraud charges filed by Chevron.
	Feb.: International tribunal established through the Hague's Permanent Court of Arbitration under rules established by the United Nations Commission on International Trade Law determines that it has jurisdiction to decide if Ecuador violated its treaty with the United States requiring it to guarantee a fair trial to Chevron in the environmental lawsuit.
	Mar. 30: 3-judge appellate panel in Ecuador denies Chevron's attempt to block enforcement of $18 billion judgment.
	May 4: Chevron files suit in the US federal court in Miami, seeking access to records of Ecuadorian bank that allegedly reflect bribes paid to a court-appointed expert in Ecuador.
	May 30: Ecuadorian plaintiffs sue Chevron in Ontario, Canada, seeking seizure of Chevron's assets to satisfy $18 billion awarded by Ecuadorian court.
	June: Ecuadorian plaintiffs file lawsuit against Chevron in Brazil seeking to attach Brazilian assets.

Information for this table was derived from the legal cases cited in the table and from Adams, 2012; Anon, 2012; Anton, 2011; Baker, 2012; Barrett, 2011, 2012; Finer et al., 2009; Garcia, 2012; Keefe, 2012; Kimerling, 1995, 2006a, 2006b, 2008; Klasfeld, 2012; Mapstone, 2012; Reddall & Garcia, 2012.

[a]The Alien Tort Claims Act was adopted as part of the Judiciary Act of 1789. It gives federal courts jurisdiction to hear a civil action brought by an alien for a "tort only, committed in violation of the law of nations or a treaty of the United States" (25 U.S.C. § 1350, 2008). One court has held that the statute "applies

only to shockingly egregious violations of universally recognized principles of international law" (*Beanal v. Freeport-McMoran*, 1997, p. 167). Another court has held that the Alien Tort Statute can be used as the basis for only claims that violate "specific, universal, and obligatory" norms that are recognized as part of the "law of nations" at the time of the statute's enactment (*Sosa v. Alvarez-Machain*, 2004, pp. 724–725, 732).

[b]*Forum non conveniens* is the power of a court to dismiss a case because another forum is considered more appropriate for the hearing of the legal matter. The court will generally not grant a dismissal if another forum is inappropriate or if there is no other forum available. Factors that the court will consider in deciding whether to dismiss a case on this basis ("Gilbert factors") include the location of the events underlying the cause of action, the residence of the parties to the action, the location of evidence and witnesses, the burden on the court, the familiarity of the forum with the relevant law, and how the dismissal would affect the parties involved. Courts may sometimes attach conditions to the dismissal, such as requiring the defendant to agree to the jurisdiction of the other court.

[c]The concept of statute of limitations refers to the maximum time that can elapse from an event for the filing of a lawsuit. The concept applies in both civil law and criminal law. A defendant in a civil lawsuit or a criminal trial may raise the statute of limitations as a defense against an action.

[d]A writ of mandamus is an order from a court to a government official, public entity, corporation, or individual to do something. As one example, a court may order a government official to fulfill his or her duties or to correct an abuse of discretion. The term "mandamus" comes from the Latin word meaning "we command." The order is also known as a writ of mandate.

[e]In general, a lawsuit involves the individual or entity bringing the lawsuit (the plaintiff), and the individual or the entity against whom/which the lawsuit is being brought (defendant). A third party with an interest in the subject matter of the lawsuit may wish to become a party to the lawsuit. That individual or entity can seek to intervene through a motion to intervene. To be successful on the motion, the third party (the moving party) must demonstrate that his or her interest would be impeded or impaired if he or she were not permitted to intervene and that his or her interests are not adequately represented by the existing parties to the lawsuit.

[f]A motion for summary judgment is a written request by either the plaintiff or the defendant to the court to grant a judgment in that party's favor, prior to the initiation of trial, based on the existing available evidence, such as that from depositions, affidavits, answers to written interrogatories (questions), and admissions of fact. The party opposing the motion must demonstrate that there are "triable issues of fact" and/or law. In deciding whether or not to grant the motion, the court must view all of the facts in favor of the party that is opposing the motion. Sometimes a judge will grant partial summary judgment, finding for the moving party on only some of the issues and requiring that the case go to trial on the remaining issues.

Epidemiologic Causation: Forensic Epidemiology Meets Popular Epidemiology: To Act or Not, That Is the Question

It has been suggested that epidemiologists would prefer to err on the side of caution and mistakenly conclude that there is no association between an exposure and a specified outcome than to err in the opposite direction and mistakenly claim that an association exists when in fact one does not (Brown, 1987). As an example, one research group that conducted a review of cancer epidemiology studies among the US populations that lived near toxic waste sites catalogued the multiple methodological deficiencies in these studies and ultimately concluded that "epidemiological studies of populations living in the vicinity of a toxic waste site have not produced evidence of a quality that most epidemiologists would consider adequate to establish a causal link between toxic waste exposures and cancer risk" (Russi, Borak, & Cullen, 2008).

Indeed, there are significant methodological difficulties associated with environmental epidemiologic studies. Because environmental health studies are often conducted without having had the benefit of direct monitoring during the period of exposure, exposure misclassification can result, whereby individuals may be erroneously classified as having been or as not having been exposed to the substance under investigation and the duration and intensity of that exposure (Buzzelli, 2007). This has led to a continual search for valid surrogates of exposure, such as proximity to the toxic site (Cutter, Hodgson, & Dow, 2001; Harner, Warner, Pierce, & Huber, 2002). Nonrepresentative samples and confounding factors, both measured and unmeasured, further complicate accurate assessment of the health risks associated with environmental exposures. Many competent, experienced epidemiologists acknowledge these limitations inherent in epidemiologic studies while simultaneously recognizing the need to make constructive use of existing knowledge:

> Epidemiologic studies, however meticulously conducted, may have inherent limitations, as all epidemiologists are aware. Epidemiology is not laboratory science but a study of the real world, and thus always subject to challenge in its ability to control for all potential effects. Especially in vulnerable study populations, exact details of the populations at risk, as well as the extents, natures, and durations of exposures, are difficult to document, and ascertainment of outcomes is limited by the quality of health services available (Breilh, Branco, Castleman, Cherniak, Christiani Christiani, Cicolella, Cifuentes, … Yassiet al., 2005, p. 217).

These issues give rise to the policy question before courts: What strength of association must be demonstrated to prompt action rather than to establish causality?[4] As one writer noted in speaking about a toxic waste dump in the United States,

> The degree of risk to human health does not need to be at statistically significant levels to require political action. The degree of risk does have to be such that a reasonable person would avoid it. Consequently, the important political test is not the findings of epidemiologists on the probability or nonrandomness of an incidence of illness but the likelihood that a reasonable person, including members of the community of calculation, would take up residence with the community at risk and drink from and bathe in water … (Couto, 1986).

Not surprisingly, then, "[w]hoever controls the definition of risk controls the rational solution to the problem at hand … Defining risk is thus an exercise in power" (Slovic, 1999, p. 699). Popular epidemiology can serve as a vehicle through which this power can be shared. Forensic epidemiology—the use of epidemiologic findings in litigation—often intersects with, and indeed constitutes one component of, what has been termed popular epidemiology. Popular epidemiology has been described as the integration of traditional epidemiologic methods with an emphasis on "basic social structural factors," and the sharing of power between the community and the epidemiologists involved (San Sebastián & Hurtig, 2005, p. 799). It is characterized by nine activities: (1) the observations of health effects and pollutants by people in the community; (2) the development of hypotheses by community members of the cause(s) of the observed health effects; (3) the sharing of information between community members; (4) discussions between community members, government representatives, and scientists about the health effects and their possible environmental causes; (5) the organization of community members in order to investigate the causes; (6) the conduct of investigations by government agencies or officials in order to respond to community concerns; (7) the enlistment of experts by the community group to investigate the possible sources of the health effects; (8) community participation in litigation efforts; and (9) the exertion of pressure on agencies and experts by the community to corroborate their findings (Brown, 1992).

In large degree, the indigenous communities impacted by Texaco's/Chevron's actions have engaged in popular epidemiology. Nevertheless, the continuing vitriolic legal battles make clear that the ability of popular epidemiology to remedy instances of environmental injustice is limited by time and money and the attainment of an equitable remedy may be illusory.

A comparison of the course of litigation and the use of epidemiologic findings in the ChevronTexaco case with that in the Pfizer Kano litigation may provide some insight into the strengths and limitations of popular epidemiology. (See Chap. 1 for a discussion of the Pfizer Kano research and litigation.) There are numerous similarities between the two situations:

- Litigation has been in process for over a decade in both cases and has not yet yielded a final result.
- The harms alleged to have been caused to residents of a developing country were committed by the US corporations.
- Those harmed attempted to have their claims heard in the US courts due to alleged corruption within the judicial systems of the respective developing countries.
- Plaintiffs relied on epidemiologic findings to support their allegations; in each case, defendants attempted on various grounds to refute those findings.
- Corporate payments were made to the governments of the affected nations—Pfizer to Nigeria and Texaco to Ecuador—leaving the recovery of damages by those individuals actually injured in doubt.
- The prospect of a monetary payment has seemingly prompted the filing of fraudulent claims against the defendant corporations.

Despite these many similarities, important differences exist between these two situations:

- There is a stunning lack of consensus among the various injured parties in the TexacoChevron situation, in comparison with the apparent relative level of consensus among the Nigerian plaintiffs.
- Individuals who were harmed as a result of Texaco's actions have been essentially ignored by nongovernmental organizations in their pursuit of a favorable ruling, unlike the participation of the Nigerian plaintiffs.
- In general, there has been relatively lesser international endorsement of and consensus around environmental rights compared to ethical principles and human rights.
- In the United States, a clear federal regulatory framework exists that enunciates the obligations of individual researchers and their institutions in conducting research involving human participants. No similar structure exists with respect to environmental impacts.

And, perhaps most significantly,

- Texaco's payment to the Government of Ecuador occurred prior to the initiation of the lawsuit against the corporation; Pfizer's payment to the Nigerian Government occurred while litigation was ongoing.
- The epidemiologic findings accepted by the Ecuadorian court that have served as the basis for its judgment against Chevron have been challenged by the defendant as fraudulent, whereas there has been relatively little debate regarding the validity of the epidemiologic findings in Pfizer Kano.
- Chevron's pursuit of a legal victory has been notably more aggressive than that of Pfizer, and is characterized by clear shifts in its legal arguments, suggesting that Chevron's only strategy is to win at any and all costs, regardless of the costs of that litigation relative to the possible costs associated with settlement.

Conclusion

Increased industrial development on a global scale is likely to expand the judicial need for and reliance on findings from epidemiologic studies of the association between adverse health outcomes and specific environmental exposures, in courts in both developing and developed countries. Because such studies are conducted in the environment and with humans, rather than in a laboratory under researcher-controlled conditions, it is difficult to account for all factors that may play a role in the development of an ultimate health outcome. That said, individuals who believe they have been harmed by specified exposures cannot wait until we have complete knowledge to file their claims and judges cannot wait to decide these cases, for the day of complete knowledge in any given circumstance may not arrive within the period of time allowable for the filing of a lawsuit[5] and, in some instances, within the individuals' lifetimes.

The Texaco–TexacoChevron–Chevron–Aguinda litigation provides a strong example of the need for rigorously conducted epidemiologic studies, community involvement and consensus-building, and education of both attorneys and judges in basic principles of epidemiology. It also underscores the need for epidemiologists to become more familiar with legal proceedings and the use of epidemiologic evidence in those proceedings, should they wish to function as an expert, whether in the capacity of only a consulting expert, or as a testifying expert as well. The conduct of the litigation reflects, perhaps to an alarming degree, the extent to which epidemiologic findings are subject to political manipulation and maneuver. The charge of fraud that has been leveled against the epidemiologists responsible for the conduct of the investigation relied upon by the Ecuadorian court for its holding suggests that epidemiologists, whether conducting research or serving as a consultant, explore and acknowledge issues of potential conflicts of interest and the advisability of assuming an advocacy role in addition to their role as a scientist. (It is beyond the scope of this chapter to explore issues relating to conflict of interest or assumption of an advocacy role and the reader is referred to Cole, 1991; Foxman, 1989; Poole & Rothman, 1990; Rothman & Poole, 1985; Weed, 1994; Yankauer, 1984.)

Notes

1. Conflicts between indigenous communities and oil companies in addition to Texaco arose in response to the companies' efforts to secure and/or exercise granted mineral and oil rights. These include efforts of the Sarayacu to prevent the Los Angeles-based Atlantic Richfield Company (ARCO) from extracting oil and of the Achuar and Shuar communities to block the similar efforts of Burlington resources, which had assumed a portion of ARCO's exploration rights in 1999 (Widener, 2007).
2. This construct has been known variously, with some variation in its composite elements across scholars, as multigenerational trauma (Danieli, 1998), historical trauma (Duran & Duran, 1995), trans-generational trauma (Felsen, 1998), intergenerational trauma (Sigal & Weinfeld, 1999), and cross-generational trauma (Lowin, 1983). Historical trauma has been defined as the "cumulative emotional and psychological wounding, over the lifespan and across generations, emanating from massive group trauma experiences" (Brave Heart, 2003, p. 7). Four mechanisms of transmission have been proposed: (1) the psychodynamic model, which posits that the child unconsciously absorbs the parent's unresolved trauma experiences; (2) the sociocultural model, which suggests that the child learns through observation of the parents and the external environment; (3) the family systems model, which anchors transmission in the family's communication dynamics and the level of enmeshment within the family; and (4) the biological model, which hypothesizes that biologic and/or genetic factors play a role in the transmission of trauma (see generally Kellermann, 2001). Symptoms noted among descendants include difficulty in interpersonal relationships, pathological mourning, social isolation, exaggerated dependence or independence, and symptoms indicative of post-traumatic stress disorder (see generally Baranowsky

et al., 1998; Barocas & Barocas, 1980; Brave Heart, 1998; Gump, 2010). These problems may be exacerbated by systemic factors such as inadequate health care access, racism, and socioeconomic conditions (Brave Heart & DeBruyn, 1998).

3. In 2008, a Chevron lobbyist advised a *Newsweek* reporter, "We can't let little countries screw around with big companies like this." A Chevron spokesman threatened, "We're going to fight this until Hell freezes over—and then we'll fight it out on the ice" (Keefe, 2012). In the context of its approach to litigation, it is of note that after defending a lawsuit filed against it by Nigerian plaintiffs seeking damages for the shooting deaths of protesters on an offshore oil platform in Nigeria, Chevron sued the plaintiffs, including widows and children, seeking reimbursement for its attorney's fees (Keefe, 2012). Chevron was unsuccessful, but the very fact of its effort demonstrates the lengths to which it will go to dissuade possibly injured parties from exercising their legal rights.
4. One writer intimated the need for judicial resolution of conflicts involving scientific conclusions in the absence of complete knowledge:

   > If the question is unambiguously scientific, then the procedure of science rather than the procedures of law are required for arriving at the truth. Where the questions cannot be answered from existing scientific knowledge or from research which could be carried out reasonably rapidly and without disproportionate expense, then the answers must be trans-scientific and the adversary procedure seems therefore to be the best alternative (Weinberg, 1972, p. 215).

5. Regardless of the country or the state, a lawsuit must be commenced within the time frame specified by law for the filing of a lawsuit. The time allowed for such filing varies with the nature of the lawsuit, e.g., personal injury, contract, etc., and also varies across jurisdictions. The prescribed time limitation for the filing of a lawsuit is known as the statute of limitations. If, for example, an individual files a lawsuit after the statute of limitations has passed, the defendant can rely on the statute of limitations as a defense and the plaintiff's case will be dismissed. That said, whether the statute of limitations has elapsed may be an issue itself in litigation.

References

Adams, D. (2012). Chevron seeks bank records in Ecuador environmental suit. Reuters, May 5. Retrieved July 11, 2012, from http://www.reuters.com/aticle/2012/05/05/us-usa-lawsuit-Chevron-idUSBRE84401A20120505.

Anon. (2009). Britain's toxic waste dumped in Africa (multimedia). *Huff Post World*, March 21. Retrieved May 16, 2012, from http://www.huffingtonpost.com/2009/02/18/britains-toxic-waste-dump_n_ 167824.html.

Anon. (2012). For the fourth time, Ecuador appellate court denies Chevron attempt to block enforcement of $18 billion judgment, says Amazon Defense Coalition. Retrieved July 11, 2012, from http://news.yahoo.com/Fourth-attempt-011010868.html.

Anon. (2010). Trafigura found guilty of exporting toxic waste. *BBC News Africa*, July 23. Retrieved May 16, 2012, from http://www.bbc.co.uk/news/world-africa-10735255.

Anton, D. K. (2011). Public international law and international civil litigation: From Ecuador to the United States and back (twice)—Chevron v. Donziger. doi: 10.1093/ijc/dyi151. Retrieved July 26, 2012, from http://ssrn.com/abstract=1960251.

Baker, D. R. (2012). Chevrons Ecuador case now reaches Canada. *Houston Chronicle*, May 31. Retrieved July 11, 2012, from http://chron.com/buisness/article/Chevron-s-Ecuador-case-now-reaches-Canada-3600649.php

Baranowsky, A. B., Young, M., Johnson-Douglas, S., Williams-Keeler, L., & McCarrey, M. (1998). PTSD transmission: A review of secondary traumatization in Holocaust survivor families. *Canadian Psychology, 39*(4), 247–256.

Barocas, H., & Barocas, C. (1980). Separation and individuation conflict in children of Holocaust survivors. *Journal of Contemporary Psychotherapy, 11*, 6–14.

Barrett, P. M. (2012). A hopeful turn in the Chevron-Ecuador fight. *Bloomberg Business Week*, May 22. Retrieved July 11, 2012, from http://www.businessweek.com/articles/2012-05-22/a-hopeful-turn-in-the-Chevron-Ecuador-fight

Barrett, P. M. (2011). Chevron looks to its home court for a comeback win. *Bloomberg Businessweek Magazine*, July 14. Retrieved July 11, 2012, from http://www.businessweek.com/Magazine/Chevron-looks-to-its-home-court-for-a-comeback-win-07142011.html

Beanal v. Freepoert-McMoran, 969 F. Supp. 362 (E.D. La. 1997).

Beck, U. (1995). *Ecological enlightenment: Essays on the politics of the risk society*. New York: Humanities.

Beck, U. (1986). *Risk society: Towards a new modernity*. New York: Sage.

Beckford, M., & Watt, H. (2009). Secret Trafigura report said "likely cause" of illness was release of toxic gas from dumped waste. The Telegraph, October 16. Retrieved May 16, 2012, from http://www.telegraph.co.uk/news/uknews/6350262/Secret-Trafigura-report-said-likely-cause-of-illness-was-release-of-toxic-gas-from -dumped-waste.html.

Bejarano, J. (2005). Largo juicio contra Texaco. El Comercio, August 25.

Biello, D. (2008). Trashed tech dumped overseas: Does the U.S. care? *Scientific American*, September 19. Retrieved May 16, 2012, from http://www.scientificamerican.com/article.cfm?id=trashed-tech-dumped-overseas

Brave Heart, M. Y. H. (1998). The return to the sacred path: Healing the historical trauma and unresolved grief response among the Lakota through a psychoeducational group intervention. *Smith College Studies in Social Work, 68*, 287–305.

Brave Heart, M. Y. H., & DeBruyn, L. M. (1998). The American Indian Holocaust: Healing historical unresolved grief. *American Indian and Alaska Native Mental Health Research, 8*(2), 60–82.

Brave Heart, M.Y.H. (2003). The historical trauma response among natives and its relationship with substance abuse: A Lakota illustration. *Journal of Psychoactive Drugs*, *36*(1), 7–13.

Breilh, J., Branco, J. C., Castleman, B. I., Cherniak, M., Christiani, D. C., Cicollela, A., et al. (2005). Texaco and its consultants (letter). *International Journal of Occupational and Environmental Health, 11*(2), 217–220.

Brown, P. (1987). Popular epidemiology: Community response to toxic waste-induced disease in Woburn, Massachusetts. *Science, Technology, & Human Values, 12*(3–4), 78–85.

Brown, P. (1992). Popular epidemiology and toxic waste contamination: Lay and professional ways of knowing. *Journal of Health and Social Behavior, 33*(3), 267–281.

Brulle, R. J., & Pellow, D. N. (2006). Environmental justice: Human health and environmental inequalities. *Annual Review of Public Health, 27*, 103–124.

Buzzelli, M. (2007). Bourdieu does environmental justice? Probing the linkages between population health and air pollution epidemiology. *Health & Place, 13*, 3–13.

Canaday, C., & Rivadeneyra, J. (2001). Initial effects of a petroleum operation on Amazonian birds: Terrestrial insectivores retreat. *Biodiversity Conservation, 10*, 567–595.

Centro de Derechos Económicos y Sociales. (2006). *Consulta previa: Ambiente y petróleo en la Amazona Ecuatoriana No. 3*. Quito, Ecuador: Author.

Cohn, P., Klotz, J., Bove, F., Berkowitz, M., & Fagliano, J. (1994). Drinking water contamination and the incidence of leukemia and non-Hodgkin's lymphoma. *Environmental Health Perspectives, 102*, 556–561.

Cole, P. (1991). The epidemiologist as an expert witness. *Journal of Clinical Epidemiology, 44*(Supp 1), 35S–39S.

Comba, P., Binchi, F., Fazzo, L., Martina, L., Menegozzo, M., Miaichilli, F., et al. (2006). Cancer mortality in an area of Campani (Italy) characterized by multiple toxic dumping sites. *Annals of the New York Academy of Science, 1076*, 449–461.

Couto, R. A. (1986). Failing health and new prescriptions: Community-based approaches to environmental risks. In C. E. Hill (Ed.), *Current health policy issues and alternatives: An applied social science perspective* (pp. 53–70). Athens, GA: University of Georgia Press.

Cutter, S., Hodgson, M. E., & Dow, K. (2001). Subsidized inequities: The spatial patterning of environmental risks and federally assisted housing. *Urban Geography, 22*(1), 29–53.

Danieli, Y. (Ed.). (1998). *International handbook of multigenerational legacies of trauma*. New York: Plenum.

DeKraay, W. H. (1978). Pesticides and lymphoma in Iowa. *Journal of the Iowa Medical Society, 1978*, 50–53.

Drost, N. (2005). *Between midnight and the rooster's crow [documentary film]*. Canada: Rocinante Productions.

Duran, E., & Duran, B. (1995). *Native American post-colonial psychology*. Albany, NY: State University of New York Press.

Evans-Campbell, T. (2008). Historical trauma in American Indian/Native Alaska communities: A multilevel framework for exploring impacts on individuals, families, and communities. *Journal of Interpersonal Violence, 23*(3), 316–338.

Fagliano, J., Berry, M., Bove, F., & Burke, T. (1990). Drinking water contamination and the incidence of leukemia: An ecologic study. *American Journal of Public Health, 80*, 1209–1212.

Felsen, I. (1998). Transgenerational transmission of the effects of the Holocaust: The North American research perspective. In Y. Danieli (Ed.), *International handbook of multigenerational legacies of trauma*. New York: Plenum.

Finer, M., Vijay, V., Ponce, F., Jenkins, C. N., & Kahn, T. R. (2009). Ecuador's Yasuní Biosphere Reserve: A brief modern history and conservation challenges. *Environmental Health Letters, 4*. doi:10.1088/1748-9326/4/3/034005.

Foxman, B. (1989). Epidemiologists and public health policy. *Journal of Clinical Epidemiology, 42*, 1107–1109.

Franzen, M. (2006). Evaluating the sustainability of hunting: A comparison of harvest profiles across three Waorani communities. *Environmental Conservation, 12*, 364–373.

Garcia, E. (2012). Ecuador plaintiffs target Chevron's assets in Brazil. Reuters, June 27. Retrieved July 11, 2012, from http://www.reuters.com/assets/print?aid=USBRE85R01I20120628

Greenpeace. (2008, February). *Toxic tech: Not in our backyard*. Amsterdam: Greenpeace International. Retrieved July 11, 2012, from http://www.greenpeace.org/international/Global/international/planet-2/report/2008/2/not-in-our-backyard.pdf

Griffith, J., Duncan, R. C., Rigan, W. B., & Pellom, A. C. (1989). Cancer mortality in US counties with hazardous waste sites and ground water pollution. *Archives of Environmental Health, 44*, 69–74.

Gump, J. P. (2010). Reality matters: The shadow of trauma on African American subjectivity. *Psychoanalytic Psychology, 27*(1), 42–54.

Hall, G., & Patrinos, A. (2005). *Indigenous peoples, poverty, and human development in Latin America: 1994–2004*. Washington, D.C.: World Bank. Retrieved July 11, 2012, from http://siteresources.worldbank.org/INTLAC/Resources/Final ExecutiveSummary_Eng_May05.pdf

Harner, J., Warner, K., Pierce, J., & Huber, T. (2002). Urban environmental justice indices. *Professional Geographer, 54*(3), 318–331.

Herbert, B. (2005, October 20). Editorials/Op-ed: Rainforest Jekyll & Hyde? *New York Times* Retrieved July 3, 2012, from http://select.nytimes.com/2005/10/20/opinion/ 20herbert.html?_r=2&oref=slogin.

Hinton, K. (2012). Shareholders slam Chevron with request for SEC investigation over Ecuador judgment. PRNewswire via COMTEX, May 14. Retrieved July 3, 2012, from http://www.texacotoxico.org/eng/node/1251.

Hurtig, A.-K., & San Sebastián, M. (2002). Geographical differences in cancer incidence in the Amazon basin of Ecuador in relation to residence near oil fields. *International Journal of Epidemiology, 31*, 1021–1027.

Hurtig, A.-K., & San Sebastián, M. (2004). Incidence of childhood leukemia and oil exploitation in the Amazon basin of Ecuador. *International Journal of Occupational and Environmental Health, 10*, 245–250.

Institute of Medicine. (1999). *Toward environmental justice: Research, education, and health policy needs*. Washington, DC: National Academy Press.

Karl, T. L. (1997). *The paradox of plenty: Oil booms and petro-states*. Berkeley, CA: University of California Press.

Karl, T. L. (1999). The perils of the petro-state: Reflections on the paradox of plenty. *Journal of International Affairs, 53*, 31–48.

Keefe, P. R. (2012). Reversal of fortune. *The New Yorker*, January 9. Retrieved July 9, 2012, from http://www.newyoyker.com/reporting/2012/01/09/120109fa_fact_Keefe? currentPage=all

Kellermann, N. P. F. (2001). Transmission of Holocaust trauma: An integrative view. *Psychiatry, 64*(3), 256–267.

Kimerling, J. (2006a). *Amazon crude*. New York: National Resource Defense Council.

Kimerling, J. (2006b). Indigenous peoples and the oil frontier in Amazonia: The case of Ecuador, ChevronTexaco, and *Aguinda v Texaco. International Law and Politics, 38*, 413–664.

Kimerling, J. (1995). Rights, responsibilities, and realities: Environmental protection law in Ecuador's Amazon oil fields. *Southwestern Journal of Law and Trade in the Americas, 2*, 293–384.

Kimerling, J. (2008). Transnational operations, bi-national injustice: Indigenous Amazonian peoples and Ecuador, ChevronTexaco, and *Aguinda v Texaco. L'Observateur des Nations Unies, 24*, 207–274.

Klasfeld, A. (2012). Ecuadoreans are two steps closer toward $18.2b Chevron judgment. *Courthouse News Service*, January 9. Retrieved July 11, 2012, from http://www.courthouse-news.com/2012/01/09/42878.htm

Leary, J. D. (2005). *Posttraumatic slave syndrome: America's legacy of enduring injury and healing*. Milwaukee, OR: Uptone.

Lowin, R. G. (1983). Cross-generation transmission of pathology in Jewish families of Holocaust survivors. California School of Professional Psychology, San Diego, CA. *Dissertation Abstracts International, 44*, 3533.

Mallin, K. (1990). Investigation of a bladder cancer cluster in Northwestern Illinois. *American Journal of Epidemiology, 132*(Suppl 1), S96–S106.

Mapstone, N. (2012). Chevron sued in Canada over Ecuador case. *Financial Times*, May 31. Retrieved July 11, 2012, from http://www.ft.com/intl/cms/s/0/e0933b16-aaa7-11e1-9331-00144feabdc0.html#axzz20Ja1DCKj

Martz, J. D. (1987). *Politics and petroleum in Ecuador*. New Brunswick, NJ: Transaction.

McAteer, E., & Pulver, S. (2009). The corporate boomerang: Shareholder transnational advocacy networks targeting oil companies in the Ecuadorian Amazon. *Global Environmental Politics, 9*, 1–30.

Menzies, P. (2009). Homeless Aboriginal men: Effects of intergenerational trauma. In J. D. Hulchanski, P. Campsie, S. Chau, S. Hwang, & E. Paradis (Eds.), *Finding home: Policy options for addressing homelessness in Canada (e-book)*. Toronto: Cities Centre, University of Toronto.

Menzies, P. (2010). Intergenerational trauma from a mental health perspective. *Native Social Work Journal, 7*, 63–85.

Nagata, D. K., & Cheng, W. J. Y. (2003). Intergenerational communication of race-related trauma by Japanese American former internees. *American Journal of Orthopsychiatry, 73*(3), 266–278.

Najem, G. R., Louria, D. B., Lavenhar, M. A., & Feuerman, M. (1985). Clusters of cancer mortality in New Jersey municipalities; with special reference to chemical toxic waste disposal sites and per capita income. *International Journal of Epidemiology, 14*, 528–537.

Nickens, H. W. (1990). A socioeconomic and historical overview of environmental contamination and minority communities. In *Proceedings of the National Minority Health Conference*, Atlanta, GA, December 4-6, 1990. Atlanta, GA: U.S. *Agency for Toxic Substances and Disease Registry*, 1992.

Poole, C., & Rothman, K. J. (1990). Epidemiologic science and public health policy (letter). *Journal of Clinical Epidemiology, 43*, 1270.

Powers, B., & Quarles, M. (2006, April 5). Texaco's waste management practices were illegal and violated industry standards. Amazon Defense Coalition. Retrieved July 3, 2012, from http://www.texacotoxico.org/eng/node/46

Reddall, B., & Garcia, E. (2012). Arbitrators say they can hear Chevron-Ecuador case. Reuters, February 28. Retrieved July 11, 2012, from http://www.reuters.com/article/2012/02/28/us-chevron-ecuador-idUSTRE81R29I20120228

Rosenthal, E. (2009). Smuggling Europe's waste to poorer countries. *New York Times*, September 27. Retrieved May 16, 2012, from http://www.nytimes.com/2009/09/27/science/earth/27waste.html?_r=1&pagewanted=print

Rothman, K. J., & Poole, C. (1985). Science and policy making. *American Journal of Public Health, 75*(4), 340–341.

Russi, M. B., Borak, J. B., & Cullen, C. R. (2008). An examination of cancer epidemiology studies among populations living close to toxic waste sites. *Environmental Health, 7*, 32. doi:10.1186/1476-069-7-32.

San Sebastián, M., Armstrong, B., Córdoba, J. A., & Stephens, C. (2001). Exposures and cancer incidence near oil fields in the Amazon basin of Ecuador. *Occupational and Environmental Medicine, 58*, 517–522.

San Sebastián, M., Armstrong, B., & Stephens, C. (2002). Outcomes of pregnancy among women living in the proximity of oil fields in the Amazon basin of Ecuador. *International Journal of Occupational and Environmental Health, 8*, 312–319.

San Sebastián, M., & Hurtig, A. K. (2005). Oil development and health in the Amazon basin of Ecuador: The popular epidemiology process. *Social Science & Medicine, 60*, 799–807.

Sawyer, S. (2004). *Crude chronicles*. Durham, NC: Duke University Press.

Sigal, J., & Weinfeld, M. (1999). Intergenerational transmission of trauma: Recent contributions form the literature of family systems approaches to treatment. *American Journal of Psychotherapy, 53*(2), 225–231.

Simons, M. (2011). The Netherlands: Court upholds fine for dumping waste in Africa. *New York Times*, December 23. Retrieved May 16, 2012, from http://www.nytimes.com/2011/12/24/world/europe/court-upholds-fine-against-trafigura-over-toxic-waste-dumping-in-africa.html?pagewanted=print

Slovic, P. (1999). Trust, emotion, sex, politics, and science: Surveying the risk-assessment battlefield. *Risk Analysis, 19*(4), 689–701.

Sosa v. Alvarez-Machain, 542 U.S. 692 (2004).

Sotero, M. M. (2006). A conceptual model of historical trauma: Implications for public health practice and research. *Journal of Health Disparities Research and Practice, 1*(1), 93–108.

Suárez, E., Morales, M., Cueva, R., Utreras, B. V., Zapata-Ríos, G., Toral, E., et al. (2009). Oil industry, wild meat trade and roads: Indirect effects of oil extraction activities in a protected area in north-eastern Ecuador. *Animal Conservation, 12*, 364–373.

Weed, D. L. (1994). Science, ethics guidelines, and advocacy in epidemiology. *Annals of Epidemiology, 4*, 166–171.

Weinberg, A. (1972). Science and trans-science. *Minerva, 10*, 109–222.

Whitbeck, L. B., Adams, G. W., Hoyt, D. R., & Chen, X. (2004). Conceptualizing and measuring historical trauma among American Indian people. *American Journal of Community Psychology, 33*(3/4), 119–130.

Jr. Whitten, N. E., & International Work Group for Indigenous Affairs (IWGIA). (1976). *Ecuadorian ethnocide and indigenous ethnogenesis: Amazonian resurgence amidst Andean colonialism*. Copenhagen: International Secretariat of IWGIA.

Widener, P. (2007). Oil conflict in Ecuador: A photographic essay. *Organization & Environment, 20*, 84–105.

Wiseman, H., Metzl, E., & Barber, J. P. (2006). Anger, guilt, and intergenerational communication of trauma in the interpersonal narratives of second generation Holocaust survivors. *American Journal of Orthopsychiatry, 76*(2), 176–184.

World Bank. (2003). Report and recommendation of the president of the International Bank for Reconstruction and Development and the International Finance Corporation to the executive directors on a country assistance strategy for the Republic of Ecuador. Retrieved July 11, 2012, from http://www-wds.worldbank.org/external/default/WDSContentServer/WDSP/IB/2003/05/07/000112742_20030507173151/Rendered/PDF/R2003000690258170EC0CAS.pdf

Yankauer, A. (1984). Science and social policy. *American Journal of Public Health, 74*, 1148–1149.

Yehuda, R., Halligan, S. L., & Grossman, R. (2001). Childhood trauma and risk for PTSD: Relationship to intergenerational effects of trauma, parental PTSD, and cortisol excretion. *Development and Psychopathology, 13*, 733–753.

40 C.F.R. § 435.32.

25 U.S.C. § 1350 (2008).

Chapter 6
Forensic Epidemiology, Forensic Pathology, Ethics and Human Rights

Bebe Loff and Stephen Cordner

The disinterest among Allied politicians and Foreign Office officials in war crimes contrasted to field investigators' sustained concerns with medical war crimes. The initiative to investigate medical war crimes was pressed by a handful of energetic medical investigators. (Weindling, 2004)

Introduction

This chapter differs from the previous chapters, as it does not deal with epidemiologists who may be called as witnesses before a court. Here the role of other forensic specialists, primarily forensic pathologists, is considered. Their adoption of epidemiological methods both to inform the evidence they provide to courts and to analyse the data that emerges from many individual death investigations has strengthened their discipline. If a forensic epidemiologist is construed as a person who relies on public health methods in criminal trials and civil litigation, then medical and scientific personnel contributing to criminal, civil or coronial systems have been undertaking forensic epidemiology for some time. Unlike most working in epidemiology, their use of epidemiological methods is a direct extension of their forensic role.

This chapter begins with a brief exploration of the historical relationship between investigation of death, death records, forensic pathology and public health. It demonstrates, through the use of case studies that emerge out of the work of a forensic institution in Australia, how modern forensic medicine has integrated an epidemiological

B. Loff (✉)
Michael Kirby Centre for Public Health and Human Rights, School of Public Health and Preventive Medicine, Monash University, Melbourne, VIC, Australia
e-mail: Bebe.Loff@Med.monash.edu.au; Bebe.Loff@monash.edu

S. Cordner
Department of Forensic Medicine, School of Public Health and Preventive Medicine, Monash University, Melbourne, VIC, Australia

S. Loue (ed.), *Forensic Epidemiology in the Global Context*,
DOI 10.1007/978-1-4614-6738-0_6, © Springer Science+Business Media New York 2013

function as a fundamental aspect of its contribution to both justice and public health. The role of forensic pathology and related disciplines in the resolution of mass deaths in war, internal conflict and disaster is examined. The importance of this work at both the level of the individual and to protecting public health is considered, as are the related ethical and human rights concerns.

An Extremely Brief History: Dissection, Cause of Death and Death Records

In 1538 Thomas Cromwell, chief minister to Henry VIII, ordered the clergy to maintain a weekly record of parish christenings, marriages, and burials, known as the "Bills of Mortality". One hundred and twenty-four years later, in 1662, John Graunt, a haberdasher, chose to make use of these records for the parishes of London, eventually publishing "Natural and political observations mentioned in a following index, and made upon the Bills of Mortality" (Rothman, 1996). In doing so Graunt became the first epidemiologist and demographer. This work presaged the significant contribution to public heath by those who continued to regard their role as identifying and recording cause of death.

When one of these slim but extraordinary volumes was put up for auction in 2010, it was described as a

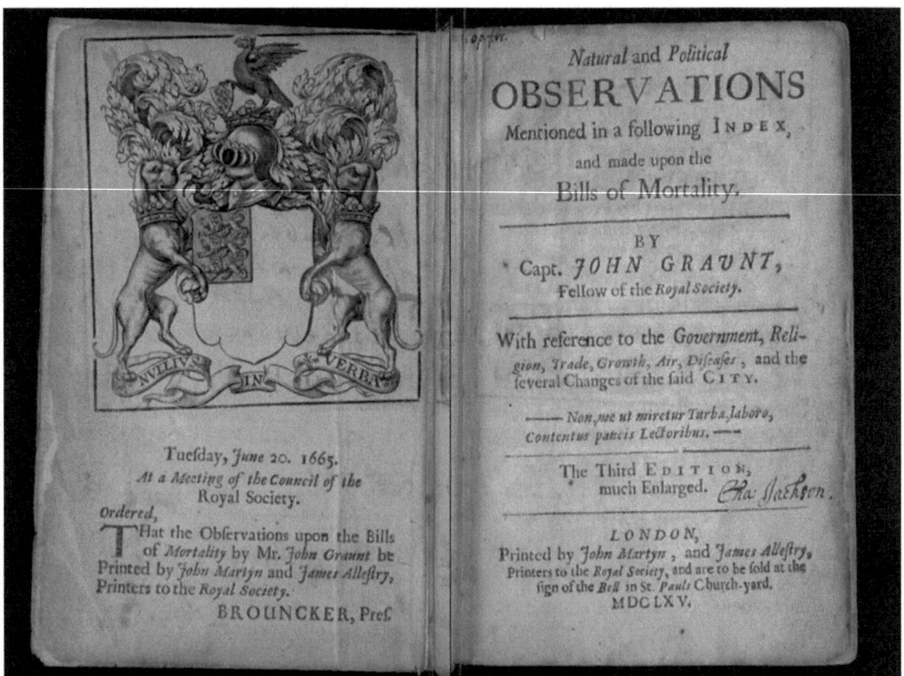

NVLLIVS IN VERBA

Tueſday, June 20. 1665.
At a Meeting of the Council of the Royal Society.
Ordered,
That the Obſervations upon the Bills of Mortality by Mr. John Graunt be Printed by John Martyn and James Alleſtry, Printers to the Royal Society.
BROUNCKER, Preſ.

Natural and Political
OBSERVATIONS
Mentioned in a following INDEX, and made upon the Bills of Mortality.
BY
Capt. JOHN GRAUNT,
Fellow of the Royal Society.
With reference to the Government, Religion, Trade, Growth, Air, Diſeaſes, and the ſeveral Changes of the ſaid CITY.
—— Non, me ut miretur Turba, laboro,
Contentus paucis Lectoribus. ——
The Third EDITION, much Enlarged.
LONDON,
Printed by John Martyn, and James Alleſtry, Printers to the Royal Society, and are to be ſold at the ſign of the Bell in St. Pauls Church-yard.
MDCLXV.

Images courtesy of European Cultural Heritage Online

> very rare first edition of the foundation of demographics and medical statistics: the beginning of studies about why people die, and the beginning of disease control (Christies, 2012).

Having made this enormous contribution to public health John Graunt returned to haberdashery, though he became and remained an active contributor to the renowned "Royal Society of London for Improving Natural Knowledge", now known simply as the Royal Society.

Historically, the investigation of deaths met several purposes. The coronial system in Britain began over 800 years ago.

> The Articles of Eyre in September, 1194, provided for the election by every English county of three knights and one clerk as "custosplacitorum coronae"—keepers of the pleas of the crown. Their main purpose was to protect the Crown's financial interests from corrupt sheriffs. In medieval times, their jurisdiction extended to treasure trove, wrecks of the sea, catches of royal fish (whales and sturgeon), and valuing the goods and chattels of felons and outlaws (Cordner & Loff, 1994, p. 799).

If it could be determined that a death was the result of a felonious act, the Crown was empowered to extract significant fines. Thus what was valued was not impartiality, but loyalty. Bias and corrupt practice among coroners, officers appointed to remedy the same problems in sheriffs, was to remain a criticism of coronial practice in England for centuries.

Somewhat later, the emergence of public systems of forensic medicine and pathology paralleled both the development of medicine as a scientific enterprise, the recognition of the medical expert, and the rise of large local government authorities, provincial municipal governments and the modern centralised state. The path by which this occurred could not be regarded as straightforward; however, the importance of strengthened public institutions in the development of forensic medicine and pathology cannot be overestimated. Thus, during the eighteenth and nineteenth centuries, medical involvement in death investigation prospered most in France and Germany, with England gaining some prominence in the latter nineteenth century.

As Katherine Watson notes,

> It was not long after the [French] Revolution that the official experts were abolished, and the whole system of medical education was reorganized along lines that stressed hands-on experience and the use of anatomy to establish knowledge about pathology, or so-called pathological anatomy. The removal of the public hospitals from clerical to state control facilitated this new form of learning: medical teachers and their students now had access to vast numbers of patients for clinical study.
>
> Crucially, the reorganized system recognized the importance of medico-legal learning by creating chairs of legal medicine at all French medical schools in December 1794. The French state dictated that forensic medicine should be amongst the compulsory subjects in a medical degree, and the Paris Morgue pioneered practical methods of instruction in forensic medicine; its directors became leading medico-legal experts. Furthermore, a law of March 1803 required judges to appoint medical experts who were graduates in medicine, who had attended a course and passed an examination in forensic medicine ….
>
> This state support helped the French to assume dominance in nineteenth-century medico-legal research (Watson, 2010 pp. 100–101).

Similarly, though a little later, forensic pathology prospered in the state supported German university system. Rudolf Virchow is an exemplar of the value of this relationship. Virchow is renowned for many things including his work in describing the cellular basis of disease and social epidemiology. Less well known is his primary role as an anatomical pathologist, and his standardisation of the conduct of an autopsy. A prosector (a person who undertakes dissections, preparing bodies for anatomical demonstrations) of the Charité Hospital in Berlin, he was appointed in 1848 to a commission sent to investigate an epidemic of "hunger-typhus" in Upper Silesia (Azar, 1997). Although the autopsies conducted by Virchow during this investigation did not lead to insights into typhus, his Report demonstrates how this experience, embedded in his work as an anatomical pathologist, was to produce insights into the social environment in which he found himself. It was this he sought to change (Taylor & Rieger, 1985). It is this approach that also informs enlightened conduct of forensic pathology today, and where the most profound ethical issues arise.

In contrast, in England, the need to standardise the provision of forensic medical evidence was relied upon as one justification in arguments for state support of medicine and medical training. Another contemporary and related development in England was the regularisation of record keeping. Edwin Chadwick, known for his contribution to Poor Law and to sanitary reform in mid-nineteenth century Britain, is less well known as an architect of the Civil Registration Act 1836, that created a central registration office for the recording of births, marriages and, in particular, for having inserted into it a requirement that cause of death be recorded (Cullen, 1974). William Farr was appointed to the new General Register Office on the recommendation of Chadwick (Schweber, 2006).

> The information compiled in this way was then used by Dr. William Farr, who joined the Register Office in 1839 as "compiler of abstracts." Farr had a gift for using the facts listed on these pieces of paper to write a series of brilliant reports that convinced governmental officials of the human cost of sickness and premature death caused by lack of proper sanitation (Davis, 1997, p. 221).

Modern Forensic Pathology

The day-to-day work of a forensic pathologist is not as it is commonly portrayed. In the popular mind the forensic pathologist is a sleuth who not only conducts post mortem examinations in mortuaries, but also actively pursues criminals and solves crimes using advanced technology and extraordinary powers of deduction. Nonetheless, and perhaps more fortunately, the modern forensic pathologist understands her/his role as the contribution to both the promotion of justice and public health.

The identification of repeated patterns in causes of death, for example, is a signal that they should be investigated beyond the pathological findings. Deaths of this kind must be addressed, not merely as a matter of justice in individual cases but, where indicated, resolved at a population level. Systematised knowledge of findings informs the evidence provided by the forensic pathologist in court, in broad-ranging coronial inquests, and in commissions of inquiry established by government to examine a matter that has engaged public interest. In some jurisdictions, databases containing individual autopsy records have been created, and data analysed, with the express intent that findings of trends in information arising from death investigations will give rise to and inform coronial inquests, evidence in criminal trials, and public health policy and programmes. In this way the forensic arm of the coronial system produces data for epidemiological analysis, carries out epidemiological research and relies on the findings when presenting evidence in a court setting.

Goodman et al. propose the following options for defining forensic epidemiology,

> The use of epidemiologic methods as part of an ongoing investigation of a health problem for which there is suspicion or evidence regarding possible intentional acts or criminal behavior as factors contributing to the health problem; or, in the alternative,
>
> The use of epidemiologic and other public health methods in conjunction with or as an adjunct to an ongoing criminal investigation (Goodman, Munson, Dammers, Lazzarini, & Barkley, 2003, p. 685).

They indicate that

> [t]he incorporation of forensic techniques into epidemiology and other public health investigative sciences illustrates the importance and interrelatedness of epidemiology to solving problems having law enforcement-related dimensions (Goodman et al., 2003, p. 685).

We suggest that these formulations, even if taken together, are too limited to capture the contribution to forensic epidemiology made by forensic medical scientists.

In a paper entitled "Grim New Role for Forensic Pathologist", Stephen Cordner and David Ranson describe the consolidation of two trends in the development of forensic medicine:

> The first is the increasing contribution of forensic pathology to prevention of injury. As early as 1915, William Brend wrote about coroners and autopsies thus "...if prevention of deaths is not now regarded as the main purpose to be served by inquests, the inquiry becomes of relatively little value". The role of the forensic pathologist in non-suspicious cases, particularly in relation to issues of public health and safety, is little understood by the general public, or the legal or medical community (Cordner & Ranson, 1997, p. SIII6).

In this paper reference is made to two quite distinct developments. The first is the creation of a National Coronial Information System in Australia, established on the basis that coroners would benefit from knowledge about a body of evidence concerning deaths found to be similar in nature including "intravenous drug deaths, suicide, medical-treatment-related deaths and health care audit, death in custody, sudden infant death and workplace deaths". The second development referred to is exemplified by the contribution of forensic pathology in systematically recording Nazi atrocity, both murder and experimentation, evidence relied on during the Nuremberg trials. More recently, forensic pathologists and related experts have been actively involved in the systematic collection of evidence in post-conflict settings and mass disasters. While this latter contribution may at first appear to be at some distance from epidemiology, as ordinarily practised, as seen below, there are some similarities. Further the contribution of this work to public health and to justice cannot be doubted.

The Victorian Institute of Forensic Medicine

The following discussion provides an analysis of the work undertaken by the range of forensically trained staff necessary to properly investigate deaths at one statutory agency—the Victorian Institute of Forensic Medicine (VIFM) in Victoria, Australia. A series of case studies are presented below that are derived from their published and unpublished data. These case studies explore the type of forensic epidemiology that is associated with the work of a forensic team employed within a state system that recognises and supports a public health role for this sector. VIFM's responsibilities are to provide independent, expert forensic medical and scientific services to the justice system, and to undertake teaching and research related to these activities. Its staff includes forensic pathologists, odontologists, anthropologists, physicians and scientists. VIFM's work provides a useful source of case studies because of the conscious inclusion of death and injury prevention as a primary legislated function and because an author (SC) is its Director and is able to provide detailed knowledge of these aspects of its work.

In 1985 the coronial jurisdiction in Victoria, Australia entered a new era. With the passage of the Coroners Act 1985 (now repealed), the function of coroners shifted

> from a traditional legal function to one that has arguably a much larger public education and prevention function. This was partly due to the coroner's ability to make recommendations or comments ("riders" is the term used in other jurisdictions) on public health and safety issues as part of their findings in order to prevent the recurrence of similar events (Bugeja & Ranson, 2003, p. 399).

According to section 19(2) of that Act, "A coroner may comment on any matter connected with the death including public health or safety or the administration of justice." The Act also established VIFM. Included among VIFM objects was the conduct research in the fields of forensic pathology, forensic science, clinical forensic medicine and associated fields.

After the introduction of the Act a number of key coronial death investigations addressed the prevention of deaths. The research relied upon for this purpose was often carried out by VIFM. Some examples are set out in the discussion that follows.

In 2008 a new Coroners Act was passed by the Victorian Parliament, which preserves a public health function. Section 8 of that Act sets out what a person should have regard to when exercising a function under the Act. This includes "the desirability of promoting public health and safety and the administration of justice". Similarly in section 64 of the Victorian Institute of Forensic Medicine Act 1985, one of VIFM's functions is to "contribute to reducing the number of preventable deaths and to promote public health and safety and the administration of justice".

Methadone Programme-Related Deaths

Methadone maintenance therapy programmes are sponsored by the state and are designed to reduce the need for addicts to use heroin or other illegal opiates. Between June 1989 and January 1990, ten people had died in Victoria, Australia within days of starting a methadone maintenance programme administered by general medical practitioners. Previously recorded methadone-related deaths had been due to high levels of self-administered methadone. Deaths in patients starting methadone programmes taking prescribed and comparatively small amounts of methadone had not been documented before.

The patients' bodies were subject to a full autopsy by forensic pathologists, with complete toxicological examination. Toxicological analysis showed that six persons had additional drugs present including two with alcohol, two with benzodiazepines and morphine, and one with benzodiazepines alone. Pathological examination involved macroscopic and microscopic examination of major organs. In each case, attention was given to evidence of needle track marks. The post mortem examinations revealed the presence of chronic persistent hepatitis in all subjects and bronchopneumonia in five. The causes of death were given as methadone toxicity or methadone toxicity in combination with bronchopneumonia. Case summaries were produced that included information from police records, statements from treating medical practitioners and pharmacists (with the assistance of the State Coroner), and the Department of Health provided information concerning the operation of the programme (Drummer, Opeskin, Syrjanen, & Cordner, 1992).

> A coroner's inquest was held in three of these methadone related deaths. The overall lack of supervision during the day, the lack of suitable counselling before and after the start of the methadone program, failure by general practitioners and pharmacists to differentiate between methadone toxicity and opiate withdrawal effects, and the relatively high starting doses were found to be factors that contributed to these deaths (Drummer et al., 1992, p. 350).

At this time the Victorian methadone maintenance programme had rapidly expanded from rehabilitation centres and hospitals to general practitioners and pharmacies. This expansion was not accompanied by a suitable increase in resources or training to ensure high quality and safe delivery systems.

As part of a coronial inquiry, VIFM was able to highlight the dangers of methadone in the first days of starting on a maintenance programme, particularly when the starting doses are relatively high and those commencing the programme have no demonstrated tolerance to opiates. Problems identified included the assessment method of persons accepted into the programme, calculation of the appropriate methadone dosage, lack of available counselling for patients and education of medical practitioners involved in the programme. In consultation with VIFM, the health ministry reformed its methadone delivery programme. Limits were introduced to the amount of methadone that could be prescribed. Medical practitioners began to be provided with training and they began prescribing lower levels of the drug to patients (Coronial Services Centre of Victoria, 2008).

Road Traffic Crashes and Drugs

Forensic medicine in Victoria has had a long involvement with road trauma and death. Victoria was the first jurisdiction in the world to legislate the compulsory wearing of seatbelts. Victoria's first police surgeon, Dr. John Birrell, made a highly significant contribution to both the development and implementation of this legislation and to recognition of the role of alcohol in transport fatalities (Coronial Services Centre of Victoria, 2008). However, the role of drugs in transport fatalities was not well understood.

Patterns of drug taking vary between jurisdictions within and between countries. A study was undertaken by VIFM staff and others of drivers killed in motor accidents in three Australia jurisdictions. The 10-year study of 3,398 drivers killed in car accidents sought to establish the incidence and extent to which drugs contributed to fatal motor vehicle accidents. The control group of drug- and alcohol-free drivers comprised 50.1 % of the study population. Cases included Victorian drivers killed in road crashes from 1990 to 1999 whose data were obtained from records kept at VIFM and the Coroner's Office. Coronial data were similarly relied upon for the states of New South Wales and Western Australia (Drummer et al., 2003).

Most of the toxicological analyses (>90 %) were conducted on blood taken from drivers at autopsy. The most common drugs (other than alcohol) found in fatally injured drivers were cannabis, benzodiazepines, amphetamine-like stimulants and opioids. Toxicology testing included testing for alcohol, amphetamines and related stimulants, benzodiazepines, cannabinoids, cocaine, opioids, and included a screen for neutral and basic psychotropic drugs. The study, conducted blind to toxicology results, found drivers positive to any psychoactive drug were significantly more likely to be culpable (i.e. more likely to have been a causative factor in the accident). Based on their findings the authors strongly suggested that the

> problem posed by drug-affected drivers is much greater than that suggested by the number of prosecutions for drug impaired driving. Indeed, standard field sobriety tests or medical evaluations tend to only detect drivers with substantial clinical impairment. As responsibility analyses suggest [in fatal road traffic accidents] impairing drug use contribute to road trauma, there is a need to recognize that recreational drugs are a likely significant cause of road trauma, and therefore there is a need to provide effective counter-measures to reduce the use of recreational drugs by drivers (Drummer et al., 2003, p. 162).

A subsequent study by the same authors used logistic regression to examine the association of key attributes such as age, gender, type of crash and drug use on the likelihood of culpability (Drummer et al., 2004). That study indicated that

> drivers killed in motor vehicle crashes and taking psychoactive drugs, particularly cannabis and strong stimulants, or two or more drugs in combination were more likely to be responsible for the crash than those taking neither drugs nor alcohol. Moreover, the combination of psychoactive drugs with alcohol further increased the likelihood that drivers caused the crash in which they died. We conclude that THC [Δ9-tetrahydrocannabinol], amphetamines and combinations of psychoactive drugs significantly increase drivers' risk of a serious road crash (Drummer et al., 2004, p. 248).

These findings have since informed evidence provided in criminal cases involving driving under the influence of drugs other than alcohol. In addition, the police, based on new legislation informed by the same research, have expanded their random roadside breath testing of drivers for alcohol to include saliva testing for methamphetamines (speed or ice), MDMA (ecstasy) and THC (the active component of cannabis).

The Great South East Australian Heat Wave and Bushfires of 2009

This case study is included as an example of epidemiological techniques required to measure the scale of some problems traditionally referred to the coronial system. When deaths are due to mechanical or visible trauma, for example car accidents or fire, the unnatural character of the death is obvious and the deaths easily identified as ones to be referred for investigation. When deaths are due to functional derangements initiated by environmental causes such as heat waves (or conversely, the cold), the unnatural character of the death is not so obvious. In addition, depending on the jurisdictional attitude to the meaning of the word "natural", such deaths may not even be regarded as unnatural. For example, deaths due to chronic alcoholism, and to the chronic effects of smoking are not regarded anywhere in the world as unnatural enough to concern the formal death investigation system.

The Black Saturday Bushfires which erupted all over Victoria, Australia on 7 February 2009 involved 4,500 km^2, destroyed 2,000 houses and a further 3,500 structures. Seventy-eight towns were directly affected by the fires and 7,500 people were rendered homeless. A total of 173 people died, 24 patients were admitted to burns units, 95 other patients admitted to hospital and 295 people were treated for burns in emergency departments and discharged (Cameron et al., 2009). All of the deaths were referred to the coroner for investigation, the main challenge for the forensic pathology service being correct identification.

In the weeks before the bushfires, Victoria (and South Australia) suffered from an even worse natural disaster as measured by lives lost: a heatwave. The estimate from Victoria's Chief Health Officer was that there were 374 excess deaths as a result of the heatwave (Department of Human Services, 2009). These were the excess deaths in the period 26 January–1 February over the average of the same period in the previous 5 years. This is likely to be an underestimate because many deaths would have occurred in the days following from heat related illness that began during the actual heatwave. The deaths involved the most vulnerable in the population: the elderly, the isolated, and those who were cognitively impaired, especially where there were other underlying illnesses. These individuals were exposed because of the relentlessness of the heat wave as seen in Table 6.1.

The diagnosis of a heat-related illness as being the cause of a death or a significant contributor to the cause of death, in a person found dead, is a conclusion based on an assessment of the circumstances in any particular case. The pathology revealed at autopsy will be the pathology of the underlying chronic illness. Where dehydration is a factor, this may be discoverable through post mortem biochemistry. In view of the fact that in many cases the death will be certified as natural by the attending physician, and a death certificate provided which may not mention any contribution from heat, epidemiological tools are required to reach a reliable conclusion as to scale of the fatal consequences of the heat wave. In this case it was the high mean temperatures that captured the relentless and oppressive nature of the insult which led to the high number of fatalities.

Table 6.1 Temperatures in Melbourne from January 26 to February 1, 2009

	Max °C	Min °C	Mean °C
Mon 26	25.5	14.4	19.9
Tues 27	36.4	16.6	26.5
Wed 28	43.4	18.8	31.1
Thu 29	44.3	25.7	35.0
Fri 30	45.1[a]	25.7	35.4[b]
Sat 31	30.5	22.5	26.5
Sun 1	33.8	20.3	27.0

[a]At the time, second hottest Victorian day ever
[b]Highest mean ever in Vic

Table 6.2 Admissions to the VIFM in the fortnight to February 8 2009, compared with two other fortnights

	Jan 26–Feb 8 2009	Jan 26–Feb 8 2008	Oct 26–Nov 8 2008
Total admissions	268	136	129
Average per day	19	10	9

The heatwave was a major disaster in its own right, and one which was completely overtaken in the public consciousness by the bushfires. It also affected VIFM's response to the bushfires. Table 6.2 shows the admissions of deceased persons to the VIFM in the fortnight leading up to the bushfires—which included the above days of the heat wave—compared with the same fortnight 12 and 3 months previously.

The number of admissions had exceeded VIFM's body storage capacity and autopsy/case management capability. Early in the week prior to February 7, a body storage contingency plan was activated so that numbers of deceased were being housed off-site. Thirty deceased from the heatwave were still awaiting examination on February 7. So, when the bushfires struck, the mortuary at the VIFM was full (with additional bodies stored off-site) and there was a significant backlog of cases, greater than normal, because of the heatwave. Disasters, not infrequently, strike in multiples.

Aboriginal Deaths in Custody

This case study is a review of forensic evidence of varying standards collected over a period of 10 years concerning deaths in custody in Australia of Aboriginal and Torres Strait Islander people. It demonstrates the need for a sound state-supported forensic pathology system that is able to provide the level of expert evidence required for just outcomes. It also provides some insight into the purpose of a forensic autopsy.

A Royal Commission into Aboriginal Deaths in Custody was established in October 1987 in response to a growing public concern about the frequency of deaths in custody of Aboriginal people and that "public explanations [about these deaths] were too evasive to discount the possibility that foul play was a factor in many of them" (Royal Commission into Aboriginal Deaths in Custody, 1991, Vol 1–1.1.2). This broad-ranging judicial inquiry represented a significant milestone for Australia, as the Commission's Report considered and made recommendations regarding not only the immediate circumstances around each death, but the factors leading to incarceration, how these factors might be addressed and incarceration prevented. Ninety-nine Aboriginal and Torres Strait Islander people died in prison, police or juvenile detention institutions between 1 January 1980 and 31 May 1989. During the course of this extensive inquiry, Commissioners were sufficiently concerned about the adequacy of the reports they received concerning the deaths of these Aboriginal and Torres Strait Islander people to request that they be reviewed. One of us (SC) was asked to conduct a review for the Commission of the forensic pathology in 27 cases. This review involved the provision of reports to the Commission on a range of parameters relating to the forensic pathology aspects of these cases. In a number of these cases the conduct of autopsies was found to be unsatisfactory.

The review noted that the forensic autopsy extends beyond the provision of "cause of death". Indeed misunderstanding of the nature and purpose of an autopsy lay at the root of many of those autopsies considered to be inadequate. Most commonly, the identification of cause of death is reasonably straightforward. The challenge for forensic pathology lies in its contribution to the reconstruction of the circumstances of death, and the onerous and more mundane tasks of recording, not only the positive but—often more importantly in the context of deaths in custody—the negative findings, so that another pathologist at another time is able to reach her/his own conclusions.

It was noted that a number of components of the forensic investigation of a death in custody must be of a suitable standard if the investigation is to be regarded as having been properly conducted. These include the following:

- Qualifications and experience of the pathologist, and the forensic team
- Investigation of the scene
- Scene photography
- Autopsy
- Autopsy photography
- Histology
- Toxicology

A number of these elements were missing from some of the cases reviewed. On seven occasions autopsies were not carried out by a qualified pathologist. On six occasions no toxicology or inadequate toxicology was performed. Samples for histology were not taken in seven cases. Photographs of autopsy findings were available in only five cases.

In 1991, the Commission made 339 recommendations to Australian governments, which aimed to reduce the rate of Aboriginal deaths in custody. The Commission found that the high number of Aboriginal deaths in custody reflected a glaring overrepresentation of Aborigines in custody generally. A number of the

Commission's recommendations concerned the practice of forensic pathology and coronial inquests. These recommendations included the following:

- The scene of death should be subject to a thorough examination including the seizure of exhibits for forensic science examination and the recording of the scene of death by means of high quality colour photography.
- Investigations into deaths in custody should be structured to provide a thorough evidentiary base for consideration by the Coroner on inquest into the cause and circumstances of the death and the quality of the care, treatment and supervision of the deceased prior to death.
- All post-mortem examinations of the deceased should be conducted by a specialist forensic pathologist wherever possible or, if a specialist forensic pathologist is not available, by a specialist pathologist qualified by experience or training to conduct such post-mortems.

Unfortunately, 10 years later, this situation had not improved, with an increase in the number of aboriginal deaths in custody (Loff & Cordner, 2001).

Fatal Head Injuries in Infants Resulting from Short Falls

What follows is a summary of a published paper that illustrates how epidemiological methods must sometimes be adopted in the course of providing evidence to a court in a criminal trial. It demonstrates how epidemiological analysis may be relied upon to inform the presentation of such evidence. The authors note that

> [t]he court, as the ultimate "finder of fact" relies on the evidence that is presented before it. The forensic pathologist may describe and determine the medical cause of death but ascertaining the intent and mechanism of death is the responsibility of the court. At times, the court may ask the forensic pathologist to provide opinions which bear upon the intent and mechanism of death. A prudent forensic pathologist, when anticipating or faced with this request, will review the scientific research literature (Ehsani, Ibrahim, Bugeja, & Cordner, 2010, p. 287).

Head injury in infants is a contentious field in paediatric forensic pathology. An accused charged with having caused the death of an infant or toddler by head injury, either from a direct blow or shaking, may claim that death was the result of a short fall. Not uncommonly, the claim is that the infant was dropped, or the toddler fell from a standing height or from a bed, for example. The question that will then need to be determined is whether it is possible for an infant or toddler to be fatally injured as the result of a short fall. Evidence in individual cases is usually insufficient to enable the court to reach a conclusion, so jury members are forced to rely on their intuitive responses.

VIFM staff undertook a rapid, focused subject review of the research literature addressing the question: "In an infant who has died of head injury, is a claim that the injury was sustained in a simple short fall credible?" They adopted an epidemiological approach rather than an analysis of the pathology to reviewing the literature.

They examined the difficulties for a pathologist who completes a rapid focused literature review during legal proceedings in response to a request for an opinion about the mechanism of a particular fatal head injury. They attempted to provide information to assist the forensic pathologist in deciding whether a claim of a short fall to account for the death of an infant or toddler is credible (Ehsani et al., 2010).

They concluded that, as few systematic reviews are available in forensic pathology, forensic pathologists must often undertake their own review of the literature. A description is provided of the process of review that is likely to be conducted. Because of its relevance to the field of forensic epidemiology, this section of the paper is quoted in full.

> The first obstacle is defining the "question." The forensic pathologist asks "In this case, is it credible that a simple short fall may have caused a significant head injury leading to death?" To answer the question requires deconstructing it to composite parts and searching the research literature for each part. The structure of the question becomes "Do simple short falls in infants cause significant head injury leading to death?" "If so, how often and under what circumstances does this occur?" and "Are the characteristics of a head injury causing death from a simple fall unique and distinguishable from other mechanisms of injury?"
>
> The second obstacle is locating, reading, understanding, appraising, comparing and integrating the available information. The time and resources the forensic pathologist can devote to this endeavor is limited, and the legal process, by nature, is time dependent. Therefore, a rapid, focused subject review of the forensic pathology research literature may be all that is possible.
>
> The third obstacle is interpreting and applying the findings from a body of information to a specific case, as research literature rarely provides information so specific that it replicates what is present in an individual case. Much research evidence applies to probabilities of occurrences in groups or populations and not in individual cases. Accurate prediction is difficult and relies on judgment regarding the magnitude of probability. Legal and scientific disciplines assign different weight to research evidence (i.e., "reasonable doubt" vs. "Level 1 Evidence"), which further confounds the issue (Ehsani et al., 2010, p. 287).

These comments raise concerns beyond those that arise in the determination of individual cause of death, which will be considered further subsequent to the presentation of the case studies. These concerns centre on the difficulties of applying evidence of a general kind to assist decision-making in an individual case.

In this instance 1,055 publications were identified for potential inclusion. Using selection criteria described in the paper, 27 publications were included in the subject review. Review studies demonstrated the inseparable relationship between the measurement of the forces from the impact of a fall and the observed injuries that result in infants. However, it was unclear how the review study authors reached their conclusions and findings were not entirely consistent. It therefore became necessary for the subject review authors to examine the diverse primary studies. The primary studies were limited by the lack of a uniform definition of what constituted a fall and specificity about the nature, height, and surface impact of the fall. Based on this subject review the authors concluded that it is very rare, but possible, for fatal head injury to occur from a short fall.

In a final reflection about the study the authors stated that the typical forensic pathologist would not have the resources to conduct a systematic review related to the question they were posing. They indicated that "[t]here may be a need for the development of a more specific approach for systematic reviews tailored to the needs of forensic pathology" (Ehsani et al., 2010, p. 297).

The Predictive Nature of Multi-stab Wound Evidence

Mr. Jeffrey Gilham was convicted in 2008 of the murder of his mother, father and brother at their home by stabbing them multiple times (15, 28 and 17 times respectively) and then setting the house alight. Mr. Gilham's account was that his brother killed his parents then set fire to the house. At this point, Mr. Gilham allegedly arrived on the scene, and chased and then killed his brother by stabbing him multiple times with the same knife used to kill his parents. At trial, the prosecution contended that the multiplicity and location of the stab injuries in all three cases were of such a similar pattern that the only possible conclusion was that there was one killer.

Expert evidence led by the prosecution in the trial was that there may be about six or eight stab wounds in a fatal stabbing, but rarely was there over ten. This evidence was provided by the pathologist on the basis of his experience. The prosecutor noted in his summing up for the jury the following:

> You might think as a matter of logic … the more stab wounds there are the fewer cases that have many. You heard Dr. C… say that it's very, very unusual for someone to be stabbed more than ten times because if you're in the centre of the chest, you only need—you certainly only need one stab wound to kill someone, and the greater the number, the fewer cases there are … There was overkill, if I can suggest that to you, ladies and gentleman so many more wounds needed than was necessary to kill any one of them, and that is an extraordinary similarity. (Gilham v. R, 2012, para. 323).

The prosecutor was asking the jury to conclude that the number of the stab wounds in the Gilham deceased (15, 28 and 17 in the mother, father and brother respectively) were all so many more than the six to eight normally seen as a maximum that this represented an "extraordinary similarity" (Table 6.3).

For the purposes of an appeal, an expert opinion was sought from SC regarding whether

- One or more aspects of the wounds ("the pattern of injury") in the three deaths were similar, and whether
- This similarity was of such significance that one could properly conclude that there was one killer of the three deceased and not two.

In order to provide this opinion it was necessary to analyse data relevant to the particular case and conduct a review of historical data:

Data from the case

- The three autopsy reports,
- Numerous articles on aspects of stab wounds,
- Excerpts of transcripts from the inquest and trial, and
- The complete transcript of the Crown's closing address

Table 6.3 A comparison of wounds inflicted*

Relative	Total number stab wounds	Stab wounds to front of chest (% total)	Stab wounds to back of chest (% total)	Dominant clustering	Number in cluster	Percentage of total wounds in cluster (%)	Wounds not to chest
Mother	15	1 (7)	13 (87)	Upper left and upper right back	9	60	Neck, L forearm
Father	28	15 (54)	7 (25)	Mid-upper chest and central chest	13	46	Face, neck, L upper arm
Brother	17	14 (82)	3 (18)	Mid-upper chest and central chest	14	82	Hand

*In this analysis, the front of the chest has been divided into eight areas, and the back of the chest into four areas. This division captures the centre of the chest as one area, maximising the prospect of seeing a pattern if the centre of the front of the chest is a site in the homicidal stabbings. Dominant clustering was defined as comprising at least 25 % of the total number of stab injuries present in one area, or two contiguous areas

Historical data

- 20 Homicide cases from nine incidents over a number of years from New South Wales and Victoria where the cause of death was from stabbing, and there were multiple deceased in each incident.
- 40 Homicide cases over more than 10 years from Victoria where the cause of death was from stabbing and where there were more than ten stab wounds.
- Other studies.

There was no body of literature that was entirely relevant. Information from nine incidents of multiple homicide (eight involving two individuals, and one involving four individuals) in New South Wales and Victoria over the previous 10 years (2000–2010) was obtained from the National Coronial Information System. This included autopsy reports. The analysis of this data found that in multiple homicides where death is due to stabbing, there are commonly a total of more than ten stab wounds, and that these stab wounds are generally concentrated in the chest. However, it did not support the assertion that there will otherwise be similarity in the pattern of injury (i.e. in the number and distribution more specifically of the stab wounds) inflicted by one person where there is a multiple homicide due to stabbing.

An analysis of 40 Victorian homicide cases was undertaken with 35 cases from 2000 to 2010 listed on the National Coroners Information System, together with 5 other VIFM cases collected manually prior to 2000. In these cases death was due to stabbing and there were ten or more stabbed and incised wounds. This study found the following:

- 8/40 had more than 28 stab wounds in total
- 16/40 had between 16 and 28 stab wounds in total
- 16/40 had between 10 and 15 stab wounds in total

It also found that stab wounds to the front (36/40) and back (27/40) of the chest are common; 25/40 had stab wounds to both the front and back of the chest.

The analysis of these 40 Victorian cases assessed a number of variables including the raw number of wounds to the chest; the number of wounds in a cluster as a percentage of the total wounds; and the number in the cluster which are parallel as a percentage of the number in the cluster. In these aspects of the Gilham deceased, it was found that similarity could not be claimed. The number of wounds in a cluster as a percentage of the total number of wounds in the deceased displayed a variation, in the three Gilham deceased, from 46 % (Father) to 60 % (Mother) to 82 % (Brother) (Table 6.3). This analysis provided a way of assessing the pattern of injury to the chest of the three deceased that had not been carried out before or during the trial.

In a sequential series of 50 Victorian homicide cases where the National Coronial Information System was searched for "multiple stab wounds", 31 (62 %) had more than ten stab wounds. In a sequential series of 165 homicidal stabbings from VIFM's database, (this series includes cases of single stab wounds), 48 (29 %) had ten or more stabbed and incised injuries (excluding incised injuries to the hands and the forearms. If injuries to the hands and forearms were included, the number would have been greater).

A Swedish study (Ormstad, Karlsson, Enkler, Law, & Rajs, 1986) found that in 142 homicidal victims of stabbing over a 10 year period in Stockholm from 1973 to 1982, after the 62 victims with one stab wound, 23 victims with ten or more stab wounds was more common than any single number between two (21 victims) and nine stab wounds. That is, 16 % of this sample had ten or more stab wounds. In a later Swedish study of 174 victims of homicidal stabbing over a 10-year period in Stockholm from 1983 to 1992 (Karlsson, 1998), it was found that 59 victims had one wound, 74 had two to nine wounds, and 41 individuals had ten or more wounds. That is, 23 % of this sample had ten or more stab wounds. (In the same paper, 30 (27 %) of the 113 perpetrators examined shortly after the homicide had evidence of sharp force injury on their hands.)

In 100 deaths from homicidal stabbing over a 30-year period in South West England, it was found that 25 individuals had more than 10 stab wounds: 11 had from 11 to 20 stab wounds, 6 had 21–30 wounds, and 8 individuals had more than 30 stab wounds. That paper noted, "As with so many aspects of forensic medicine great circumspection is required in drawing conclusions from the number of wounds found at autopsy in death from stabbing" (Hunt & Cowling, 1991, p. 111). In 62 non-firearm homicides autopsied at St Pancras mortuary in London between 1992 and 2001, there were 36 cases of stabbing; 20 % of these had more than ten stab wounds (Henderson, Morgan, Patel, & Tiplady, 2005).

The above research indicated that the "extraordinary similarity" claimed by the prosecution of the number of stab wounds in the Gilham deceased was in fact quite common in stabbing deaths generally, and therefore of little significance in concluding whether there were one or two killers. Further, there was no distinctive quality to the pattern of injury in these cases that would lead to the conclusion that one person was responsible for the three deaths. Importantly, the call to the jury to rely on their logic may well have resulted in a wrongful conviction.

There were a number of grounds of appeal, and on 2 December 2011 the New South Wales Court of Appeal quashed Mr. Jeffrey Gilham's conviction for the murder of his parents, and on 25 June, 2012 the Court acquitted him (*Gilham v. R*, 2012).

Some Ethical Issues

The Ethical Significance of Autopsy

> It is generally agreed that an autopsy is a procedure of considerable ethical significance as it interferes with the body (Cordner, Linehan, El Nageh, Wells, & McKelvie, 1999, p. 39).

In this chapter, the "autopsy" has been discussed dispassionately, indeed merely as a source of evidence to be relied upon by courts, and as data for public health purposes. To overlook the significance of the autopsy itself, as an interference with the body of a person recently deceased, and its impact on the next of kin, would itself be a moral failing. The autopsy is at the heart of forensic pathology. The seriousness and consequences of the procedure demands that it be undertaken with proper authority, care and respect, and that to the greatest extent possible, it should meet the purposes for which it is being carried out and those purposes should be carefully considered.

Understandably, very few people think about autopsies, and to the extent they do, they do not like them. It is difficult for many people to look past the mechanics of doing autopsies to their true underpinnings and the benefits that may flow from their performance. It is also difficult to think clearly about autopsies because of the inherent sensitivities concerning the status of a dead body. Clarity about these matters is essential in establishing a forensic pathology service, a task that in recent times has fallen to the authorities in Ontario, Canada. A substantial paper prepared for the 2007 Inquiry into Pediatric Forensic Pathology in Ontario sets out the basis for a conception of forensic pathology that requires a forensic pathology service to realise as many of the possible benefits of autopsies as possible within resource constraints, and in accordance with the law and community standards (Cordner, McKelvie, Leahy, & Ranson, 2008).

It is insufficient to perform an autopsy with the sole result a brief report sent to the coroner who makes an in-chambers finding that is then filed with the autopsy report. Despite the autopsy having taken place, effectively no useful purpose has been served. Families may receive a pro forma sheet of paper, but no reconciliation of the autopsy findings is made with the questions the family may have, no health issues for the family raised by the autopsy are discussed, no implications of a continuing educational kind for the deceased's medical attendants are explored, and no opportunities are offered to the relatives to donate tissue from the deceased for transplantation or research. To this list should be added the valuable uses of autopsy-generated information, including learning from the death to prevent re-occurrence of the particular circumstances of that death. Much of this learning will require the tools of epidemiology and it is the obligation of the forensic autopsy provider to use them.

If these functions are possible, and no attempt to perform them is made by the autopsy service provider, it may be concluded that the service is inadequate (Cordner et al., 2008).

Adequacy of Investigation in Each Case

It is clear that in order for the contributions of forensic medical teams to public health and to justice to be of value, each individual case must be thoroughly investigated. The autopsy must be carried out in such a way that the findings are of sufficient quality for presentation as evidence to a court, and together with relevant data are entered into a structured database so that they are available for epidemiological and other research.

Rudolf Virchow recognised quite early the need to standardise the constituent elements of an autopsy. The basic aims of a forensic autopsy as expressed in the contemporary literature are as follows:

- To discover, describe and record all the pathological processes present in the deceased and, where necessary, the identifying characteristics of the deceased.
- To relate these processes to the known medical history of the deceased, to draw conclusions about the cause of symptoms and signs observed in life and then to draw conclusions about the cause of death and other medical and non-medical factors contributing to death.
- To contribute to the reconstruction of the circumstances surrounding the death. Where these circumstances are important or likely to be in dispute, this will require consideration of the scene of the death as well as the relevant autopsy observations, many of which may be of trivial medical consequence.
- In accordance with good medical practice, to record all the relevant observations and negative findings, and to retain specimens, so that another pathologist at another time is in as good a position as possible to come to his or her own conclusions about the death. This will often involve reliance on good quality, preferably colour, photography (Cordner & McKelvie, 2002, p. 877).

Generally speaking, in the case of a forensic investigation of a death, this will require the following:

- The pathologist and forensic team have suitable qualifications and experience
- The scene be visited, examined and a photographic record made
- The autopsy be carried out systematically and carefully, with accompanying autopsy photography
- Appropriate histological and toxicological tests are carried out.

Throughout this process an awareness of the requirements of the law is as important as the duty to be alert to population level issues.

Duty to Be Alert to Population Level Issues

Both the forensic team and coroners have a duty, where possible, to determine the cause of death in the individual case. This duty should be extended to the consideration of whether individual cases have broader ramifications. This should not be thought of merely as a discretionary addition to what is often conceived of as the prime, if not the sole, function: identification of the cause of death in the service of coronial inquests and criminal prosecutions. The duty should be framed and regarded as a positive duty with findings from epidemiological and other forms of analysis made available to parties who have an interest in and responsibility for resolving identified problems.

Whether harm is intentionally inflicted, the result of systemic problems or lack of understanding is a matter of public interest. The public has an interest in both being made aware of the nature of these problems and having them resolved. The extent to which a forensic service will be able to fulfill such a duty will depend on whether this duty is recognised and accepted by the service, the broader community, and the State with the provision of adequate resources allocated specifically for this purpose. This function does not properly belong to a court, whose role does not include the conduct of medical or epidemiological research, but the evaluation of such research when it is presented as evidence. It ought to be allocated to a body with the requisite interests, skills and aptitude. This means that staff with skills in epidemiological and biostatistical research should be regarded as key and necessary staff in forensic medical services.

Conduct of Expert Witnesses

Justice finds it difficult to select from competing and conflicting evidence presented by numbers of expert witnesses. While expert witnesses are supposed to provide courts with independent and impartial evidence, views of experts will often conflict. This problem is not confined to forensic pathology or epidemiology. Conflict in expert opinion may be genuine, the result of conscious or unconscious partisanship in favour of a client, and/or clients may choose an expert who is known to hold a particular view. This can cause undue expense and delay in resolving a matter and, of course, lead to unjust outcomes.

Clearly expert witnesses should give their evidence in good faith, and experts should consider themselves to be assisting the court rather than performing any sort of partisan role. These matters have been considered in many jurisdictions and a variety of rules have emerged to govern the behaviour of expert witnesses and those who instruct them. For example, it may be required of parties to an action that they not instruct their experts to present a particular view. Pretrial meetings of experts and the preparation of joint reports (to the extent that agreement is possible) in meetings where clients are not present may be mandated. Expert witnesses may be court appointed rather than appointed by the parties. During hearings the judge may order that all expert evidence be presented in a block so that juries are better able to consider conflicting expert evidence. These and many other rules may be implemented to promote the likelihood of impartiality and clarity in the expert evidence presented to a court.

Pontificating Without an Evidence Base

Impartiality is one concern; another is the quality of the evidence that forensic pathologists and other forensic experts are able to rely upon to underpin their views. In the Gilham case above, it became clear the forensic evidence provided by some of the forensic pathologists, while based on experience, was not founded in fact. In other words, the pathologists were misled by placing too much reliance on perceptions informed only by their experience. Without conducting actual research, these pathologists stated to the court that there was similarity in the pattern of stab wounds, and one of them said that from this understanding the conclusion would follow (i.e. that the accused was a multiple murderer). The evidence provided at the appeal by another forensic pathologist acting for the defence and the product of systematic research showed that this was not correct and formed the basis of critical comment of the prosecution by the Court of Criminal Appeal when it acquitted Mr. Gilham.

The opportunity to conduct research to substantiate an assertion does not always exist. In such cases, where a view is based on experience not evidence, great care should be exercised by experts. If experience-based evidence is proffered, juries should be carefully cautioned.

It is undoubtedly true that there is clearly a need for more systematic epidemiological research based on forensic data. Significantly, however, it is not possible to predict the nature of all issues that will come before a court. In anticipation of such cases, as recognised by the authors of the analysis of fatal head injuries in infants from short falls, attention should be given to the development of a method for undertaking systematic reviews that is both rigorous and meet the needs of the expert forensic pathology witness and justice.

Looking at the Facts Not Just the Stats

> Of course the leading Australian case on expert evidence going wrong is that of Michael and Lindy Chamberlain who were convicted on 29 October, 1982 in respect of the alleged murder of Azaria Chamberlain at Ayers Rock on 17 August, 1980 (Porter, 1995, p. 53).

Though not necessarily an example of misapplication of statistical data, the best known case in Australia, that of Lindy Chamberlain and the death of her infant daughter Azaria on 17 August 1980, is an example of terrible injustice arising from the misapplication of scientific knowledge. After a second coronial hearing Lindy Chamberlain was committed for trial for the murder of her daughter. She was tried, found guilty and given a life sentence. Despite being released in 1985, the matter was not finally resolved until the *fourth* coronial inquest announced its findings into Azaria Chamberlain's death on 12 June 2012. The Coroner found that a dingo, a native Australian dog, had been responsible for Azaria's death.

Scientific experts gave evidence concerning a spray of an infant's arterial blood under the dashboard of the Chamberlain's car. This was eventually found to be a sand and bituminous compound sprayed underneath the car to deaden road noise. A procession of experts declared that a sharp instrument such as scissors, not the teeth of a dingo, had been caused the damage identified to the baby's clothes. It was later found, as a consequence of research, that the damage to the jump suit was indeed consistent with canine teeth. The prosecutor had also stated it was inconceivable that a dingo would take a baby. The expert evidence was completely at odds with the evidence of eye witnesses, but it was nonetheless (and sadly) preferred.

Chamberlain, a Seventh Day Adventist, had endured media attack fanned by the sometimes hysterical, condemnation of people all over the world, in turn caused in part by fictions about ritual slaughter of infants among followers of this religion, and because of her apparently calm demeanour.

In Australia, this case led to a reconsideration of forensic practice, in particular a not altogether successful attempt to ensure that defence counsel were able to access high quality forensic advice. This case is also one of many that serve as an example of the truism that courts have difficulty preventing injustice when presented with poor expert evidence (Chamberlain Innocence Committee, 1985; Royal Commission of Inquiry into Chamberlain Convictions, 1987).

Potential for Misinterpretation of Evidence

Most lawyers do not understand science or epidemiology. Terms such as null hypothesis, determinants, statistical association, confidence intervals and logistical regression are likely to have little or no meaning—or a soporific effect. Even the difference between prevalence and incidence is likely to be difficult for many lawyers to comprehend immediately. The use of such terms is likely to add to confusion rather than clarity. Similarly, those with a scientific or health-related background, including epidemiologists, are unlikely to have more than a lay understanding of court processes, rules of evidence or the legal meanings of various terms. This lack of common language and analytic framework can cause difficulties, both for the advocate who is attempting to elicit evidence and the witness who is attempting to provide it. The process of cross-examination may be an excellent tool for working out who has the better opinion when the differences are agreed and narrow. In other circumstances, such a process may lead to confusion, as one party seeks to muddy the waters, or there needs to be a level of education introduced into the proceedings before rational discussion can properly be had. In other words, greater consideration may need to be given to innovative ways of presenting expert evidence and sorting out where the correct views lie.

Those employed in forensic medical and scientific services in Australia may receive training in the giving of evidence and, with experience, soon become familiar with legal procedures, language and court processes. Skills are also developed in delivering the information they regard as important to a case. Nonetheless, the "clash of cultures" is a matter that all parties must be alert to, and address actively if just outcomes are to be achieved. It may be that judges need to become much more actively involved in this aspect of their trials.

Coronial Findings

Some have expressed concern that insufficient attention is given to the implementation of coroners' recommendations in the realm of public health (Bugeja & Ranson, 2005). While this concern has validity, it is also reasonable to suggest that caution ought to be exercised before implementation of recommendations made by a coroner or court. Neither coroners nor judges are expert in public health or epidemiology. Cases come before courts in an ad hoc fashion, rather than through a systematic examination of public health matters where criminal or civil fault might be attributed. Independent research to address the problem that is before the court may not have been carried out. Although issues may be identified that require resolution, they may not be those identified by health ministries, for example, as being in need of immediate attention. The need to respond to problems singled out in this manner may cause an unnecessary skewing of budgets and priorities.

On the other hand, it would be wrong to suggest that coroners' recommendations ought to be ignored. Where population level issues are identified by courts, those with an interest in, and the capacity to address them, should be required to respond within a reasonable period. The response may indicate that recommendations will not be pursued and the reasons for this, or that they are being considered with some indication as to what is being, or will be done.

Obligation of the State to Facilitate Epidemiological Research Derived from Autopsy Data

Data collected by forensic pathologists are a valuable resource, both to them when presenting evidence, and to the community. Unless there is a commitment by the State to ensure that such data is properly collected and rigorous analysis carried out, this will not happen.

Forensic Epidemiology in the International Context

In this part the role of forensic teams in assisting in the resolution of mass deaths in war, internal conflict and disaster is examined. Again the importance of this work at both the level of the individual and to protecting health and human rights is considered. This new role for the forensic medical sciences emerged at the end of the Second World War.

> WW2 saw the first investigations of war crimes by pathologist led teams. Surprisingly it was the Nazi investigation in 1943 of the Soviet murder of thousands of Polish officers at Katyn, Ukraine that introduced the use of international scientific teams to war crimes investigations. Though an exercise in anti-Soviet propaganda (as was the subsequent Soviet investigation of the massacres that blamed, unsurprisingly, the Nazis) it demonstrated through mass grave excavation, autopsy and analysis of bullets and shell cases that the Soviets had carried out mass killings three years earlier (Hanson, 2008, p. 18).

British pathologist, Keith Mant, investigated Nazi war crimes between 1945 and 1948. He, John Thompson (a neurophysiologist and US citizen in the Royal Canadian Air Force Office seconded to British scientific intelligence) and Leo Alexander (a psychiatrist and neurologist who was a Viennese Jew who had moved to the United States in 1933 and who had assisted Telford Taylor and drafted the Nuremberg Code) "provided crucial impetus to the new wave of investigation, arrest and trial" (Weindling, 2004, at p. 88) that led to the Medical Trial at Nuremberg.

> Thompson's concept of a medical war crime linked revelations of medical atrocities to war crimes investigations, and provided a basis for prosecutions. The investigators [*Thompson, Mant and Alexander*] tied the human experiments to German war aims: they reconstructed how prisoners were wounded, subjected to pressure and freezing, and to drugs for experimental purposes (Weindling, 2004, pp. 88–89).

Keith Mant joined the Royal Army Medical Corps in 1944. In 1945 he was made the officer in charge of the pathology section in the team investigating war crimes in North Western Europe. Initially his role had been to determine whether Allied airmen

> had died from injuries on crashing or whether the Germans executed the airmen after capture. Over three years he examined over 150 corpses, often from unmarked graves, and found 49 were executed by a Genickschuss—shooting through the neck or the back of the head (Weindling, 2004, p. 117).

Keith Mant then extended his investigations to examine cases for the "Special Operations Executive" that had supported resistance activities and dropped combat personnel behind enemy lines. This led to his examination of medical abuses at Ravensbrück. In 1946

> he became secretary of the International Scientific Commission for Medical War Crimes, which aimed to collect and evaluate details of all human experiments. Survivors' evidence was reinforced by war crimes investigators, who corroborated testimony by means of documents and affidavits, so that witness statements should not be dismissed in court as inadequate hearsay or exaggeration (Weindling, 2004, p. 63).

He interviewed medically qualified Nazis who had been SS members or had worked for the SS conducting their so-called medical experiments. He interviewed survivors and undertook exhumations:

> The planned British trial of medical atrocities at Ravensbrück was the first of the zonal trials to emerge from the flurry of interest in medical war crimes. Mant's careful investigations were crucial. As Ravensbrück was in the Soviet zone, Mant worked by interrogating

> captured camp staff, and by tracing survivors, collecting their testimonies and by medical appraisal of their wounds. He also studied documents, some held by Polish organizations and others captured from the Germans. Between June and October 1946 he collected evidence on human experiments in France, Belgium, Denmark, Sweden and Norway. He interrogated the self-styled "Rabbits", documenting their wounds and combining humane sympathy with clinical precision. On 24–28 June 1946 Mant and Lépine took affidavits from JaninaIwanska and Helena Piasecka. These affidavits were reproduced as part of the series of American war crimes documents, and were used at the Nuremberg Medical Trial on 2 January 1947. Mant then went to Hirson in northern France to collect a witness statement from Denise Fresnel, who was the doctor in Block 8. A number of Ravensbrück survivors had found refuge in Sweden, and Norwegian prisoners supplied significant testimony. Mant took a deposition from Sofia Maczka on 15–16 April 1946 with the assistance of the British consul, Stockholm—this document was also to be used at the Nuremberg Medical Trial. On 11 July 1946 Mant's convoy reached Lund where he interviewed Irena StanislawaSuchon. On 15–19 July he was in Stockholm. After attending the International Scientific War Commission in Paris from 31 July to 2 August 1946, on 9 August he went to Brussels to collect further evidence. On 20 August 1946 Mant visited the formidable Sylvia Salvesen in Oslo; Gerald Draper (the hawkish chief British prosecuting lawyer) had already interrogated her about the RavensbrückRevier. Salvesen was to be a powerful and articulate witness (Weindling, 2004, pp. 115–116).

Subsequently

> [h]e extended the investigation to Auschwitz, taking on board sterilization and infertility experiments by Carl Clauberg and twin experiments by Mengele, and analysing the German motives. Drawing on the testimonies of concentration camp survivors, Mant listed no fewer than 12 categories of experiments, which he attributed to war priorities (as typhus experiments, war gases, war surgery), racial theories or to the whims of Himmler (Weindling, 2004, pp. 112–113).

There is undoubtedly a great deal more to be said. Readers who are interested in further detail are referred to the excellent text by Paul Weindling titled *Nazi Medicine and the Nuremberg Trials*. However, what emerges is a clear story of the methodical (and determined) collection of data intended to be relied upon for forensic purposes, and oral evidence from victims and perpetrators. This data has been analysed systematically in order to determine, not only individual cause of death and injury, but patterns of behaviour that were attributable not to a group of deranged doctors, but to a regime in which these doctors and other staff willingly and intentionally played a part.

Since then, forensic experts have unfortunately been required to investigate other mass atrocities and gather evidence to enable to prosecution of war crimes.

In addition to determining the identity of those killed, forensic teams may be required to analyse the

> statistical aspects of the atrocities, including the recognition of patterns within the evidence, comparing differences between mass graves resulting from related atrocities and highlighting rare experiences or events. Likewise, the formulation of a demographic profile based on age, sex, ancestry, and stature is potentially important for determining the presence of biological group characteristics and thus is often included among the responsibilities of the forensic team (Jessee & Anderson, n.d., para. 11).

The use of epidemiological methods has been recognised as an element of the forensic investigation of international human rights violations. This is demonstrated

Table 6.4 Experts involved in investigations of mass atrocities

Medicine/health care	Science	Other professionals
Forensic pathology	Anthropology/osteology	Crime scene examiners
Clinical forensic medicine	Molecular biology (DNA)	Evidence handlers
Forensic odontology	Radiography	Photographers
Medical epidemiology	Archaeology	Interviewers
	Ballistics	Liaison
	Firearms and toolmark examiners	Police
	Entomology	Ordinance experts
		Mortuary technicians
		Logistics and administration
		Fingerprints experts

(Italics added)

in Table 6.4 reproduced here, which outlines the wide range of experts who may be involved in investigating a mass atrocity (Cordner & McKelvie, 2002).

The necessary contribution of many forensic disciplines was recognised in response to the catastrophic events of 9/11.

> Identification of WTC [World Trade Centre] victim remains was the responsibility of the New York City Office of Chief Medical Examiner (OCME), which is one of the largest and most sophisticated in the country. Yet, its resources and scope of experience had to be expanded. The New York State Police Department (NYSP) was responsible for DNA analysis of reference samples. Several private DNA laboratories also tested samples, and software vendors helped to develop data analysis and compatibility tools. The NYSP and the OCME asked the National Institute of Justice (NIJ) to convene a group of scientific and medical experts [the Kinship and Data Analysis Panel (KADAP)] to advise them in the DNA identification effort. KADAP included experts in forensics; bioinformatics; and molecular, medical, statistical, and population genetics. The KADAP's charge was to assist the OCME in the development of procedures, standards of evidence, and processes related to the DNA identification effort. The final determination of a specific identification rested with the OCME (Biesecker et al., 2005, p. 1122).

(The complex data collection processes and statistical analyses undertaken for identification purposes during the aftermath of 9/11 are well described in the paper by Biesecker et al. (2005)).

Similarly, following armed conflict (and natural disasters) there are ethical and human rights norms requiring the identification of the remains of victims, if not also legal imperatives. International humanitarian law recognises a right for families to know the fate of their missing relatives (Additional Protocol I to the Geneva Conventions, 1977: Article 32). Additional Protocol I applies to international armed conflicts. The right is not explicitly referred to in Additional Protocol II which applies to internal violence, but the International Committee of the Red Cross believes that, if the right exists in international conflicts it is hard to see how it does not also exist in circumstances of internal violence.

In 1998, the Secretary General of the United Nations referred to the "right to know". This was in a report describing the programme established in the Former Yugoslavia

> for the excavation of mass graves and exhumation of mortal remains for the purpose of identifying deceased missing persons, returning the remains to the families concerned and thereby responding to the right of families to know the truth about the fate of their loved ones (Commission on Human Rights, 1998, para. I.D.3.)

If there is a right to know the fate of those missing in war or internal violence, then for the right to have any content it must mean the following:

- Families have a right to know whether the missing relative is dead or alive.
- If the relative is dead, families have a right to know something about how the death came about, including the cause of death.

(See below for the practical consequences of this being implemented by the ICRC). This right to know is the humanitarian parallel of what is more readily recognised as a legal imperative: the need for identification of the dead in criminal proceedings for war crimes. While identification in the form of names attached to human remains may be desirable for the purpose of criminal prosecutions, it is not necessary. The International Criminal Tribunal for the Former Yugoslavia only needed demographic information about the dead for its purposes. Its Deputy Prosecutor at the time said as much when the ICTY auspiced forensic teams in Bosnia "to determine the cause and manner of death and the demographic profile of the victims …" (Blewitt, 1997, p. 288), thus explicitly omitting the need to attach names to those whose remains were to be exhumed.

Nonetheless, for an identification to be made, in addition to the collection of ante-mortem data, and the application of anthropological and pathological approaches, DNA based methods for human identification may be used to identify the victims of armed conflicts. The interpretation of DNA data is based on an assessment of the statistical probability that the DNA of the unidentified person matches DNA derived from family members. If the only family member available is a half sibling for example, or the genetic matter is degraded, co-mingled with other genetic matter, or little is available for DNA analysis, great reliance will be placed on statistical calculations of the likelihood that a missing person has been identified. Matching reports are issued when the statistical probability of a family link is at least 99.95 % (Budowle, Bieber, & Eisenberg, 2005).

The identification of victims of war crimes through their DNA is now relied on in the investigation and prosecution of war crimes for both the dead and the living. The first prominent application of genetic analysis in this context was in the investigation of the missing in Argentina by the National Commission on the Disappearance of Persons (King, 1991).

The International Committee of the Red Cross (ICRC) has been tracing the whereabouts of people since the Franco-Prussian War of 1870. Their Central Tracing Agency has developed different facets since then including well-known measures such as delivering correspondence and providing food packages to prisoners of war. During the Second World War the services of this Agency were greatly extended. A more recent development emerging from this traditional role is the

ICRC's programme of "The Missing". Morris Tidball-Binz, the forensic coordinator for the ICRC has stated that there has been

> insufficient recognition of the importance of ensuring proper management of the dead and of caring for the needs of the bereaved, coupled with the frequent collapse of forensic services in the aftermath of catastrophes, (contribute to) perpetuating the tragedy and trauma suffered by survivors forever unable properly to bury and mourn their dead (Tidball-Binz, 2007, p. 421).

In 1996 then US President Bill Clinton established an entity now known as the International Commission on Missing Persons (ICMP). It describes its role as being

> to ensure the cooperation of governments in locating and identifying those who have disappeared during armed conflict or as a result of human rights violations (ICMP, 2008, About ICMP, para. 1).

Its first contribution to the identification of the missing has been in the aftermath of war in the former Yugoslavia.

> Since November 2001, ICMP has developed a database of 89,086 relatives of 29,109 missing people, and more than 36,000 bone samples taken from mortal remains exhumed from clandestine graves in the countries of former Yugoslavia. … ICMP currently operates the world's largest high-throughput DNA human identification facility (ICMP, 2008, About ICMP, para. 3).

Irrespective of the recognised problems with use of DNA evidence in addition to those described above, ICMP indicates in a 2010 report of their work in Kosovo

> The use of DNA permits an accurate accounting of the overall number of missing persons and can also reveal mistakes made by previous, less reliable means [of identification] (ICMP, 2010, p. 6).

They also point out, the more organisations that are present, serving different purposes with uncoordinated and inconsistent means of gathering data on the missing, the harder it will be to form a uniform and reliable identification process. In 2006 the Pan American Health Organization, World Health Organization, International Federation of Red Cross and Red Crescent Societies and the ICRC published guidelines for the management of the dead entitled *Management of Dead Bodies after Disasters: A Field Manual for First Responders*, which contains advice for non-specialists for the dignified management of the dead in catastrophes and for the care of bereaved relatives. It includes instructions for the information to be collected to help identify the missing.

It has become clear that in order to deal effectively with crimes committed during wars and armed conflicts the coordinated contribution of all of the disciplines within forensic medicine and science are needed. Without the evidence that such forensic investigation is able to produce, the conduct of war crimes trials is potentially much diminished. Furthermore, and in parallel with this, the humanitarian needs of the families of the missing require that those killed during war and internal violence to be identified.

This chapter is dedicated to the memory of professor Keith Mant (1919–2000) (with thanks to Paul Weindling).

References

Additional Protocol I to the Geneva Conventions. (1977). <http://www.icrc.org/ihl.nsf/FULL/470?OpenDocument>.

Azar, H. A. (1997). Rudolf Virchow, not just a pathologist: A re-examination of the report on the typhus epidemic in Upper Silesia. *Annals of Diagnostic Pathology, 1*(1), 65–71. doi:10.1016/S1092-9134(97)80010-X.

Biesecker, L., Bailey-Wilson, J. E., Ballantyne, J., Baum, H., Bieber, F. R., Brenner, C., et al. (2005). DNA identifications after the 9/11 World Trade Center attack. *Science, 310*(5751), 1122–1123. doi:10.1126/science.1116608.

Blewitt, G. (1997). The role of forensic investigations in genocide prosecutions before an International Criminal tribunal. *Medicine, Science, and the Law, 37*(4), 284–288.

Budowle, B., Bieber, F. R., & Eisenberg, A. (2005). Forensic aspects of mass disasters: Strategic considerations for DNA-based human identification. *Legal Medicine, 7*(4), 230–243. doi:10.1016/j.legalmed.2005.01.001.

Bugeja, L., & Ranson, D. (2003). Coroners' recommendations: Do they lead to positive public health outcomes? *Journal of Law and Medicine, 10*(4), 399–400.

Bugeja, L., & Ranson, D. (2005). Coroners' recommendations: A lost opportunity. *Journal of Law and Medicine, 13*(2), 173–175.

Cameron, P., Mitra, B., Fitzgerald, M., Scheinkestel, C., Stripp, A., Batey, C., et al. (2009). Black Saturday: The immediate impact of the February 2009 bushfires in Victoria, Australia. *Medical Journal of Australia, 191*(1), 11–16.

Chamberlain Innocence Committee. (1985). *New forensic evidence in support of an inquiry into the convictions of M. and L. Chamberlain*. Sydney: Chamberlain Innocence Committee. Retrieved August 15, 2012, from http://www.lindychamberlain.com/files/Blue_Book.pdf

Christies. (2012). GRAUNT, John. (1620–1674). *Natural and political observations mentioned in a following index and made upon the bills of mortality...with reference to the government, religion, trade, growth, ayre, diseases, and the several changes of the said city*. London: Tho: Roycroft, for John Martin, James Allestry, and Tho: Dicas, 1662. Retrieved July 13, 2012, from http://www.christies.com/LotFinder/lot_details.aspx?intObjectID=5388544, from http://www.christies.com/LotFinder/lot_details.aspx?intObjectID=5388544

Commission on Human Rights. (1998). *Question of the human rights of all persons subjected to any form of detention or imprisonment. Human rights and forensic science*. Report of the Secretary-GeneralE/CN.4/1998/32.5 January 1998. Retrieved August 15, 2012, from http://www.unhchr.ch/Huridocda/Huridoca.nsf/TestFrame/35154209d0ceb78fc125660c00550688?Opendocument

Cordner, S., Linehan, B., El Nageh, M., Wells, D., & McKelvie, H. (1999). *Ethical practice in laboratory medicine and forensic pathology* (WHO Regional Publications, Eastern Mediterranean Series). Alexandria, Egypt: WHO Regional Office for the Eastern Mediterranean.

Cordner, S., & Loff, B. (1994). 800 Years of coroners: Have they a future? *The Lancet, 344*(8925), 799–801. doi:10.1016/S0140-6736(94)92348-5.

Cordner, S., & McKelvie, H. (2002). Developing standards in international forensic work to identify missing persons. *International Review of the Red Cross, 84*(848), 867–884. doi:10.1017/S1560775500104213.

Cordner, S., McKelvie, H., Leahy, F., & Ranson, D. (2008). Model forensic pathology service. In K. Roach (Ed.), *Controversies and models in paediatric forensic pathology independent research studies* (Prepared for inquiry into pediatric forensic pathology in Ontario, Vol. 1, pp. 168–170). ON, Canada: Ontario Ministry of the Attorney General, Queens Printer for Ontario.

Cordner, S., & Ranson, D. (1997). Grim new role for forensic pathologist. *The Lancet, 350*(Suppl. 3), SIII6. doi:10.1016/S0140-6736(97)90039-8.

Coronial Services Centre of Victoria. (2008). *Mortui vivos docent: Celebrating 20 years of the Coronial Services Centre of Victoria, 1988–2008*. Melbourne, Australia: Victorian Institute of Forensic Medicine.

Cullen, M. (1974). The making of the Civil Registration Act of 1836. *The Journal of Ecclesiastical History, 25*(1), 39–59. doi:10.1017/S002204690004505X.

Davis, G. (1997). Mind your manners: Part I: History of death certification and manner of death classification. *The American Journal of Forensic Medicine and Pathology, 18*(3), 219–223.

Department of Human Services. (2009, January). *Heatwave in Victoria: An assessment of health impacts*. Melbourne, Australia: Victorian Government.

Drummer, O., Gerostamoulos, J., Batziris, H., Chu, M., Caplehorn, J., Robertson, M., et al. (2003). The incidence of drugs in drivers killed in Australian road traffic crashes. *Forensic Science International, 134*(2–3), 154–162. doi:10.1016/S0379-0738(03)00134-8.

Drummer, O., Gerostamoulos, J., Batziris, H., Chu, M., Caplehorn, J., Robertson, M., et al. (2004). The involvement of drugs in drivers of motor vehicles killed in Australian road traffic crashes. *Accident Analysis and Prevention, 36*(2), 239–248.

Drummer, O., Opeskin, K., Syrjanen, M., & Cordner, S. (1992). Methadone toxicity causing death in ten subjects starting on a methadone maintenance program. *The American Journal of Forensic Medicine and Pathology, 13*(4), 346–350.

Ehsani, J., Ibrahim, J., Bugeja, L., & Cordner, S. (2010). The role of epidemiology in determining if a simple short fall can cause fatal head injury in an infant: A subject review and reflection. *The American Journal of Forensic Medicine and Pathology, 31*(3), 287–298. doi:10.1097/PAF.0b013e3181db7eb5.

Gilham v R (2012) NSWCCA 131. Court of Criminal Appeal, New South Wales. Retrieved July 28, 2012, from http://www.caselaw.nsw.gov.au/action/PJUDG?jgmtid=159326

Goodman, R., Munson, J., Dammers, K., Lazzarini, Z., & Barkley, J. (2003). Forensic epidemiology: Law at the intersection of public health and criminal investigations. *The Journal of Law, Medicine & Ethics, 31*(4), 684–700. doi:10.1111/j.1748-720X.2003.tb00135.x.

Hanson, I. (2008). Forensic archaeology: Approaches to international investigations. In M. Oxenham (Ed.), *Forensic approaches to death, disaster and abuse* (pp. 17–28). Queensland, Australia: Australian Academic Press.

Henderson, J., Morgan, S., Patel, F., & Tiplady, M. (2005). Patterns of non-firearm homicide. *Journal of Clinical Forensic Medicine, 12*(3), 128–132. doi:10.1016/j.jcfm.2004.10.011.

Hunt, A., & Cowling, R. (1991). Murder by stabbing. *Forensic Science International, 52*(1), 107–112. doi:10.1016/0379-0738(91)90102-O.

International Commission on Missing Persons (ICMP). (2008). *About ICMP*. Retrieved August 15, 2012, from http://www.ic-mp.org/about-icmp/

International Commission on Missing Persons (ICMP). (2010). *The situation in Kosovo: A stock taking*. Sarajevo: ICMP. Retrieved August 15, 2012, from http://www.ic-mp.org/wp-content/uploads/2007/11/icmp-dg-264-4-doc-general.pdf

Jessee, E., & Anderson, K. (n.d.). *Forensic evidence in international criminal trials*. Retrieved August 15, 2012, from http://www.sharedhumanity.org/LibraryArticle.php?heading=Forensic%20Evidence%20in%20International%20Criminal%20Trials

Karlsson, T. (1998). Sharp force homicides in the Stockholm area, 1983–1992. *Forensic Science International, 94*(1–2), 129–139. doi:10.1016/S0379-0738(98)00067-X.

King, M.-C. (1991). An application of DNA sequencing to a human rights problem. In T. Friedman (Ed.), *Molecular genetic medicine* (Vol. 1, pp. 117–128). San Diego, CA: Academic.

Loff, B., & Cordner, S. (2001). Death rate of aborigines in prison is increasing. *The Lancet, 357*(9265), 1348. doi:10.1016/S0140-6736(00)04546-3.

Ormstad, K., Karlsson, T., Enkler, L., Law, B., & Rajs, J. (1986). Patterns in sharp force fatalities—A comprehensive forensic medical study. *Journal of Forensic Sciences, 31*(2), 529–542.

Porter, C. (1995). The evidence of experts. *Australian Journal of Forensic Sciences, 27*(2), 53–58. doi:10.1080/00450619509411328.

Rothman, K. (1996). Lessons from John Graunt. *The Lancet, 347*(8993), 37–39. doi:10.1016/S0140-6736(96)91562-7.

Royal Commission into Aboriginal Deaths in Custody. (1991). *National report vol. 1-1.1 Indigenous Law Resources, Australasian Legal Information Institute*. Retrieved August 15, 2012, from http://www.austlii.edu.au/au/other/IndigLRes/rciadic/national/vol1/7.html

Royal Commission of Inquiry into Chamberlain Convictions. (1987). *Report of the Commissioner the Hon. Mr. Justice T.R. Morling/Royal Commission of Inquiry into Chamberlain Convictions*. Canberra: Government Printer.

Schweber, L. (2006). *Disciplining statistics: Demography and vital statistics in France and England 1830–1835* (p. 106). London: Duke University Press.

Taylor, R., & Rieger, A. (1985). Medicine as social science: Rudolf Virchow on the typhus epidemic in Upper Silesia. *International Journal of Health Services, 15*(4), 547–559.

Tidball-Binz, M. (2007). Managing the dead in catastrophes: Guiding principles and practical recommendations for first responders. *International Review of the Red Cross, 89*(866), 421–442. doi:10.1017/S1816383107001130.

Watson, K. (2010). *Forensic medicine in Western society: A history* (pp. 100–101). Oxon: Routledge.

Weindling, P. (2004). *Nazi medicine and the Nuremberg trials: From medical war crimes to informed consent*. New York: Palgrave Macmillan.

About the Contributors

Domnița Oana Bădărău received her training in bioethics while a Fogarty fellow in the Department of Bioethics, Case Western Reserve University, with a focus on research ethics. Prior to this, she studied economics, international economic relations, and law at Alexandru Ioan Cuza University in Iasi, Romania. Currently she is a Research Assistant at the Institute for Biomedical Ethics at the University of Basel, where she is pursuing research related to autonomy, competency, and decision making during her Ph.D. studies in pediatric oncology. Her research interests include clinical ethics and decision-making processes, international research ethics, global justice, cultural sensitivity, and gender inequities in health care.

Stephen Cordner is the Professor of forensic medicine at Monash University, Melbourne, Australia, and also the Director of the Victorian Institute of Forensic Medicine in Australia. The Institute is Victoria's statutory provider of forensic pathology and clinical forensic medicine services. In 2003 he spent a year with the International Committee of the Red Cross in Geneva, Switzerland, as its consultant in forensic pathology during the implementation of its project entitled "The Missing." This project addresses not only missing individuals, many of whom are dead, during war or internal violence, but also the families of the missing individuals.

Beatrice-Gabriela Ioan is an associate professor in the Department of Legal Medicine, Medical Deontology and Bioethics and the coordinator of the Department of Behavioral Sciences of the Gr. T. Popa University of Medicine and Pharmacy of Iasi, Romania. She holds degrees in medicine (1993), psychology (2002), law (2012), medical sciences, and bioethics (2004). Dr. Ioan serves on various councils and committees, including the Bureau of the Steering Committee on Bioethics (DH-BIO) of the Council of Europe and the Superior Commission of Discipline and the Bioethics Commission of the Romanian College of Physicians. Dr. Ioan is also the deputy editor in chief of the *Romanian Journal of Bioethics* and an associate editor of the *Journal of Immigrant and Minority Health*.

She is the author/coauthor of 11 books, 20 book chapters, and more than 60 scientific papers in the fields of legal medicine and bioethics.

S. Loue (ed.), *Forensic Epidemiology in the Global Context*,
DOI 10.1007/978-1-4614-6738-0, © Springer Science+Business Media New York 2013

Brandy L. Johnson, J.D., is an attorney at the law firm of Feirich/Mager/Green/Ryan in Carbondale, Illinois. She holds a degree in law from Southern Illinois University School of Law and an undergraduate degree in political science from Southern Illinois University-Carbondale. She is licensed to practice law in Illinois and Missouri and has authored appellate briefs to the United States Supreme Court, the United States Court of Appeals for the Eighth Circuit, the Missouri Supreme Court, the Missouri Court of Appeals for the Southern District of Missouri, the Missouri Court of Appeals for the Eastern District of Missouri, the Illinois Court of Appeals for the Fifth District, and the Missouri Labor and Industrial Relations Commission. Mrs. Johnson concentrates her practice in workers' compensation and employment discrimination and also has experience in the areas of tort litigation, including premises liability, personal injury, and insurance law. She serves as an appointee to the Illinois State Bar Association's Standing Committee for Disability Law and is a member of the Missouri State Bar Association's Workers' Compensation Commission. Mrs. Johnson has published articles in numerous journals and is of high demand as a speaker nationwide on issues pertaining to workers' compensation.

Bebe Loff is a lawyer and Director of the Michael Kirby Centre for Public Health and Human Rights in the School of Public Health and Preventive Medicine at Monash University, Australia. Prior to this position, she directed the legislative programs of Ministers of Health in her state and was a policy adviser to an attorney general. She has worked with a number of United Nations agencies and in community-based legal services.

Sana Loue, J.D., Ph.D., M.P.H., M.S.S.A., M.A., is a Professor at Case Western Reserve University. She holds a primary appointment in the Department of Bioethics in the School of Medicine, with secondary appointments in the Departments of Epidemiology and Biostatistics, Psychiatry, and Global Health and at the Mandel School of Applied Social Sciences, the university's school of social work. Dr. Loue's empirical research focuses on gender, sexuality, HIV risk, mental illness, and family violence. Dr. Loue has served as a consulting forensic epidemiologist in lawsuits involving infectious disease, pharmaceutical products, and product defects. Dr. Loue has presented her work related to forensic epidemiology nationally and internationally and has contributed to various journals on the subject, including the *Journal of Legal Medicine*. She is the author or the editor of 30 books, including *Forensic Epidemiology: Integrating Epidemiology and Law Enforcement* (Jones & Bartlett, 2009), *Case Studies in Forensic Epidemiology* (Kluwer Academic, 2002), and *Forensic Epidemiology: A Comprehensive Guide for Legal and Epidemiology Professionals* (Southern Illinois University Press, 1999).

Dr. Claire McIvor started her academic career in 2002 when she took up a lectureship at Durham University. She is now a Senior Lecturer in Law at Birmingham Law School. She holds degrees from Queen's University Belfast (L.L.B. in Common and Civil Law with French) and Durham University (M.Jur. and Ph.D.). Her main teaching and research interests lie in the field of tort law and medical law, and she has published numerous articles in leading law journals. She is the author of *Third Party Liability in Tort* (Hart Publishing, 2006) and she is currently completing a monograph on Vicarious Liability in Tort.

Ryan C. Turnage, J.D., is an attorney at the law firm of Rynearson, Suess, Schnurbusch & Champion, LLC in St. Louis, Missouri. He holds a degree in law from Saint Louis University School of Law and undergraduate degrees in political science and English from Saint Louis University. He is licensed to practice law in Missouri. Mr. Turnage's practice concentrates on insurance defense, insurance coverage, contract disputes, and family law. He is currently a member of The Missouri Bar's 2012 Leadership Academy and is a 2012 recipient of the "John R. Essner Young Lawyer of the Year Award" from Legal Services of Eastern Missouri where he serves as a volunteer lawyer.

Jennifer L. Woulfe, J.D., is an attorney at the law firm of Rynearson, Suess, Schnurbusch & Champion, LLC in St. Louis, Missouri. She received both her law degree and her undergraduate degree in finance from Saint Louis University School of Law. She is licensed to practice law in Illinois and Missouri. Ms. Woulfe concentrates her practice on premises liability, personal injury, and insurance law. She has published an article in the *Saint Louis University Public Law Review*.

Index

S. Loue (ed.), *Forensic Epidemiology in the Global Context*,
DOI 10.1007/978-1-4614-6738-0, © Springer Science+Business Media New York 2013

MIX
Papier aus verantwortungsvollen Quellen
Paper from responsible sources
FSC® C105338

If you have any concerns about our products,
you can contact us on
ProductSafety@springernature.com

In case Publisher is established outside the EU,
the EU authorized representative is:
Springer Nature Customer Service Center GmbH
Europaplatz 3, 69115 Heidelberg, Germany

Printed by Libri Plureos GmbH
in Hamburg, Germany